Rivalry

Rivalry

In business, science, among nations

REUVEN BRENNER

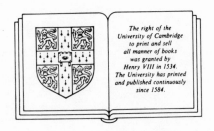

CAMBRIDGE UNIVERSITY PRESS
Cambridge

New York   New Rochelle   Melbourne   Sydney

Published by the Press Syndicate of the University of Cambridge
The Pitt Building, Trumpington Street, Cambridge CB2 1RP
32 East 57th Street, New York, NY 10022, USA
10 Stamford Road, Oakleigh, Melbourne 3166, Australia

First published 1987

Printed in the United States of America

Library of Congress Cataloging-in-Publication Data
Brenner, Reuven.
Rivalry: in business, science, among nations.
1. Competition.   2. Industrial organization (Economic
theory)   3. Risk.   4. Decision-making.   I. Title.
HD41.B743   1987   338.6'048   86-24415

British Library Cataloguing in Publication Data
Brenner, Reuven
Rivalry: in business, science, among nations.
1. Competition
I. Title
338.6'048   HF1436

ISBN 0 521 33187 0

To those who were and are entrepreneurs in our family: My beloved grandmother and father who were, and my father-in-law, who is.

Contents

Preface

This book looks at the behavior of enterprises, the organization of markets, the structure of industries (particularly scientific ones) by putting the entrepreneurs' and the decision makers' perceptions at center stage. This departure point provides a unifying viewpoint, leads to a close relationship between facts and interpretation, and enables insights for formulation of policies promoting innovations.

The book does not deal with "markets," "capital," or "technology," but looks at the human being and the society in which he lives in order to understand the decisions to compete or not to compete, to bet on new ventures or not, to reorganize the firm or not, and so forth. This departure point stands in sharp contrast with the usual ones treated in the field of "industrial organization," where firms are frequently treated as a simple-minded "brain," a decision-making unit that has not much to do but adjust output and prices of one or two products to very simple imagined changes.

So the questions raised will be: What do "firms" do and for what end? How do they compete? Do they always have the motivation to compete? What role exactly do entrepreneurs and managers play? How can they increase productivity and profits?

Since some answers are given to this last question, a brief clarifying note is necessary. Since increased profits and increased productivity will be linked to bets on new ideas and greater efforts, and to provoking fear, stress, envy, and suffering among subordinates, the reader may be puzzled and ask: What do "economics" in general, productivity and profits in particular, have to do with "fear," "envy," and "stress"? Aren't they psychological concepts outside the realm of economics?

The answers will be clear: As suggested in my two previous books, *History – the Human Gamble* and *Betting on Ideas,* I don't believe that the separation into "psychological" and "economic" reactions can be made. There are just human reactions. Also, as suggested there, profits and productivity are due to something, and that "something" can be related to "fear" and "stress" – on the whole there are no free lunches within my view of the world.

Following these brief introductory remarks one may be afraid of reading any further. For, in the past, the reader may have glimpsed at the psycholog-

ix

ical literature and become buried in its jargon (an ancient word which means the twittering of geese – so attributing its use to a group is not meant to be complimentary). He may also have glimpsed at the economic literature and gotten lost in its mathematical jargon. So what can the reader expect from a combination of these two approaches!

Let the answer be clear: I intend to use only plain English and try to avoid as much as possible any technical, bombastic words. It is not so much a question of reaching a larger audience, but I found that as one gets deeper and deeper into the essential behind the world of business – which is human behavior – one is virtually forced to use a simpler language. The specialized terms just do not carry the burden that must be carried by words describing human behavior. [Mathematical translations of these everyday words are presented for two reasons only: either to check the consistency of the arguments or to show, for specialists, the difference between my approach and the traditional ones (mainly in appendixes).] But I realize that by writing in clear, simple English and by avoiding using jargon and pompous language, I risk being misinterpreted – paradoxical as this may sound. The reason is that some readers may infer that the straightforward language suggests a simplistic approach, the sad fact being that today most social scientists consider a nonpersonal, lethargic, witless prose as evidence of seriousness. I choose to bear this risk.

The first chapter summarizes and extends the model of risk taking and decision making presented in the previous books and shows how it can be applied to explaining the behavior of decision makers within enterprises. Since my view of human behavior is different from the one assumed in economic models, the vocabulary pertinent to the subject of competition, "entrepreneurs," "profits," "risk," "uncertainty," "productivity," and others must be first redefined. These words have a different meaning here than in the traditional literature, although they seem to correspond to their everyday, commonsense use. For example: "Profits" are associated with innovations and uncertainty; "productivity" too is associated with the new ideas and managerial talents (rather than being an unexplained residual). Once the views are presented and the appropriate simple vocabulary precisely defined, then the behavior of enterprises is examined.

The model is not just descriptive, but has also predictive power, among others on the willingness of individuals to undertake ventures they have previously shunned – this prediction is confronted with the stubborn facts in the second chapter.

Chapter 3 returns to the model to redefine "competition." In contrast to the now customary definition (which was not Adam Smith's) that uses the criterion of lack of power over prices to identify this concept, the one that can be given within my approach is the following: Businessmen compete with *ideas* to find a combination of customers and services with respect to which they have an advantage over those whom they *perceive* as their competitors. The model thus enables a definition of competition that reminds one of Adam Smith's and Schumpeter's. Since competition implies new ideas, innovations in particular, a *secured* monopolistic position implies their absence. The elaboration of this view and the examination of facts, which leads us to a reexamination of antitrust laws, suggest that the pricing, concentration, and other criteria used to infer noncompetitive behavior are inaccurate. Instead, the accused firm's relative rate of innovation (as measured by the fraction of sales of new products in the firm's total revenues) is suggested as the appropriate measure for inferring noncompetitive behavior.

Chapters 4 and 5 examine in detail facets of just two competitive strategies: advertising and inventions, in science in particular. Chapter 6 shows how the same model that illuminates the behavior of privately owned enterprises sheds light on the origins and behavior of those owned by the state. Chapter 7 puts the whole picture together and examines the behavior of entrepreneurs and the role of governments within a broad, historical perspective.

Thus, as one can infer from this brief outline, many things traditionally treated in the field of industrial organization are left out (at the same time themes that traditionally have been neglected are introduced), for several reasons: First, to put in everything achieves a less truthful rather than a more truthful result. As Jonathan Hughes once put it: "The broad picture is always the most simple one – once one decides how to paint the picture." Second, since the views presented here have not much to do with the fashionable theses of the moment, it was easy to leave things out. Third, sources discarded when making up my mind are not discussed because this process is of no interest to the reader, while the final viewpoint may be. Last, but not least, the ideas expressed here, sometimes in detail, are simple and should be obvious – at least that is my perception. Therefore I don't think that there will be any difficulty understanding them. The difficulty may be more in discarding old ideas to which one is accustomed. Discarding them was not easy and I neither expect nor wish for easy surrenders from others.

I am indebted to William Baumol, Ronald Bodkin, Dennis Carlton, Greg Marchildon, Timur Kuran, Ian MacMillan, Douglass C. North, Jeffrey B. Nugent, Frederic Pryor, T.W. Schultz, as well as to my colleagues and students at the Université de Montréal for helpful suggestions. I greatly appreciate the work of my production editor, Judi Steinig, and the staff at Cambridge University Press. Special thanks are due to one of my students, Alain Plouffe, for his excellent research assistance. I am also grateful to the dedicated secretarial assistance provided by Ghislaine Gaudichon and Louise Beaulieu at the Centre de recherche et développement en économique.

The research has been supported by a grant from the Social Sciences and Humanities Research Council of Canada, which I thank.

Calm times teach few lessons.
Adversity is a Great Teacher.

Otto Eckstein

CHAPTER 1

Theory of the entrepreneurial firm

From time to time it is probably necessary to detach oneself from the technicalities of the argument and to ask quite naively what it is all about.

F.A. Hayek, *Economics and Knowledge*

As mathematics penetrated economic analysis during the nineteenth century, a structural, static, rather than a behavioral, dynamic view of enterprises and of markets became widespread. This viewpoint reduced the entrepreneurs to the level of arithmeticians and eliminated all social and cultural context. The viewpoint presented here restores the balance and shows how to understand numerous facets of the behavior of enterprises by looking at the entrepreneurs and other decision makers behind them.[1]

1   What is a "market"?

One of the cornerstones of economic analysis is the concept of "the market" within which demand and supply curves are drawn and the equilibrium price, to which a firm in a competitive industry adjusts itself, is calculated. The definition of the market involves two steps: The first is to identify the purchasers, and the second to identify the group of sellers who are or could potentially serve these purchasers. The output, that is, the product together with its good substitutes, defines the relevant market. How to handle this definition in practice? Can it be handled?

Consider the following examples[2]:

1. Dry cleaning was once a growth industry. In the age of wool garments the boom was on. Yet 30 years later the industry was in decline. The good substitutes did not come from better ways of cleaning, but from the invention of synthetic fibers and chemical additives that have cut the need for dry cleaning. If the dry-cleaning industry was in trouble, it may have been because the decision makers in the industry assumed themselves to be in the "dry-cleaning market" rather than in the "cleaning market."

2. The film companies in Hollywood were once a growth industry. All of

them got into trouble and some disappeared with TV's inroads. Again, the substitutes did not come from movies produced elsewhere or better movies, but from the invention of TV. If the movie industry was in trouble, it may have been because the decision makers in this industry assumed themselves to be in the "movie business," when, in fact, they were in the entertainment business. Hollywood's managers scorned and rejected TV instead of perceiving the opportunity.

3. "Crude oil" was first, largely, a patent medicine. Before this fad ran out, the demand was expanded by the use of oil in kerosene lamps. During this time, oil companies competed with each other and against gaslight trying to improve the lamps. Then Edison invented his lamp, which would have greatly reduced the demand for oil. But at the same time kerosene started to be used in space heaters, preventing the decline. Later two further innovations occurred, *neither* originated by the oil industry. Coal-burning domestic central heating systems made the space heater obsolete, but the industry received a still persisting boost from the invention of the internal combustion engine. In the 1920s came the central oil heater (again an *outsider's* invention), and later the war helped the industry (facts that may lead one to suspect that the managers of the oil companies had more luck than innovative spirit). Centralized oil heating later ran into competition from natural gas. Even though the oil companies owned the gas, the industry did *not* originate the natural gas revolution (which was originated by the newly formed transmission companies, against the advice and resistance of the oil companies. The managers of these companies were ex-oil pipeline executives who were unable to persuade their companies on the profitability of the new opportunities). As in the previous examples, the managers of the oil industry perceived themselves to be in the "oil" market rather than the "heating," "light," or "transportation" business.

4. Gillette has had the lion's share of the world shaving products business since the turn of the century when King C. Gillette invented the disposable razor blade (in 1895), following a suggestion of a fellow inventor to come up with a product that once used, is thrown away. On this idea the corporation was built, and its dominant position secured by patents. Yet Bic, a European *pen* manufacturer threatens the entire Gillette franchise with the idea of a disposable razor.

These examples illustrate much more than the difficulties of handling the definition of markets and of the measurement of demand and supply curves in practice (later we shall look at them from other perspectives). But first let us see what light they shed on the concept of "the market," as defined in the first paragraph.

The definition includes a reference to "good substitutes." But "good substitutes" perceived by whom? In the previous examples, outsiders perceived them while the managers of dry-cleaning, movie, and oil businesses did not. If so, how can "the market" be defined? There will be as many definitions as perceptions. Numerous views will exist on what "the market," "the demand," and "the supply" curves are, and these notions are all subjectively defined. The actual quantities exchanged and the price at which they are exchanged will depend on all these perceptions, some erroneous, others not. The difficulty with the definition of markets arises because of *innovations*, innovations that change the number and quality of goods perceived as good substitutes, and because of different perceptions of demands for new products.[3]

Of course, one may give an objective, "product-oriented" definition of markets. But what for? In the aforementioned cases some entrepreneurs realized that there is no demand for crude oil, gasoline, or dry cleaning, but only for having light, driving a car, and having clean clothes. Indeed, one can argue that the narrow, product-oriented view has led some managers in the previously mentioned industries astray. Thus, if one wants to understand "the market mechanism" one must try to look at it from the point of view of decision makers participating in the market, or intending to do so, and see how such decisions are made, how people form or change their perceptions. Only by examining these questions, which are related to people's willingness to take risks and innovate, can one start and hope to shed light on how the world of business "works." This is the approach pursued in this study: There will be no aggregations, no supply curves, no demand curves. Only individuals trying to "mind" their business – literally speaking.

Briefly, as the story unfolds, it will become clear that the traditional notions of "markets," of "costs," of "profits," and of "production functions" are neither useful nor interesting (moreover, they are not even well defined). The approach pursued here will suggest both that the useful set of questions concerns inventions, innovations, entrepreneurship, and competition (but the latter will be defined here differently than in neoclassical economics), and that predictions about them can be made.

> The true characteristic of economic and social systems can only be
> discovered in periods of stress.
> 　　　　　　　　　　　Otto Eckstein, *The Great Recession*

2　　Decision making and the goal of enterprises

Frequently, in economic theory, an arbitrary distinction is made between the theory of households, which are assumed to maximize their utility, and the theory of firms, where the entrepreneur or the decision maker is assumed to maximize profits. Although attacks on this latter hypothesis have been frequent, no one, to my knowledge, has suggested a uniform approach toward all aspects of human behavior, including the behavior of business firms.[4] But such an approach is pursued here, continuing the line of argument presented in my two earlier books, where it has been used to examine numerous aspects of human behavior on small and large scales.[5]

Summarized briefly (the formalization of the views appears in the appendix to this chapter) the views suggest that bets on new ideas are triggered when the customary ways of behavior, failing to produce the expected results, lead to the perception of a loss in one's relative standing in a society. One can define this drive, this adaptive behavior, as being due to "fear of being hindered by others," "ambition," or "envy" (recall Mandeville's "Envy itself and Vanity/Were Ministers of Industry"). The perception of leapfrogging (i.e., of being outdone by one's fellows) leads to the following type of behavior:

- People may start to participate in games of chance that they have previously shunned.
- They may commit a crime, or an act not in accordance with existing customs.
- They may bet on new (i.e., noncustomary) ideas in general, on innovations and entrepreneurial acts in particular.

And the contrary: When aspirations are more than fulfilled, and people unexpectedly outrank their "fellows," they:

- Tend to take out insurance that they previously shunned.
- May avoid committing a crime that they contemplated before.
- May avoid implementing new ideas.

When aspirations are realized, not much can be said but that people will imitate rather than innovate and will pursue the beaten tracks. The three predictions are derived by assuming that people try to do their best when facing uncertain prospects and that the wealth distribution within the group of people with whom comparisons are made is pyramidal. That is, there are a few people on the top, some more in the middle, and larger and larger numbers below (additional assumptions will be discussed below).[6]

At first sight this departure point may seem unusual. In fact it is not and bears resemblance to Simon's view (1959). His view was that the behavior of "firms" should be examined through the prism of observations obtained in psychological studies where the following conclusions have been reached:

(a) Where performance falls short of the level of aspiration, search behavior (particularly search for new alternatives of action) is induced.
(b) At the same time, the level of aspiration begins to adjust itself downward until goals reach levels that are practically attainable.
(c) If the two mechanisms just listed operate too slowly to adapt aspirations to performance, emotional behavior – apathy or aggression, for example – will replace rational adaptive behavior. (p. 87)

Simon also notes that "the aspiration level defines a natural zero point in the scale of utility" (p. 87) and that "in most psychological theories the motive to act stems from *drives* and action terminates when the drive is satisfied" (p. 86). Although Simon has neither formalized these views nor tried to examine them systematically, the similarity in the departure points is evident. The difference is in objectives: In the preface to his book, Simon (1957) states that his goal is to construct a set of tools – a set of concepts and a vocabulary – suitable for *describing* an organization and the way in which it works.[7] My goal is different: Not only do I *not* want to build a new vocabulary, I want to eliminate existing ones. Furthermore, my goal is not only to describe events but to examine them from a viewpoint that has predictive power and then to see whether or not the stubborn facts contradict the predictions.

Entrepreneurs and their profits

As noted above, I do not intend to build a vocabulary. Instead this section will show what is the precise definition that can be given to some well-known words within this view of human behavior. The view's mathematical translation, so far as the bet on new ideas is considered, is the following: Let W_1 represent the wealth one aspired to and expected to achieve, and $\alpha(W > W_1)$ the fraction of people who would be richer. Let W_0 represent one's realized wealth and $\alpha(W > W_0)$ the respective percentage of richer people. $U(W_0, \alpha(W > W_0) \mid \alpha(W > W_1))$ denotes one's utility (a precise formulation of the conditional statement can be found in the appendix to this chapter). It is assumed that as one's wealth increases, so does one's utility (when other people's wealth, with whom comparisons are made, remains constant). But one's utility diminishes if one's wealth stays constant, whereas everybody with whom comparisons are made is becoming significantly richer. The intuition behind this formulation and the deeper philosophical implications are discussed elsewhere – here only some of its practical implications will be explored.[8]

Let P denote the amount invested in developing an idea, which, besides the direct costs of investment in time and other resources, also includes the resources spent in trying to discover the potential demand. Let H denote the increase in wealth that one expects to gain by selling the idea. With a probability p, the potential innovator or entrepreneur guesses that he will lose the amount P. The condition under which an individual becomes an innovator or an entrepreneur, that is, bets on a new idea is (omitting the conditional statements):

$$U(W_0, \alpha(W \geq W_0)) \leq pU(W_0 - P, \alpha(W \geq W_0 - P)) + (1 - p)U(W_0 + H,$$
$$\alpha(W \geq W_0 + H)) \tag{1}$$

where p, H, and P all represent *subjective* judgments by individuals and it is impossible both to determine whether one is right or wrong, and to r like comparisons among individuals. The costs and benefits are subjective and exist only in the decision maker's mind.

Suppose then that W_0 represented the wealth and $\alpha(W \geq W_0)$ the status one aspired to, and that at this level of wealth, one avoided implementing a particular idea. That is, suppose the inequality in equation (1) is reversed. What changes can lead to a change of mind? What changes can now reverse the inequality?

There are several possibilities:

1. The individual may perceive that the cost of investing in developing and implementing an idea may have significantly diminished, or that the gains from this idea may have significantly increased. This is a trivial statement; the nontrivial question is what happened in the society that could have led to this change in perceptions. This issue will be discussed in Chapter 3, where such changes will be linked to those in relative prices, and in the last chapter, where they will be linked with broader considerations.

2. The individual is, or is suddenly threatened to be, outranked within a hierarchy. Taking the risk one was previously reluctant to take (which is here equivalent to the creative, entrepreneurial act) may restore or even improve one's position. To put it simply: For those who suddenly fell behind, the incentives to begin ''thinking'' (i.e., to bet on new ideas) increase. As Samuel Johnson wrote a long time ago: ''The mind is seldom quickened to very rigorous operations but by pain, or the dread of pain.''[9]

Let us turn now to the definitions that can be given to some words within this model: An ''entrepreneur'' is an individual who bets on novel (i.e., non-customary) ideas and tries to implement them.[10] This view of the act and the model that led to this definition enable one to infer two things: First, that discussions on entrepreneurship cannot be made without reference to the social and legal environment (since the definition refers to customs), and second, that a distinction can be made between ''risky'' and ''uncertain'' states.[11] Let us see how.

When circumstances are expected to be stable, traditions shape people's aspirations and expectations. The outcomes of the customary ways of action are properly incorporated and discounted in the notion of ''wealth.'' In particular, no changes in perceptions (of gains, costs, or probabilities) can be assumed to occur (since they would contradict the assumption of stability). Thus, although people may be involved in acts such as gambling on games of chance or buying defective products, the effects of these outcomes are already taken into account and their occurrence does not alter people's willingness to undertake entrepreneurial acts. Such situations can be defined as ''risky.''

Of course, even in these circumstances misfortune may strike and one can ask: Would not individuals thus affected become entrepreneurs or criminals? The answer is that if customs or redistributive taxes existed that led to expectations that these individuals would either be compensated for the loss, or severely punished if they deviated from tradition, the entrepreneurial act would be less likely to be undertaken. The model provides some good reasons for such customs or such systems of taxation to evolve (eventually – as indeed they did)[12] since within it they are the responses that maintain stability.[13]

But if, for reasons beyond human control, some societies have been subject to frequent significant shocks, preventing the accumulation of institutional dust (in the form of such customs and redistributive policies), entrepreneurial bets will be more frequent. For two reasons: First, the shocks cause disorder, significantly altering some people's position in the wealth distribution; and second, they alter the perceptions of costs and benefits associated with the implementation of various ideas. Thus, in these circumstances, people are more likely to undertake acts never done by either themselves or anyone else before. A certain group of people, those whose lives have been disordered (as the evidence discussed later suggests), pin their hopes on precisely this instability in the institutions of their society and seize the opportunity for getting richer. Such states can be defined as "uncertain," since people bet on and implement ideas that did not come to life before. (Although they may have "crossed people's minds" – note that this expression has a literal interpretation within the model.)

The distinction between "risky" and "uncertain" situations also enables one to see what is the meaning of "profits," and how profits are associated with "uncertainty." When only risky activities are undertaken, the outcomes, being already discounted, can only lead to relatively minor fluctuations in one's relative wealth. Thus, no innovations are expected to occur and, if one could measure profits properly, one should find them equal to zero. In contrast, the bet on new ideas involves, by definition, the creation of new "wealth" when a lucky hit is made, and such "hits" bring profits.[14]

This view suggests that the meaning of "profit maximization" and the behavior that will characterize firms will become radically different from what they are in the traditional theories of the firm. According to it, profits can be increased either when entrepreneurs make lucky hits or when managers succeed in giving the proper incentives to employees to bet more frequently on new ideas (or just by chance – but that is under no one's control). The behavior of firms is characterized by the individual who calculates risks and makes the decisions. The surviving entrepreneurs, managers (and hence their firms), are those who either have made relatively fewer mistakes or who have been lucky (*ceteris paribus,* i.e., neglecting, for the moment, the effects of political intervention).

In contrast, the traditional economic theories view the firm as performing a simple arithmetic calculation, which, as Baumol (1968) puts it, "becomes a passive calculator that reacts mechanically to changes imposed on it by fortuitous and external developments. . . . One hears of no clever ruses, ingenious schemes, brilliant innovations, of no charisma or of any of the other stuff of which outstanding entrepreneurship is made. . . . The model is essentially an instrument of optimality analysis of well-defined problems, and it is precisely such . . . problems which need no entrepreneur for their solution" (p. 67) and, one should add, no economists either. Even when the language of game theory has been adopted to examine the behavior of firms, no additional insights are gained. Within game theory a criterion of "rationality" is defined, a term that within my model is without interest since the model deals with dynamic circumstances, when people "change their minds," whereas "rationality," as defined in game theory in particular, refers to static circumstances. Moreover game theory says something about strategic competence *only*. But such competence is of no help in the analysis of situations when changes in risk-taking propensity are the determinants of outcomes. And when are they not?[15]

Motivations of owners and managers

At first sight it would seem that the definitions and descriptions given above could mainly fit enterprises where the decision maker is also the owner of the enterprise, but not when ownership and control of the firm's activities are separated. But as will be argued below, this is not the case – the previous definitions can be used in the context of any enterprise.

Consider first the owner: If one assumes that he tries to do his best, one assumes that he tries to do it with respect to any decision, in his business in particular – the individual does not have two "utility" functions, one explaining his decisions at home and the other at work. However, this statement does not imply that the owner will at all times pursue new ideas, which within this model represent the only way to make profits.[16] If a person achieves the status to which he or she aspired or, by chance, exceeds it, this person stops betting on new ideas and insures himself. If no outside shocks occur, an enterprise that has such an individual at its helm will be characterized from then on by a stable level of difference between revenues and measured costs. The meaning within the model of statements such as "this firm could not do better," or "could not further raise profits" (i.e., profits are "maximized") is only that under *this* entrepreneur's leadership it could not. What an enterprise lacks within this model is not opportunities but imagination and audacity. Opportunities are not "given" in this model, but taken, seized. Thus, the problem of the firm must be identified with that of the entrepreneur interacting with given institutional features of a society.

The characterization of enterprises where control and ownership are separated is not significantly different.[17] Suppose that the decision makers' income within such an enterprise depends on its performance, an index for which is the difference between revenues and measured costs. This implies that their wealth also depends on this measure, and, so long as they try to do the best for themselves, they will also try to do their best to increase the aforementioned difference.

How can the owners infer whether or not the decision makers in the enterprise they own indeed do their best? There are two possible ways: The owners must make comparisons either with past experience that shaped anticipations or with outside standards of comparison (for example, a competitor's experience).[18] But the managers know that too and realize that if their performance falls short either of the owners' expectations or of their competitor's performance, their ''heads may roll,'' wiping out reputation and wealth. This interaction imposes on managers the necessity to make comparisons both with other firms' performances and with the firm's past, customary, performance. Thus, one obtains a behavior pattern of decision makers within such enterprises that is not really different from that of an entrepreneurial firm.

At the same time, the following reservations must be made when interpreting such behavior. Let us assume that the owners have received (and anticipated) a 10 percent return on their venture, a rate that owners in comparable enterprises have also received. In this case the 10 percent will determine both the owners' and the managers' behavior, and define the customary level of profits. Decision makers choosing careers in this sector estimate their wealth by relying on this figure.

What happens if suddenly the rate of return in just *one* enterprise drops to 5 percent (or in all the others it increases to 15 percent)? The owners can give two interpretations to this alteration: Either that their decision makers met with a stroke of bad luck or that the decision makers made an erroneous decision. If they adopt the first interpretation, they may give to the decision makers another chance. In the other case, they may either try to replace the managers (or a takeover will be attempted) or give them another chance. There may be good reasons for providing people additional chances, since they will bet on new ideas and thus learn if they are set back significantly by either a misfortune or an error.

Suppose that an individual finds himself at the helm of such an enterprise (where management and ownership are separated), and his aspirations were achieved at a certain level of wealth (derived in part from income received for his services for the enterprise). What happens if unexpectedly (due to good luck) the measured profits of the enterprise increase and the decision maker, being compensated, achieves a significantly higher level of wealth? The views presented here predict that the decision maker will try to "insure" himself, and that customary, cautious strategies will characterize such an enterprise from then on. This observation is not novel: Levitt (1960), for example, wrote:

The belief that profits are assured by expanding and more affluent population is dear to the heart of every industry. It takes the edge off the apprehensions everybody understandably feels about the future. If consumers are multiplying and also buying more of your product or service, you can face the future with considerably more comfort than if the market is shrinking. An expanding market keeps the manufacturer from having to think very hard or imaginatively. If thinking is an intellectual response to a problem, then the absence of a problem leads to the absence of thinking (p. 48).

These arguments do not imply that an enterprise whose profits are rising will necessarily be characterized by conservative, unimaginative behavior. The previous discussions just suggest that the behavior depends, in part, on the personal characteristics of the decision maker, who happens to be at the top of the enterprise at that point in time. If the wealth derived from the enterprise exceeds the decision maker's aspirations, conservative behavior results; but if the decision maker's aspirations are not yet satisfied even by the higher level of wealth, he will continue to bet on new ventures.

Consider now an alternative, hypothetical situation: Suppose that profits fall, or are expected to (because of a threat of entry, for example). What will decision makers do? As in the previous discussion, no unequivocal answer can be given. The reaction depends on the decision makers' realized wealth and the status it defines (which depends on the enterprise's current and future performance) relative to the status they aspired to. If it exceeded it, the enterprise will not pursue new ventures. But if the enterprise's performance is perceived to be significantly threatened (and thus the wealth the decision makers expected to derive from it significantly lowered), decision makers may decide to pursue new ventures. The reactions are, however, not automatic or mechanical.

Thus, within this model, individuals – call them "leaders" if you want – play a central role in explaining the behavior of enterprises. Also, the *fluctuations* in the history of the enterprise of its decision makers may provide a clue as to its future performance. In this sense, the empirical examinations that are required to falsify my views must be undertaken in a "historical" context.[19] Ahistorical examinations are inappropriate. It is useful for the moment to illustrate these arguments by the goal of General Motors' new chief executive, Roger B. Smith, and the reaction to it: " 'I'll stop panting' when GM attains a 10% profit margin, he says. That is the bench mark that has stuck in every GM executive's mind since it was last attained in 1965." Executives within the company recognize their problems may be due to those early successes, which led to the quite widespread attitude that being the best, further "intellectual risk taking" was to be discouraged. Some suggest that this "in-breed thinking" may turn out to be Mr. Smith's biggest obstacle in revitaliz-ing the company. At Ford of Canada, Arthur Hanton, its vice-president, said that the company's two successive years of after-tax losses ($86 million in 1980), and a steadily declining market share, led to a radical departure in the company's hierarchical structure, decision-making process, and strategies: "It's not an overstatement to say the trauma of those losses represented a religious experience for us."[20]

In conclusion, the goal of enterprises within this model is *not* "profit max-imization" (a term, that as shown later, has never been precisely defined) but something much more complex, depending, in part, on the entrepreneurs' and decision makers' perceptions and personalities. Enterprises are characterized by calculating risks and by making decisions, sometimes erroneous, some-times correct ones. The surviving and flourishing enterprises are those in which either fewer mistakes were made, their decision makers stumbled on some good ideas and seized the opportunity, or fortune smiled upon them.[21]

Profit maximization, production, and cost functions – are they irrelevant concepts?

It is relatively easy to criticize and attack theories. It is more difficult to provide alternative ones and reexamine a wide range of facts within their light. Many studies therefore just chose the first step. But, although criticism may have been justified, these types of studies may have little effect since without providing an alternative, the criticized approach still remains the only game in town. Still it is important to review a sample of the criticism on the theory of the firm and show how the approach pursued here provides not only answers but a workable alternative.

Traditionally, a firm is assumed to maximize the residual share – the prof-its. But "who" is this firm that is making the maximization is not made clear. The theory leaves unsolved the question of whether short- or long-run profits are maximized. Long-run profit maximization implies maximization of the enterprise's current and future income stream. But how far into the future? And, since such a calculation requires predictions about future events that are inherently uncertain, probabilities and attitudes toward risks must be taken into account. But whose? And since risks are involved, one needs a theory with predictive power telling us how such attitudes are formed and change. Traditional theories of the firm do not address these issues, and do not have a theory explaining attitudes toward risks that has predictive power.[22] But this issue can be addressed within the framework presented here.

If the answer to the aforementioned questions is that the entrepreneurs and other decision makers provide the clue to the firms' behavior, then "utility" rather than profits will be maximized, as indeed Simon (1959) noted:

The entrepreneur may obtain all kinds of "psychic income" from the firm, quite apart from monetary rewards. If he is to maximize his utility, then he will sometimes balance a loss of profits against an increase in psychic income. But if we allow "psychic income," the criterion of profit maximization loses all of its definiteness. . . . The entrepreneur may not care to maximize, but may simply want to earn a return that he regards as satisfactory. (p. 85)

Moreover, once the notion of expectations and uncertainty is taken into account, the fact that only *subjective* interpretations can be given to the variables manipulated by firms comes to the fore, as Machlup (1946) emphasized a long time ago:

It should hardly be necessary to mention that all the relevant magnitudes involved – costs, revenue, profit – are subjective – that is, perceived or fancied by the men whose decisions or actions are to be explained . . . rather than "objective". . . . Marginal analysis of the firm should not be understood to imply anything but subjective estimates, guesses and hunches. (pp. 521–2)

Similar observations can also be frequently found in Buchanan's, Kirzner's, and others' writings.[23]

There have been a number of economists who made the observation that firms do not maximize profits and that new insights can be gained by looking at the motivations of individuals who make decisions in the firm. As already noted, Simon (1957, 1959) and Baumol (1968) make this observation. But they are not the only ones: Becker's *Economics of Discrimination,* Williamson's *The Economics of Discretionary Behaviour: Managerial Objectives in a Theory of the Firm,* Marris's *The Economic Theory of Managerial Capitalism,* and Leibenstein's *General X-Efficiency* pursue this line of argument.[24] Yet, as Baumol (1968) has pointed out, though these types of models may serve some objective, they do not take us a whit further in the analysis of entrepreneurship, of risk taking:

For example, consider what Oliver Williamson has described as the "managerial discretion models," in which the businessman is taken to maximize the number of persons he employs, or sales, or still another objective distinct from profits. True, this businessman has (somewhere outside of the confines of the model) made a choice which was no mere matter of calculation. He has decided . . . to assign priority to some goal other than profit. But having made this choice he becomes, no less than the profit maximizer, a calculating robot, a programmed mechanical component in the automatic system that constitutes the firm. . . . Nor can the "practical pertinence" of the decision variables make the difference in carving out a place for the entrepreneur. Maximization models have recently been developed in which, instead of prices and outputs, the decision variables are the firm's real investment program, or its financial mix . . ., or the attributes of a new product to be launched by the company. These decisions seem to smell more of the ingredients of entrepreneurship. But . . . their calculations are again mechanistic and automatic and call for no display of entrepreneurial initiative. (p. 68)

Instead, Baumol suggests pursuing an approach that would consider *neither* the means the entrepreneur employs nor the process whereby he arrives at his decisions but examines instead his attitudes toward risks and the payoffs of his activity (p. 70). These features characterize the departure point here.

But if all these observations have been made, how did economists deal with the criticism? How did they define "profits," "production," and "cost" functions, and deal with the distinction between "uncertainty" and "risk"?

Although some economists have argued that no distinction should be made between "uncertainty" and "risk," others have argued the opposite position, without, however, indicating how. Keynes's (1921) *Treatise on Probability* makes such an unsuccessful attempt. Yet in spite of the devastating criticism of the book, Keynes did not seem to change his mind that such distinction is meaningful, and the idea surfaces a number of times in the *General Theory* published 15 years later[25]:

Thus if the animal spirits are dimmed and the spontaneous optimism falters, leaving us to depend on nothing but a mathematical expectation, enterprise will fade and die. (p. 162)

We are . . . reminding ourselves that human decisions affecting the future, whether personal or political or economic, cannot depend on strict mathematical expectation, since the basis for making such calculations does not exist; and that it is our innate rage to activity which makes the wheels go round, our rational selves choosing between the alternatives as best as we are able, calculating where we can, but often falling back for our motive on whim or sentiment or chance. (pp. 162–3)

Knight (1921) too makes the relationship between profits and uncertainty and argues that only the latter concept, rather than risk, can be related to "pure profits," an opinion that is accurate within the model.[26] For most economists, "profits" are associated with "noncontractual costs." These amounts are equal to the difference between total receipts and total contractual costs, and are received by the owner of the entrepreneurial capacity. Friedman (1975) adds some notes to this definition:

This term [profits] is, however, somewhat misleading. The actual non-contractual costs can never be determined in advance. They can be known only after the event and may be affected by all sorts of random or accidental occurrences, mistakes on the part of the firm, and so on. It is therefore important to distinguish between actual non-contractual costs and expected non-contractual costs. The difference between actual and expected non-contractual costs constitutes "profits" or "pure profits" – an unanticipated residual arising from uncertainty. Expected non-contractual costs, on the other hand, are to be regarded as a "rent" or "quasi-rent" to entrepreneurial capacity. They are to be regarded as the motivating force behind the firm's decisions. (p. 99)

He then adds: "More precisely, expected utility corresponding to the probability distribution of non-contractual costs is what the firm is to be regarded as maximizing" (p. 99).[27] But this argument, if brought to its logical conclusion, would imply a discussion on whose utility is being maximized, whose expectations and perceptions of probability distributions are concerned, what are "the firm's" attitudes toward risk, and how to redefine the vocabulary, since only subjective concepts are involved. Friedman never discusses these issues. But, as the next quote shows, Friedman seemed to be well aware of the fact that in making the aforementioned definitions he was only playing with words:

. . . implicit in the view we are adopting [is] the notion that each individual can, as a formal matter, be regarded as owning two types of resources: (1) His resources viewed exclusively as "hired" resources – what his resources would be if he were not to form his own firm. . . . (2) A resource that reflects the difference between the productivity of his resources viewed solely as hired resources and their productivity when owned by his firm – we may call this "Mr. X's entrepreneurial capacity." . . . It should be emphasized that this distinction between the two types of resources is purely formal. Giving names to our ignorance may be useful; it does not dispel the ignorance. A really satisfactory theory would do more than say there must be something other than hired resources; it would say what the essential characteristics of the "something other" are. (p. 95)[28]

The model and arguments presented here provide exactly such a theory and avoids this kind of vocabulary, which only leads to the illusion that our ignorance has been dispelled.

Part of the literature about industrial organization and the theory of the firm deals with production and cost functions and attempts to find their shapes. Let us examine again what is hiding behind its technical vocabulary and these examinations. Few studies deal in depth with this issue, Friedman (1975) being an exception. He states:

The individual's entrepreneurial capacity can . . . be specified by a production function, showing the maximum quantity of a product *he* is capable of producing under given conditions with given quantities of "hired" resources (including any he "hires" from himself). Thus if X_i represents the quantity of product produced by individual i, and $a, b, c, \ldots$ the quantities of various factors he uses, we can conceive of $X_i = f_i$ $(a, b, c \ldots)$ as the production function attached to the individual. (p. 98)

In other words, what a "production function" represents is how an entrepreneur or a manager *perceives* the way to produce a certain good. Can an outsider "objectively" estimate such a function? The answer is NO. For notice that in its definition one of the factors of production is the amount the "entrepreneur" or the "manager" hires from "himself" – a concept that is not observable. The only thing outsiders can perceive is whether or not the difference between revenues and costs are lower or higher in one enterprise than in another that produces the same good. This observation can be inferred by making *comparisons* with the performance of other enterprises within the same sector. Moreover, the risk-taking ability is viewed as a factor of production too, assumed to be separated from one's entrepreneurial talent. In contrast, according to the views presented here, this separation cannot be done.

What can one learn from the aforementioned comparison if the aforementioned difference is lower? Two interpretations are possible: either that the decision makers in the enterprise with the lower profitability made an error or that they are satisfied with a lower measurable rate of return on their performance. What can outsiders then recommend? To try to correct the error in the first case and, unless a historical perspective is taken nothing clearcut can be recommended in the second case. For, a priori, it is unclear on what grounds one can recommend that people should be pushed to be either more ambitious or make more efforts. Thus, the statement frequently used in economic analysis "that some outcomes are inefficient" has no interesting interpretation within my view of the world. It either implies the obvious, that is, that errors were made (but to err is human) or that some people are not as ambitious or as driven as others. That's how the previous technical language used to describe some features of the firm can be translated to a language that describes everyday human behavior.

What then do the many estimates of "production functions" made by economists reflect? They merely reflect correlations between averages, averaging out individual characteristics of each firm, the entrepreneurial talent employed by them in particular. Needless to repeat that by doing so, no light can be shed either on a firm's behavior or on competition (a subject discussed in Chapter 3).

Since a cost function is derived from a firm's production function, its interpretation is subject to the same reservations as made above. It cannot be quantified in the way economists do for the simple reason that the compensation for one of the factors of production, as Friedman noted, refers to "the resources one hires from oneself" (including the entrepreneur's ability to take risks) – which is *never* measurable. Costs – it will be recalled – are defined as forgone opportunities – but can outsiders know what individuals imagine to be the alternative uses of their skills? Such alternatives exist only in the entrepreneurs' and decision makers' minds. The only thing one can learn when looking at the expenditures of an enterprise is whether or not they were high or low relative to either anticipations or to those of other enterprises producing similar goods. But, as suggested above, numerous interpretations can be given to a significant difference, if such a difference is found. These observations too are not entirely novel: Stocking and Watkins (1948) noted that "business costs are not uniformly defined or easily determined. They are as variable as human judgement and accounting practice. What the businessman chooses to treat as costs, under whatever accounting category he may record the expenditure or in whatever accounting period he may reach to recover the outlay, depends on managerial judgement'' (p. 105).[29] Before continuing with the theoretical discussion, it may be useful to illustrate parts of it by looking at some statements that Henry Ford made in his autobiography:

Our policy is to reduce the price, extend the operations, and improve the article. You will notice that the reduction in price comes first. We have never considered any costs as fixed. Therefore we first reduce the price to the point where we believe more sales will result. Then we go ahead and try to make the prices. . . . The more usual way is to take the costs and then determine the price, and although that method may be scientific in the narrow sense, it is not scientific in the broad sense, because what earthly use is it to know the cost if it tells you that you cannot manufacture at a price at which the article can be sold? But more to the point is the fact that although one may calculate what a cost is . . . no one knows what a cost ought to be. One of the ways of discovering . . . is to name a price so low *as to force* everybody in the place to the highest point of efficiency. . . . We make more discoveries concerning manufacturing and selling under this forced method than by any method of leisurely investigation. (pp. 146–7, italics added)

Although Ford uses a somewhat imprecise language, the view of human behavior presented here provides a justification for the possible success of his operating philosophy. Ford's lower price imposes a choice on his subordinates of either becoming more innovative, making greater efforts, or losing their jobs. Ford's idea that at $500 he could sell millions of cars was a bet, but a bet perceived to be *realistic* enough to challenge his subordinates[30] (at $250 the idea may have been perceived as ''crazy''). It may be also useful to note a feature of the period that led to Ford's bet since it is linked with some of the broader implications of the model. In 1906, fearing that the ''motorcar mania'' would incite the poor to envy the rich, Woodrow Wilson suggested that the automobile might carry socialism to America. It was a year later that Ford announced his mission, which could solve this problem: building a car that anyone making a decent income could buy.[31]

3   What do firms do?

Let us now recapitulate and see how some features of the behavior of enterprises can be characterized within the view of human nature proposed here.

What do enterprises do? In order to answer this question one had to clarify first what is hiding behind the word ''enterprise.'' The word is defined by the law: The law establishes their rights and obligations, and laws and customs will determine their behavior. But in what sense precisely can one speak about their ''behavior''?

Suppose that a family owns a restaurant and that only family members run it. If one attributes predictable behavior to this firm, it means that one attributes predictable behavior to whoever is making the final decision in the family. Thus, if one assumes that families have some goals, one must assume that such firms serve as one of the *means* for achieving that goal. Yet the economic literature (with few exceptions) assumes that households and firms have different motivations and does not try to use a uniform departure point to examine their behavior. But such an approach has been suggested in the previous sections.

Why did households decide to cooperate and sell something to other people? To put it simply, some people may have believed that they had an idea that they could sell and thus get richer. Or, to paraphrase Manne, one can say that every business gets organized in order to *exploit some ideas*.[32] The idea may have been either a novel one or just an adaptation of one that worked before. Such ideas may come to life when a number of individuals cooperate directly, each making a contribution: One may be the entrepreneur who offers the idea, the other may provide the managerial ability, while the third may gamble on the venture and provide the needed financial resources. Such organizations may eventually become relatively large, and the owners (shareholders, for example) may no longer have direct control over those who make decisions within the corporation. But, as suggested until now, the deeper process underlying the behavior of such organizations can be discussed in terms similar to that used for simpler ones.

Any enterprise must have a few individuals, whether the entrepreneur or the chief executive, who assume responsibility: They are the people who bet on new ideas and implement them whether in management, technologies, or strategies promoting their business. This view enabled one to perceive how profits can be associated with chance, uncertainty, and some specific institutional features of society. Let us now see how additional words, such as "productivity" and "teamwork," pertinent to the behavior of enterprises, can be defined without this framework.

Betting on new ideas and implementing them involves the creation of new wealth when lucky hits are made: An outsider (an accountant or an economist) would measure an increase in profits. But profits can be increased not only if the entrepreneur bets on a new idea but also if he or a manager finds ways for their *subordinates* to bet more frequently on new ideas; let us call this induced increased betting activity an increased "productivity."[33] How can managers do that? The view of human behavior suggested here points toward several strategies: One is having significant differences in the wages of similarly trained individuals and having fewer positions at the higher wages. Such a wage structure could provide incentives for some individuals who are ambitious and fear falling behind to gamble on novel ideas. For, at one point in their life cycle, their expectations may be frustrated. Assume that one expected to achieve a higher-paying job (or a job with greater status) at the age of 30 or 40 with some probability. One's aspirations took into account this probability. But suppose that the individual suddenly realizes that his chances to fulfill his expectations have significantly diminished. What will such an individual do? According to the view of human behavior presented here, this individual may make greater efforts and gamble more frequently on new ideas. Thus the feasibility of leapfrogging within a hierarchy provides incentives for increasing productivity.[34] A method of promoting new ideas within such a structure is – paradoxical as it may first seem – to encourage peers to first deflate these ideas. This peer reaction, by frustrating the subordinates' expectations, may lead them to work harder. Such strategy seems to be used not only by "America's Best-Run Companies" [as documented in Peters and Waterman (1982)] but also by some presidents of the United States who want their secretary of state to be more effective, as the next statements suggest:

We don't kill ideas, but we *do* deflect them. We bet on people. . . . You invariably have to kill a program at least once before it succeeds. That's how you get down to the fanatics, those who are really emotionally committed to find a way – any way – to make it work. (p. 230)

while Kissinger (1982) in his memoirs said that Nixon was convinced that his special talents would flourish under conditions of personal insecurity, and that Nixon saw to it that he developed some doubts about his standing with him. The model suggests, however, that these strategies may backfire and lead not only to originality but to other noncustomary behavior as well (of a criminal nature) among the individuals who are under pressure – more about that in the next section and chapters.

These arguments already suggest what "teamwork" implies within this model, and why it induces the contractual form called "the firm." Some managers may find the proper incentives for some employees to bet more frequently on new ideas and thus to become more productive. However, these incentives may work for some people and not for others. Thus, people's productivity may increase under some managers' schemes and strategies, but not under others' (as an intuitive example consider how differently orchestras perform under different conductors). In this sense one can speak about the productivity of a team, and see the motivation for the contractual form that characterizes firms: The managers must *know* their employees in order to find out how to motivate them to become more "entrepreneurial." No price mechanism can substitute for this continuous *interaction* within a team and for the perception of the leapfrogging process, which is at the heart of the emergence of new ideas and thus the increased "productivity."[35] The observed wage and price structures represent only one facet of this deeper, entrepreneurial process that takes place. The next section elaborates this interaction between hierarchy and productivity.

4 Hierarchy, leapfrogging, and productivity

Within the views presented here, risk taking, productivity, and leapfrogging within a hierarchical structure are *inseparable* concepts. The hierarchy in the enterprise and society, within which mobility is perceived as feasible, and thus leapfrogging occurs, provides the motivation for betting on new ideas and making greater efforts. At the same time continuous efforts will be made to prevent some from jumping ahead and thus try to maintain stability. If successful, such attempts maintain productivity at existing levels. At times, this stability is achieved through subtle forms, as the next studies illustrate.

In a series of classic studies of the behavior of workers conducted between 1927 and 1932 at the Western Electric Company's Hawthorne Works in Chicago, researchers found that the men conformed to a "norm" of output, which was achieved by a variety of social interactions in the workplace, and represented a group of workers' conception of a fair day's work. By what mechanism exactly was stability maintained? If one turned out "too much work," he was called a "ratebuster," a "cyclone," and given an unfriendly gesture (a "binging," that is, an as hard as possible pat on one's upper arm). At the same time, there were also reactions against the "saboteurs" who turned out too little work.[36] These interactions increased the subjective costs and diminished the subjective benefits associated with mobility and maintained stable productivity.

Can managers and entrepreneurs change this rigid structure and increase productivity and profits? The evidence presented next suggests how they may try, but that it is not easy (more evidence will be presented in the next chapters, 5 in particular, although in a different context).

A Xerox advertisement says that "Productivity is a manager who helps subordinates grow." In the previous case either there were no such managers or the managers decided that the norms achieved were the best possible (compared with performance in other sectors) and no nonconformist behavior was to be encouraged since such encouragement could also have backfired. Indeed, some case studies have found that pitting workers against each other backfires at times, disrupting a team. A European bank gave managers bonuses to encourage competition among them. The bank found out that a manager steered customers to rival banks rather than to another branch. A Los Angeles insurance company ranked offices according to how frequently they distributed disability payments on time. One of the consequences of this altered ranking system was that when one office got a claim that was meant for another, workers used the mail rather than the telephone to redirect the information in attempts to lower the performance of another office.[37] In the monthly publication of the U.S. Chamber of Commerce, there was an article on the seven deadly sins of management, dealing with envy, among others. Envy was said to be found sometimes in superiors toward their more talented and efficient subordinates or among colleagues who, from envy, band together in cliques against the more talented man.[38] These patterns of behavior are by no means novel: In the Bible (Genesis 26:14–15) one reads: "For he had possession of flocks, and possession of herds . . . and the Philistines envied him. For all the wells which his father's servants had digged . . . the Philistines had stopped them, and filled them with earth." According to Schoeck (1969), envy of a neighbor's herd of cattle and an assault on his water supply are the order of the day in many villages in South America today.[39] Thus, although perceptions of inequality and the feasibility of leapfrogging are *necessary* to promote innovative acts, one must also be aware of its dangers – more facts in the next chapters.

These are not the only dangers that face entrepreneurs and managers who try to increase productivity and profits. According to Drucker (1984), the only thing common to the companies who were J.P. Morgan's clients 80 years ago and who performed poorly was that each level of management was paid 130 percent more than the next rank (the other companies who performed better had more gradual increases associated with ranks). How can one interpret this evidence? Note that the judgment for one's performance can only be made by comparisons with other performances. If the customary increases between ranks were, let say, of a 50 percent magnitude between ranks, the noncustomary, significant increases above them may be interpreted by those falling behind as a sign of "greed" and "dishonesty" of the superior ranks, provoking "criminal" rather than entrepreneurial acts.[40] The consequent acts of sabotage or of provision of lower level of efforts will lead to the measurement of lower productivity. Thus, although within the view of human behavior presented here hierarchy is a *necessary* condition to promote innovations (as is the feasibility of leapfrogging), a change to a steeper pyramidal structure ("steeper" relative to customary ones) may be dangerous too. This conclusion too is not exactly novel and has been made in much broader contexts since ancient times. Pythagoreans believed that "the eternal fact of inevitable inequality underlies everything and is the basis for social institutions. Society is made up of individuals differing in virtue and other qualities, some of whom are naturally rulers, some naturally subjects. . . . The perfectly harmonious and truly well-ordered state is achieved by the cooperation of both classes (rulers and ruled), each within its proper sphere" [as quoted in Spengler (1968), p. 221], while according to Aristotle if "inequality becomes extreme (i.e., when 'unequals' are not treated in proportion to the inequality existing between them), and men become aware of this inequality, government becomes unstable and revolution tends to result" [as quoted in Spengler (1968, p. 272)].

In conclusion, the views presented here provide some suggestions on how managers and entrepreneurs can increase productivity and profits: Impose a hierarchical structure, which should be neither too rigid nor too steep. Progress through the hierarchy should not be automatic and predictable, but both management and subordinates must perceive some threats from either insiders or outsiders.[41] The roles of hierarchy and of the feasibility of leapfrogging suggest why it is not the wage structure that plays a decisive role within these views, but rather the way this structure is perceived: Whether or not one can jump within it and whether or not it significantly departs from customary ones. Note, however, that by implementing such strategies, entrepreneurs and managers walk on a tightrope since the same strategies may lower productivity and profits rather than increase them (since leapfrogging may cause criminal acts too, and a too "mild" hierarchy relative to the one existing in other enterprises may diminish the subordinates' propensity to bet on new ideas).[42] If these recommendations seem slightly vague, they should be. I don't look for pseudoclarity, but only for as much clarity and precision as the subject – human behavior – permits.

5   Where is the demand curve?

Let us return now to the notion of the market where the arguments started. Within the standard, neoclassical analysis, markets are always characterized by demand-and-supply curves. It is assumed that the prices in the "long run" impose some "normal" valuation upon the contribution of the entrepreneur (but which, as already pointed out, has never been defined), and then some static, equilibrium conditions are described.[43] Such a case presented no problem of "market" definition (or of demand) since it was assumed that equally efficient sellers sell a single homogeneous product for which there are (by assumption) no close substitutes and that nobody is trying to invent some.

Within the model presented here, this whole exercise is meaningless. For in "static," "stable" circumstances, the word "entrepreneur" cannot be even defined. In static circumstances, by definition, there are no new ideas. The same goods and services are produced over and over, generation after generation, by the same method. One can only speak about imitators and memory in such models but not of either entrepreneurs or creativity. (Such exercises, however, are not totally without interest, and some of their implications may be useful for examining features of relatively stagnant societies, in particular those that we call "primitive.")[44]

Once one abandons the assumptions of static equilibrium, much of the structure built on demand-and-supply analysis seems to crumble for the simple reason that "the demand" can no longer be well defined once inventions are taken into account. When entrepreneurs implement new ideas and offer new products, they make *a guess* of what might be the demand out there and their perceptions differ. They may be wrong, in which case they will lose part of their wealth, or they may be right. Only some entrepreneurs perceive the demand for the new product; others obviously either don't or think that at the cost at which they can produce it, they may lose. Until now several examples were given to illustrate how in such a changing world some entrepreneurs perceived demands that others did not – the history of Ford, of the managers of Hollywood's studios, of the dry-cleaning industry, and of those involved in various facets of the oil industry, showed the two possibilities. The lesson is clear: Demand may be perceived, discovered; but it is impossible to define the supply (or average and marginal costs) for different hypothetical outputs without making reference to perceptions of demand. This conclusion is not exactly novel: Friedman (1955) remarked that "the existence of specialized resources [the entrepreneur?] not only complicates the definition of optimum size; even more important, it makes it impossible to define the average cost of a particular firm or different hypothetical outputs independently of conditions of demand" (p. 233) – the missing word in this statement is *"perceptions"* before the words "conditions of demand."[45]

Economists have been aware of the difficulties of handling the definition of markets in practice, but without linking them to innovations. Posner (1976), for example, discusses the failure of antitrust law to develop a sensible approach to product market definition. He criticizes the law because of its failure either to consider substitution in production or to apply correctly principles of substitution in consumption. Yet to argue that the notion of cross-elasticities (since they are assumed to measure "good substitutes") should play a central role in the analysis is not entirely satisfactory for two reasons: First, as will be argued in Chapter 3, the law should be concerned about effects on innovations rather than definitions of markets; second, the calculation of cross-elasticities is very difficult, if at all feasible. Let us see why.

The definition of cross-elasticity of demand is the percentage of change in the quantity of X demanded divided by the percentage of change in the price of Y. To calculate this measure, one must assume "all other things remaining the same," in particular the price of X. Also, there must be no change in the nonprice variables [such as level of advertising, other firms' changing prices in reaction to Y's changed behavior, etc. (see Needham 1979)]. But suppose that in spite of these formidable difficulties some figure is obtained for cross-elasticities. The problem still remains how to decide which goods are to be regarded as "the same," which as "different," and which firms are members of the "same" industry. Economic theory provides no answer to the question of the dividing line between "good" and "not so good" substitutes – locating the dividing line is a matter of opinion.[46]

Yet, in spite of this reservation, Needham (1979) argues that using the substitutability criterion may be useful:

> The task, if one is interested in behavior, is to discover which firms take each other's behavior into account. . . . The use of cross-elasticity measures of substitutability is simply a method of discovering the degree to which firms are affected by each others' pricing behavior, in order to infer which firms are likely to take each other into account in deciding upon their individual policies. (pp. 81–2, italics added).

The problem with this view is that cross-elasticities will rarely, if ever, provide a measure for such a perception. Consider the examples given earlier in this chapter: Bic suddenly decided to compete with Gillette, the chemical industry with the dry-cleaning industry, and, frequently, outsiders to industries compete with established firms [see Jewkes et al. (1958)]. Could an economist measuring cross-elasticities guess that Bic was looking at Gillette? Hardly (not to mention that Gillette certainly did not seem to look then, but seemed preoccupied with patenting its idea. Thus, from Gillette's perspective the cross-elasticities certainly seemed different). Briefly, cross-elasticities may not be very useful in understanding a firm's behavior. What one must try to understand is both the circumstances that induce people to innovate and to take risks and the way their perceptions are formed.

What did other economists say on the subject of markets and for what purpose? Marshall either ignored the problem or dealt with it only in the geographic sense. Robinson and Chamberlin either avoided the problem, mentioned cross-elasticities, or spoke of using "common sense" in the definition [Whose? As Posner's (1976) critique on the decisions made in numerous antitrust cases suggests, there is not much agreement on who uses such sense]. In practice, economists have used the elasticity of demand in order both to define the boundaries of an industry and to measure the degree of product differentiation, and thus classify market structures [see Stigler's (1968) survey].

But recognizing the practical problems mentioned earlier, Boyer (1979) suggested a different definition:

> I propose to define an industry from the point of view of a single firm: to a firm, its industry is the smallest group of sellers such that, were all members of the group to collude, bringing additional members into the collusive group would give the firm only minimal short term advantage. In a sense, a firm sees its industry as the ideal collusive group. (p. 92)

This definition of an "industry" is subject to the same reservations as the previous ones concerning markets. No theorizing can better show the weakness of this definition than the examples given in this chapter: Gillette and Bic, the dry-cleaning and the chemical industry, and so on are not exactly of the type one would think as belonging to "ideal collusive groups." Also, note that the definition refers to individual "firms." But who *is* this "firm"? Why would the entrepreneur want to collude? Why not knock out the competitor with a bright new idea? Boyer, like others discussing issues related to the definition of markets, does not raise these questions since he does not approach the problem of the behavior of firms from the perspective pursued here, that is, of understanding some basic aspects of human nature. Since market definition was not an end in itself, but was used as a tool for examining whether or not some firms possess monopoly power, the subject will be raised again both in Chapter 3 once the view on monopoly within the departure point proposed here becomes clear, and, implicitly, in Chapter 5, where innovations are examined.

Let us now make a few further clarifying comments on the reasons for the different view of demand curves proposed here relative to the one presented in the traditional literature. First, the "law of demand" is derived for well-defined products. But how can one define a demand curve for a product that does not yet exist? The only way one can define it is as done in the chapter: guesses in some people's minds. One cannot say that although this may be interesting, it is a "marginal" case and the "important" questions can be treated within the traditional framework. For, "growth," "development," and "technological change" are about *new* ideas, *new* products, and it is their emergence that one should try to explain rather than how resources are allocated in a "static" world (i.e., in a world where no new products are introduced). Whether per capita wealth is *increasing* or not is determined by the rate of innovations, not the way given resources are allocated. At this point, it may be useful to recall that while the theory of the firm was developed to shed light on the process of competition, initially, in Adam Smith's *The Wealth of Nations,* competition and economic growth were indeed two aspects of the *same* process, rather than two different ones as within the subsequently elaborated neoclassical approach – more on this point will be said in Chapter 3.[47]

In conclusion, the assumptions underlying the "law of demand," a "law" to which entrepreneurs are supposed to respond, are restrictive. The downward-sloping demand curve is derived by assuming that "real income" remains *constant* when relative prices change. But when one resource or another becomes scarcer, the assumption that real income is held constant already means that somehow a compensation has been made to everybody (or "on average") for the diminished wealth. Unfortunately, only in myths and fairy tales do people receive such compensations. In practice, if they want to restore their wealth, they must make *greater efforts* and *innovate* (through the process described in this chapter). But not only does the theoretical concept of the law of demand rely on more than what first meets one's eyes, the empirical verifications too become suspect. For suppose that there was a significant increase in the relative price of a commodity on which people spent a relatively large fraction of their income. Then average wealth per capita drops and the wealth distribution changes. If one observes a decreased demand for the commodity whose relative price has increased, one will *not* be able to attribute this decrease to the law of demand since real income has *not* stayed constant[48] (making one skeptical about efforts for finding "demand curves").

These reservations point to the radically different approach taken here to industrial organization, to the type of empirical analyses done in the latter chapters, and to the nature of the questions that will be raised there. But before continuing it may be useful to illustrate some of the views on "markets," and "demands" presented here with a few further examples. Some people may still remember that the "corner grocery store" was once a flourishing industry.[49] The big food chains of the 1930s narrowly escaped being driven out by the intrusion of independent supermarkets. The first supermarket was opened in 1930 (in Jamaica, Long Island), and by 1933 supermarkets were flourishing in California, Ohio, and Pennsylvania. But the established chains' reaction was that they were "cheapies," promoted by "unethical opportunists" and, as one of their executives expressed it, it was "hard to believe that people will drive for miles to shop for foods and sacrifice the personal service chains have perfected and to which Mrs. Consumer is accustomed." As late as 1936, the National Wholesale Grocers Association said there was nothing to fear since the supermarkets had only limited appeal. Is there any meaning in drawing demand curves in this market where the *perceptions* of the entrepreneurs and managers who produced the services within it differed so significantly? The entrepreneurs and managers decide how much to produce and of what quality according to the way *they* perceive the demand. This is how demand curves are *discovered,* and, in this sense, "the market" is created by some entrepreneurs. Can one discuss the supermarkets' specific features without referring to the "unethical opportunists" who came up with the idea? Or can one discuss the market for cars without referring to Ford's perceptions? Or consider the following sequence of events. In 1980 there were three large firms in the disposable diaper market in the United States: Johnson & Johnson, Procter & Gamble, and Kimberly-Clark. In 1980 the latter two introduced fitted diapers with elasticized legs ("Luvs" and "Huggies," respectively) and knocked the first company out of this market. The new idea was a bet: The latter two firms could not know with precision the demand for the new product, that is, how valuable and time saving this innovation was for parents and whether or not parents were willing to give up Johnson & Johnson's reliability for the new untried product (until

1980 parents paid a premium for Johnson's brand name). But they made a lucky hit: Anyone with young children will appreciate the time saved by the new product, for instead of changing both diapers and clothes frequently, it is enough to do the former less frequently. Let us turn to another example: Church & Dwight Co., maker of Arm & Hammer baking soda, went through 5,000 questionnaires that, among others, asked people what their "refrigerator needs" were. Most consumers could not really think of any. About 100 said it would be nice to use baking soda to maintain fresh odor. With this discouraging evidence, Arm & Hammer went ahead in 1972 and advertised the virtues of baking soda. Within a year more than half of American households had the boxes open in their refrigerators.[50] Both examples show that "the market" is discovered and the estimated demand curves seem nothing more than reflections of guesses made by entrepreneurs. *Demand is thus discovered, although not created* – the implication of this statement for advertising is examined in Chapter 4.

6   Conclusions

A number of viewpoints on the issues raised until now have already been discussed extensively in Brenner (1983, Chapter 1; 1985, Chapter 2), where comparisons are made with Knight's, Schultz's, Hoselitz's, Schumpeter's, the Austrians', and other opinions. For readers acquainted with their viewpoints, the model presented here may not come as a total surprise, in spite of the fact that none of the writers mentioned above succeeded either to give precision to their views or to provide a viewpoint open to verification. Yet in their writings entrepreneurs play central roles in understanding the behavior of firms and the organization of industries. They also linked entrepreneurs with disequilibrium and uncertainty, and profits with uncertainty and chance, links that are accurate within the model presented here. But none of them linked the arguments with the disorder caused by the leapfrogging process, which plays the central role within my views.[51]

There have been numerous other writers who criticized the static analysis of neoclassical economics and wrote books, such as Nelson and Winter (1982), *An Evolutionary Theory of Economic Change.* Yet, surprisingly, they state that the emphasis in their analysis is on larger systems, not on the individual actors. By stating the problem in this fashion they eliminate this central question: Who is making the change if not the individual who is coming up with new ideas? How are institutions, or larger systems, changed if not when the people operating within them bet on the ideas of one individual or another? Buchanan (1979) has stated the criticism in similar words: "By imposing the condition that no participant in the economic process can independently influence the outcome of their process, all 'social' content is squeezed out of individual behavior in market organization. The individual responds to a set of externally determined, exogenous variables, and his choice problem again becomes purely mechanical. The basic flaw in this model is not its lack of correspondence with observed reality; no model of predictive value exhibits this. Its flaw lies in its conversion of individual choice behavior from a social-institutional context to a physical-computational one" (p. 28). Hannah (1984) restates the same criticism in different words in his inaugural lecture at the London School of Economics titled "Entrepreneurs and the Social Sciences" in these words: "I am constantly surprised as I read the offerings of scholars in these fields, and in other social sciences, by the damage *artificial* departmental boundaries have created for the scientific study of this (i.e., entrepreneurial), social and economic phenomenon. The kind of questions on which I would expect business historians to be able to throw some light overlap quite naturally with questions to which industrial economists or industrial sociologists address themselves." (p. 219, italics added).

But it should be noted that although the fashionable mathematical models in economics have not given any precise roles to entrepreneurs and managers, numerous empirical studies have attributed a wide range of evidence to their specific skills. It has been found that executives' and managers' salaries and bonuses are strongly correlated with both the assets of the enterprise and its profitability. The first was interpreted as suggesting that larger enterprises need greater entrepreneurial talent, and such talent is compensated, whereas the second correlation was thought to indicate that managers too (and not only owners) are concerned with profits.[52] The evidence that persistent adverse deviations from trend profitability tend to shorten the corporate presidents' tenure reinforces this interpretation. The role of entrepreneurial talent was also noted in the context of mergers and acquisitions. Friedman (1958) attributes them to the fact that they infuse superior management into companies suffering from talent or motivational deficiencies. One firm may have two or three unusually creative engineers, but no distribution network, whereas another may have a good network but unimaginative engineers. After examining 28 cases of mergers, Lynch (1971) too concludes that the improved performance following acquisition is less likely to result from the traditionally discussed economies in the combined use of physical resources than from the use of managerial talents.[53] Silver (1984) argues and presents extensive evidence to suggest that the onset of vertical integration can often be understood in terms of entrepreneurial efforts associated with the implementation of new ideas.[54] Frequently, entrepreneurship, innovation, and profits have been linked too. Demsetz (1973) argued that the greater profitability of leading firms may have little or nothing to do with economies of scale (in the conventional sense, due to technology) and that this view may lead to an inaccurate chain of causation. Instead he suggests that within some firms innovations have been made that reduced costs or led to the introduction of new products and thus led to higher profits. A statistical analysis will then discover a positive correlation between size and profitability. But both can be attributed to the superior talents used, as Peltzman's (1977) examinations suggest.[55] Others, probably remembering Mark Twain's observation that statistics can be used the way a drunk uses a lamppost, to lean on rather than for illumination, have directly described the history of some entrepreneurs; Hughes's *The Vital Few* probably provides the best example of this genre. Indeed, behind the statistical abstractions verifying various facets of entrepreneurship, interesting personal histories are always hidden, as the evidence in the next chapter too will suggest.

Let us conclude briefly: Entrepreneurs and the perception of leapfrogging play the central role in understanding the behavior of enterprises and the structure of organization. The entrepreneurs, their ideas, their willingness to implement new ones, and *not* "larger systems," are the pivot on which many things turn (to paraphrase J.B. Say). But entrepreneurs are individuals, shaped by culture, mores, and chance. Their ideas and behavior must be put in a historical context. Attempts to do so can be seen in Brenner (1983, 1985) where such evidence as Jewish and other minorities' entrepreneurship, innovations during the Industrial Revolution and in agriculture in general, and patents in the United States are discussed in such contexts. The next chapters complement the pictures by discussing additional evidence.

Before examining it, a final methodological point: The fact that I try to explain here the behavior of firms, competition, and numerous other features of the world of business from the same departure point that in the previous books was used to examine gambling, crime, creativity, wars, features of primitive societies, of the Middle Ages, and other topics, may seem, at first sight, absurd. How can the vast variety of human experience across countries and time be examined from a unified, simple departure point? The answer seems simple: I make a conceptual separation between the static "initial conditions," which represent the complicated state of the world (defined by the perplexingly complex customs, traditions) and some simple, universal "laws of movement" that determine people's deviations from it (thus creativity among them). Whether or not this separation will prove to be useful in the social sciences, time will tell: This and the previous books show the relationship between fact and interpretation based on this departure point. How convincing the relationship is, the readers will decide.

CHAPTER 2

Who are the entrepreneurs? (or, don't confuse brains with a bull market)

REUVEN BRENNER
AND GABRIELLE A. BRENNER

> Failure is what I fear. Fear is what will prevent it.
> Walter Fiveson, an entrepreneur

From words to facts. In previous studies a wide range of evidence on entrepreneurship has been examined: from data on minorities who have been discriminated against, to data on the emergence of the entrepreneurial trait within some well-defined historical circumstances (the Industrial Revolution), to a detailed examination of the relationship between patents (taken as a crude proxy for "novel ideas") and changes in people's position in the distribution of wealth.[1] The picture that emerged from all the verifications are similar: Within groups that suddenly fell behind, or following periods of deepening depressions, the entrepreneurial trait surfaced (although not always directed toward business, but sometimes toward criminal activities too – as indeed one should expect).

The facts presented in this and in some of the following chapters complement the pictures provided in Brenner (1983, 1985) and also regroup additional, scattered, at times forgotten evidence on entrepreneurship gathered by researchers in numerous disciplines. Before discussing them let's reemphasize some crucial points in the model presented in the previous chapter in order to justify the search for the type of evidence presented next.

First, the model suggests that not "the poor" but those who perceive themselves threatened and *falling behind* in wealth and status will tend to bet on novel ideas. This implication of the model immediately suggests that one must look at the problem in a historical perspective – both the history of the individual and that of the society within which his expectations were shaped matter. Second, the discussion covers both self-made men and individuals within corporations. Within the framework suggested here this does not constitute a problem since, as shown, the hierarchy within a corporation imposes on the individuals working within it the same type of incentives that others derive from a perception of a pyramidal distribution of wealth outside the

29

corporation. In both cases, the perception of falling behind one's "fellows," and the feasibility of jumping ahead, induces individuals to be more driven.

1   Adversity and entrepreneurship

In a study of 23 entrepreneurs, Joshua Ronen (1983) has found that one of the main factors that pushed people to become entrepreneurs was not only "a relative unattractiveness of known alternative employment opportunities" (p. 139) but:

In some cases, the prime push was a dark fear (experience of the depression!) of having to go on living without money. Or else, the urgent need for financial independence. . . . Some said that the original entrepreneurial decision was taken out of sheer brutal need, *in the midst of relative wealth*. (pp. 39–40, italics added)

This quote suggests, if indeed people's words can sometimes be trusted, that part of the reason for the entrepreneurial gamble was to raise the entrepreneur's relative wealth. Similar conclusions were reached by Collins, Moore, and Unwalla (1964) in their book *The Enterprising Man*, a study of 150 Michigan entrepreneurs. They found that a "remarkably large number" among them stated that they became entrepreneurs because of poverty. Even those who came from relatively affluent families indicated that the family was experiencing *relatively* hard times when they became entrepreneurs. An additional characteristic of some of the Michigan entrepreneurs was that they experienced as children either the loss of a parent by either death or divorce or estrangement from a parent. Hannah (1984) found similar evidence: "Among a group of 189 innovative American entrepreneurs at the turn of the century . . . more than a quarter had had highly unsatisfactory relationship with absent or bullying fathers (Sarachek 1978). These entrepreneurs were, moreover, the most socially mobile, the most self-made in the whole group, implying that drive is related to such experience of adversity" (p. 226). Silver (1983) too concludes that frequently the "future entrepreneur's father either died early or was absent from family life often" (p. 31) and that in general "those who don't suffer . . . are not likely to become entrepreneurs" (p. 37).[2]

To prevent anybody from jumping to logical conclusions and policy implications and becoming indifferent (or even happy) when perceiving someone's wealth or customary family life being destroyed, it should be immediately noted that another group of researchers have found that suddenly diminished wealth and "broken homes" (due to separation, divorce, prolonged absence of a parent, etc.) were also found to be correlated with increased criminal acts among those who suffered, the offspring in particular [see Carr-Saunders (1942), Glueck and Glueck (1950), Carr-Hill and Stern (1979), and Braithwaite (1979)].

Their conclusion was that these and other forms of "maladjustment" provoke criminal acts (Walker 1965) – but according to Collins's et al. in the earlier mentioned *The Enterprising Man,* viewed as the seminal study of psychiatric characteristics of entrepreneurs, these same types of maladjustments seemed to be the key to success too.[3] The relationship between these findings and the views presented in the previous chapter is straightforward: Since parents provide insurance to their offspring, the diminished amount provided when any of the events mentioned earlier occurs implies that from the offsprings' viewpoint, they became worse off relative to their peers [for theory and facts making the relationship between "wealth," insurance, and family structure, see Brenner (1983)]. One could have expected that in such circumstances, the offspring will bet more frequently on new ideas, entrepreneurial or criminal.

In a 1975 study, Albert Shapero, a psychologist, concluded that the specific conditions for venturing into entrepreneurial acts can be spelled out:

The simplest route is falling on hard times. Most entrepreneurs are . . . displaced persons who have been dislodged from some nice, familiar niche, and tilted off course. Sometimes they are [displaced persons] in the most literal sense; political refugees often produce a surge of company formations in their adopted country. The French refugees who left North Africa for France, the East Germans who escaped to West Germany and the Cubans who fled to Miami are all known for their entrepreneurial energy. (p. 75)

Hannah (1984) emphasizes similar findings in Britain, noting that "what is less well-known is how historically deep rooted the dependence on immigrant entrepreneurs has been in the strategically important growth sectors from Lord Hirst (born Hirsch, a Jewish refugee from Prussian militarism, who came to Britain at the age of 17 in 1880) in the electrical industry, to the modern chemical sector" [see Reader (1970, 1975)]. Wiener (1981) notices additional evidence: By the end of the 1950s "the most efficient firms in Britain were predominantly enterprises that had been started by immigrants as early as 1940, and were controlled by minorities (Quakers and Jews, chiefly)" (p. 203) – more about the British evidence will be said later. The evidence on Jewish and other immigrants' group behavior in other countries is examined in detail elsewhere (Brenner 1983).[4] Chiswick's (1978) evidence should also be noted: He found that in the United States *all* immigrant groups, holding schooling and work experience constant, have higher incomes than the rest of the population (this in spite of the fact that they start by working for lower wages than similarly trained American-born workers). Chiswick attributes the observation to "entrepreneurship," without further discussion. In a recently published book, Andrew Malcolm (1985) attributes Canada's vitality to its modern wave of immigration. Although at first immigration was carefully restricted to the British Isles and northern Europe, under a liberalized law in the 1960s the constraints were changed and a broad mix of immigrants from the Commonwealth were admitted. According to Malcolm, the immigrants and Canadians' reaction to their presence provide the energies that started to "fuel Canada's imagination."

In a study of entrepreneurial activity in the Swedish industry between 1919–39, Dahmèn (1970) has collected data on the social origins of entrepreneurs and found that two-thirds of the known founders of new firms in the engineering industry came from blue-collar backgrounds (p. 237) and that the years of depression, 1922 and 1932, showed an increase in the number of new firms. He attributes the phenomenon to the large number of *newly* unemployed who were pressed to take the entrepreneurial gamble, a gamble that they previously shunned (pp. 249–50, 273).[5] His explanation is that:

Managers, engineers and high-level executives were reluctant to accept [the great entrepreneurial risks] and generally preferred to remain in salaried positions. While these groups . . . had better opportunities than the blue-collar groups to raise the necessary beginning capital, they also had relatively less to gain and more to lose as independent entrepreneurs. (pp. 241–2)

Additional evidence comes from detailed case studies carried out for different time periods, for different industries. Chapman and Marquis (1912) have studied the social origins of firm owners in the Lancashire cotton industry. They found that 63 percent of the loom owners and 84 percent of the mill managers had first been wage earners in the industry, and belonged to the poorest class: They were also disproportionately represented among the entrepreneurs.

In his 1979 book titled *Stalemates in Technology,* Gerhard Mensch has tried to examine when "basic innovations" appeared [where he defines basic innovations as "the source from which new products and services spring and in turn create new markets and new industrial branches to supply them" (p. 122)]. His first finding was that basic innovations appearing in each 10-year period between 1740 and 1955 fluctuate dramatically around a time trend. There were definite periods of clustering, especially in the mid 1820s, mid 1880s, and mid 1930s, which did correspond to the deepening depressions of the periods 1814–24, 1870–86, and 1925–39. He concludes that "surges in basic innovations will come during the periods when stagnation is most pressing, that is in times of depression" (p. 131), and his explanation is that: "A certain group in society pin their hopes on precisely this . . . instability in the institutional structure" (p. 9), that is, when the established orders crumbled, people whose position was or is perceived to be threatened, bet on new ideas.[6] It should also be pointed out that the phenomenon of "geniuses" (in literature and the arts in particular) appearing in clusters has been observed since antiquity, and that the possibility that these occurrences are due to either chance or genetics is infinitesimal.[7]

Cyert and March (1955) found this evidence: Firms with a suddenly declining share of markets strove more vigorously to increase their sales than firms whose shares of the market were steady or increasing. An examination over a 10-year period in five large firms reveals that resistance to a general upward trend in research and development expenditures operates only in years following decreases in both dollar sales and net profits. Why? Cyert's and March's (1956) answer is that people do not seem to bet on new directions "until some form of shock (such as failing to meet its goals) forces a kind of search behavior on the organization" (p. 54). They also note that a review of the literature on budgeting reveals that such reactions are typical: They are called expenditure revisions by "brute force." Cyert and March contrast these findings with the implications of the traditional theories of the firm. Although according to these theories if the opportunities "existed" for increasing profits, the firm should have exploited them previously, these findings suggest that new ideas are implemented only after some negative shock occurs.

A warning must be made again to prevent readers from jumping to logical conclusions and policy implications and deciding that since things must get worse before they become better, let us make them worse and thus promote innovations, productivity, and entrepreneurship. Evidence exists that the same circumstances that have led to more innovative behavior within some firms induced illegal acts in others: Both Palmer (1972) and Asch and Seneca (1976) found that an unsatisfactory *relative* profit performance increases the probability of collusion. These observations are not novel: Stocking and Watkins (1948) argued a long time ago that cartels are *Kinder der Not,* children of distress, and presented some detailed case studies too, and David Landes (1950) in his statistical study of French crises concluded that "it has always been more or less the rule in French industry to meet falling profits by first adulterating or otherwise changing the product. . . . Unfortunately, in times of crises, the deviation of a few has generally been sufficient to make even those manufacturers with the best intentions follow suit" (pp. 205–6).[8] More evidence on noncustomary reactions is presented in the next chapters.

With these reservations in mind, let us continue the examination of evidence on entrepreneurship. In a study of the machine tool industry, Brown (1957) found that at any given time each firm had a "shelf of design ideas . . . which was made up of anything from completed plans for a new machine to ideas which have not yet entered the formative stage" (p. 409), but these ideas were further developed and used only when the demand for machine tools *fell,* that is, when the firms' anticipation of sales was not realized. Mack's (1941) conclusion was that:

> It seems generally true that, particularly after a long depression, technological change will have taken a jump . . . [because] when business slows down, the engineering staff *attempts to justify its employment* by developing designs that look promising. (p. 292, italics added)

More recently, Klein (1977), in case studies of the commercial aircraft and aircraft engines industries, notes that the top managers gambled on innovations reluctantly. They introduced them only after a series of misfortunes plagued the company: First a test plane crashed killing foreign dignitaries; then there was the commercial failure of the Boeing Strato Cruiser in 1949, which resulted in a $50 million loss. Thus, Klein concludes that "Boeing's success . . . resulted . . . from the necessity to survive in a highly uncertain environment and from the ability to turn misfortune into opportunities" (p. 129). The now successful Northern Telecom's history provides one further illustration of this argument. This is the Canadian-owned firm whose technical ties with an American firm were significantly affected by a U.S. antitrust decree. But as stated in a recent *Wall Street Journal* article: "Once the sleepy manufacturing acme of Canada's largest telephone utility, Northern has become a major force in North America's telecommunication market by combining solid research and product development with a marketing flair uncommon in the utility business."[9] The article was written on the occasion of the recent AT&T breakup and Edmund Fitzgerald, Northern's president, is quoted as saying that "Western [Electric] is in the early stages of going through what Northern already has gone through."

Before turning to discuss a different set of facts, let's sketch the history of some entrepreneurs, a history that disappears in the previous abstract summary of aggregates. Milton Reynolds went into the automobile business before he was 20.[10] By 26 he was on the verge of making a fortune, but lost it all in the stock market. In 1925, he went into the prefabricated housing business in Florida, succeeded, but lost everything in a hurricane that swept away a cargo ship full of his entire stock of unassembled houses. At the age of 35 he ventured into the manufacture and sale of stock-quotation boards to brokerage firms, succeeded – until the Crash. He was back in business again with a printing shop turning out sign printing machines for department store display advertising. He succeeded [by *raising* the machine's price from $595 to $2,475, his view being that with some products "the more you can sell something for, the easier you can sell it"]. It was in 1945 during a trip to Argentina that he stumbled on a new, popular novelty – the ball point pen – unknown at the time in the United States. But it was patented. To circumvent the patent he came up with a pen that fed the ink by means of gravity – an idea that could not be patented.[11] The rest of Reynolds's story is well known and appears in Chapter 4 in another context.[12]

Procter (of Procter & Gamble) had come to America following these events: In London, on a Monday, he had opened a woolen goods shop.[13] The next morning he unlocked the door to discover that burglars had stolen every item in the store. Promising his creditors to send payment on his debts, he left with his wife to try his luck in Louisville, Kentucky. Unable to afford anything better, they took a flatboat down the Ohio River, on which his wife was stricken with cholera and died in Cincinnati. John Dowling, branded a real estate superstar by Randall Smith (1983), attributes his success to the fact that his father, a lawyer, died of a heart attack at the age of 45 leaving his wife without support to raise five boys aged 2 to 12. His mother had to move to a blue-collar neighborhood and work. These events induced in him a deep insecurity that has driven him ever since. John Houseman, one of the most successful producers and directors in show business of our time, launched his career after his financial ruin as a grain trader in the 1930 Great Crash (Lardner 1983). Barbara Proctor, a very successful founder of an advertising agency, founded her company only after being fired by her previous employer (Gottschalk 1983); and Fred Smith, the entrepreneur who established Federal Express, revealed in the CBS "60 Minutes" program that he was on the brink of bankruptcy more than 10 years ago. What saved him was his trip to Las Vegas where he won $50,000. (He did not gamble either before or after this event.) The richest businessman identified in Britain between 1860 and 1980 was Sir John Elterman. He was worth £55 million in 1916, and even in the depression of 1933 when he died, the value of his estate for probate purposes was still £37 million (Rubinstein 1984), an amount sufficient to compare him with the richest today (the Westminsters, Sainburys). Yet his father was a German immigrant who died when his son was nine, leaving £600.

Gottschalk (1981) deals with the problem of the young 30-year-old rising executives and suggests that because of the glut of their peers, they find their careers advancing at a slower rate than expected (expectations based on the sixties). This leads to a lot of frustration even among those earning $50,000 (but who may have expected $70,000 and the status associated with it by that time in their life cycle). This observation leads Eric Flamhultz, a UCLA professor of management [quoted by Gottschalk (1981)], to predict that "more and more business school graduates will become entrepreneurs . . . as they get fed up with waiting for advancement in big corporations." In a different context, Harry Levinson (1970) makes a related point. In his book, *Executive Stress,* he cites a study conducted by Joe Stockford of the California Institute of Technology, where 1,100 men in managerial and professional positions were surveyed. Five out of six reported a period of frustration in their mid-thirties (and one in six did not seem to recover fully). According to Stockfoıᵤ "this is the critical age . . . when a man comes face to face with reality and finds that reality doesn't measure up to his dreams."[14] A 1985 Gallup poll surveyed a cross section of small businessmen running companies with sales of less than $50 million [see Graham (1985)]. The sample included 153 entrepreneurs who headed young, rapidly growing companies and 258 owners and managers of well-established companies with modest growth rates. Their responses were compared with those of 207 top-level executives from Fortune

500 companies. The study reveals that corporate businessmen were outstanding students (with 83 percent ranking at least above average academically in college). In contrast, 59 percent of the entrepreneurs achieved such distinction, and 38 percent were average or below-average students. Of the corporate executives 94 percent completed four years of college, compared with 76 percent of the entrepreneurs, who also attended less prestigious schools. Of the entrepreneurs 16 percent were suspended or expelled from school, compared with 8 percent of their big-business counterparts. Almost one-third of the entrepreneurs had been fired, compared with 9 percent of the corporate executives. Finally recall the argument made in Chapter 1 implying that one can examine firms where ownership and management are separated and where they are not from the same perspective. The question was whether or not the management in the first type of firm succeeded in providing a system of incentives for internal entrepreneurship and innovations. If the management did, one should not expect differences in the behavior of entrepreneurial firms and "intrapreneurial" ones (i.e., where internal entrepreneurship is present) – only the organizational setting is different. Roberts's (1968) findings that those who headed new ventures within the corporation appeared similar in all key characteristics to founders of new companies fail to contradict this view.

The evidence presented until now not only does not contradict some of the predictions made in Chapter 1, but it raises further doubts on assumptions frequently made in the literature dealing with the behavior of enterprises. Much is made of the fact that some companies are big, have a lot of "capital" (another undefined word), and the "small" man has no chance of competing.[15] The fact that penniless immigrants, fired or bankrupt individuals seem to be frequently the driving force behind businesses that turn out to be successful requires revisions in this view of the world (in the chapter on innovations, R & D, and the role of the state, this point will be raised again).[16] It suggests that people may get some start, some financing, if they have some good ideas. Indeed, according to the views presented in Chapter 1 it is not so much money that prevents one from carrying out an entrepreneurial act but a stable, ordered way of life. This observation is by no means novel and can be found in Schumpeter's (1919) writings:

Actually among the obstacles in the way of the rise of an industrial family, eventual lack of capital is the least. If it is otherwise in good condition, the family will find that in normal times capital is virtually thrust upon it. Indeed, one may say, with Marshall, that the size of an enterprise . . . tends to adapt itself to the ability of the entrepreneur [pp. 157–8]. . . . But in considering this process of expansion, we come upon another reason for the varying success of business dynasties. Such expansion is not simply a matter of saving and efficient routine work. What it implies is precisely departure from routine. Most members of the class are handicaped in this respect. They can follow suit only when someone else has already demonstrated success in practice. Such success requires a capacity for making decisions and the vision to evaluate forcefully the elements in a given situation that are relevant to the achievement of success, while ignoring all others. The rarity of such qualifications explains why competition does not function immediately even when there are no outward barriers . . . and this circumstance . . . explains the size of the profits that often eventuate from such success. This is the typical pattern by which industrial fortunes were made in the nineteenth century, and by which they are made even today. (pp. 158–9)

But Schumpeter never discusses how one explains within one view of human nature both the mobility and the immobility.[17] It is also interesting to note that in a lesser-known essay (*The History of Astronomy*) Adam Smith expressed a somewhat similar view of human nature, stating that people "have seldom had the curiosity to inquire by what process of intermediate events a change is brought about. Because the passage of the thought from the one object to the other is by custom become quite smooth and easy" (pp. 44–5), and that "it is well known that custom deadens the vivacity of both pain and pleasure, abates the grief we should feel for the one and weakens the joy we should derive from the other. The pain is supported without agony, and the pleasure enjoyed without rapture: because custom and the frequent repetition of any object comes at last to form and bend the mind or organ to that habitual mood and disposition which fits them to receive its impression, without undergoing any violent change" (p. 37).[18]

2   Luck, wealth, and diminished entrepreneurship

Additional predictions of the views presented in Chapter 1 concern the behavior of entrepreneurs who have succeeded beyond expectations, and who have grown accustomed to being relatively rich: They will tend to become less entrepreneurial ("entrepreneurial" as defined here. If one defines the word as simply indicating whether or not one owns a business, the term will have different implications).

From his interviews with successful entrepreneurs, Ronen (1983) concluded that "few . . . are willing to take any great risk . . . they pay . . . attention to the *downside risk*" (p. 144, italics added). Thus, one does not find in this study the portrait of the entrepreneur as a consistently compulsive risk taker, but more of a man who, after succeeding in a gamble, starts to husband prudently his new fortune. Ronen's conclusion is that:

The strong impression emerges that the willingness to undertake ventures where risk is specifically viewed as the possibility of ruin shrivels away with the accumulation of accomplishment (or wealth). Perhaps . . . success can bring about the demise of entrepreneurship. (p. 145)

Evans (1959) too noted that unexpected, big success frequently diminished entrepreneurship. When it happened, the entrepreneurs were unwilling to consider either the production of substitutes or the modification of their products. Some of his illustrations are illuminating: The entrepreneur of the Erie Steam Shovel Company, having done extremely well with a line of earth-moving equipment, was very reluctant to modify designs to meet rising competition. He is reported to have said: "When Henry Ford changes his model T we'll change our shovel." The reference to Ford is appropriate: He too was very reluctant to alter his product, a reluctance that had very bad consequences for his company. Edison, having developed a direct-current lighting system, flatly refused to have his firm have anything to do with alternating current. Although the Du Pont enterprise had been built up through the production of high-grade black powder, Henry Du Pont opposed having anything to do with the new competing product – dynamite. Marcus Samuel (1853–1927), a Jew born in the East End of London, created in the late nineteenth century one of the world's leading oil companies, Shell. In 1895 Samuel bought a great country estate; in 1902 he became lord mayor of London and devoted attention to ceremonial public duties. The result was that Henry Deterding, who controlled Royal Dutch, first proposed a merger willing to accept a minority position. Samuel did not respond. A few years later, with Shell's loss of impetus, he was forced to agree to a merger with 60 : 40 Dutch control. Recently, in a book on the decline of British entrepreneurship, Wiener (1981) contrasts Samuel's attitude with that of Gerson Bleichröder, one of the leading Jewish entrepreneurs of Bismarcks's Prussia. He notes that "despite his political services to Bismarck, Bleichröder's social acceptance was much more problematical, although his economic energies (perhaps partly for that very reason) never flagged" (p. 203).

Another of Ronen's findings, which further undermines the image of the entrepreneur as a permanent risk taker, is that there are *no* differences between risk-taking activities of entrepreneurs and managers (who already succeeded): They all aim at minimizing the risks of losing large sums of money. The difference between entrepreneur-owners and managers comes to the fore only in a different context. When comparisons were made between owner-controlled and management-controlled firms, one of the results was that the returns in the latter case exhibit less fluctuation. Some economists have interpreted this result as implying that managers are more averse to risk. Yet when accountants looked at the facts, their interpretation was different: They have attributed the smaller degree of fluctuations to different accounting techniques (the one chosen by managers being defined as "income smoothing"), rather than different earnings-generating process [see Kamin and Ronen (1978)]. The explanation for the difference in the choice of accounting technique used seems straightforward. Income-smoothing technique is defined as a dampening of fluctuations of income around a predetermined "desirable" trend – deemed by management as the underlying time pattern of income used by investors to predict earnings.[19] Owners don't have an incentive to play with such techniques, but managers do. For suppose that because of good luck the returns in one management-controlled enterprise turn out to be higher than expected for a few consecutive periods. The stockholders and the competitors perceive that and may revise their behavior: The stockholders may start to judge the performance of the managers relative to the higher returns rather than the previous trend, whereas some competitors who fell behind may start betting on new strategies. Both reactions would force the managers of the company to react and to deviate from the beaten tracks. The income-smoothing technique prevents, to some extent, this chain reaction and maintains a greater degree of stability.[20]

In a broader context Levitt and Albertine (1983) (quoting a study of McKinsey and Co.) concluded that nowadays it is still true that the elite of America's entrepreneurial talent is composed of self-made people, often from lower-middle class backgrounds; Beard [quoted by C.W. Mills (1945)] found that among 11 great U.S. entrepreneurs of the nineteenth century, only two built their fortune on inheritance; Taussig and Joslyn (1932) in their study of the American business elite found that success in business without any inheritance or financial help from friends was the rule (p. 161); and Wohl (1953) quotes a study from 1852 of the 1,257 men with property worth more than $50,000 in Massachusetts, which shows that out of the 1,092 whose initial wealth could be traced, 775 (or 70 percent) began as poor, whereas 342 either inherited or married "wealth" (p. 393). Wohl also notes that studies for New York and Philadelphia showed similar patterns (p. 694). Stamp (1926a,b), another participant in the debate on the relationship between wealth, class, and entrepreneurship that was so popular in the 1920s and 1930s, quotes Haensel on the subject[21]:

Only in a few instances of settled property is wealth kept through successive generations. . . . The German proverb "the third critical generation" compares our Lancashire saying: "clogs to clogs in three generations" – has proved to be true after a particular study of wealthy people in Hamburg over three generations. (p. 687)

Haensel also found that among very wealthy men, the wealth was seldom inherited: It was mostly acquired by self-made men. A similar finding is presented by Rubinstein (1981), who concludes that: "Few of the descendants of the very wealthy *improved* upon the size of their ancestor's estate. . . . This strongly suggests that the incentives to continue in the entrepreneurial paths of the founder of the dynasty's fortunes simply disappeared" (p. 135).

Wiener's (1981) earlier-mentioned book thus summarizes evidence from England:

Samuel's career pattern [summarized above] was repeated over and over again: The vigorous, unpolished outsider achieves a business (or professional) triumph, trades his winnings for a knighthood . . . and a country estate, and soon becomes absorbed in the rituals of his new position, while his business touch slips away . . . sometimes successful industrialists left business altogether; other times they stayed in business, but viewed it ever more as a social duty rather than an economic opportunity. . . . P. Sargent Florence observed in 1953 that for the hereditary manager "the pecuniary incentive to large-scale expansion . . . may be weak, since the family . . . [is] already well established. The transpecuniary objects are often stability and a conventional standard of life . . . rather than making one's way farther up the ladder." (p. 147)

Similar conclusions have been reached in completely different contexts. Recall the examples given in Chapter 1 on the lack of innovations among the decision makers of some established enterprises in the energy sector, the movie industry, and so forth. That evidence is part of a larger pattern: Grabowski and Mueller (1975) argued that most corporations experience a kind of "life cycle." First, a firm is innovative and succeeds. Then a period of maturity sets in, when managers expand in accustomed ways. Not surprisingly, they found that for the 759 U.S. corporations they classified as "mature" or "non-mature," the returns on measured investment were significantly higher for the latter. Their interpretation is that the managers in the mature corporations make the persistent error of reinvesting too large a percentage of their internal funds. But Grabowski and Mueller do not draw their arguments to their logical conclusion and ask what characteristic of human nature leads once successful people or people working within the "establishment" to close their eyes, fail to perceive new opportunities, thus making what Grabowski and Mueller view as persistent errors. The views presented here provide an answer, which also suggests that it is unfortunate to call the managers' attitude "erroneous" – the attitude is typical of *all* people who have not been subject to some unfortunate, unexpected shocks. That's how we all are: not quite perfect.

The public's perception that heirs to great wealth will "waste" the inherited money (unless restricted by law) is clearly reflected in the events that led to changes in the federal inheritance taxes in the United States. Dalton (1925) (basing his summary on H.E. Read's *Abolition of Inheritance,* 1918) wrote:

Marshall Field died in 1906. His immense fortune, estimated at one hundred and twenty-five million dollars, passed into the hands of trustees for his grandsons, then twelve and ten years old respectively, to be held by them, on the account of their incapacity, until they should become fifty years old. The public was suddenly shaken from . . . an old opinion . . . that great fortunes are quickly dissolved in the hands of heirs and, therefore, not dangerous. This will, according to Mr. Read, was the cause of great discussion in the American press and of President Roosevelt's message to congress in December 1907, advocating a graduated Federal inheritance tax. (p. 153)

Dalton's, and the public's perception that people who either expect to inherit or inherit great wealth waste money is by no means novel. Aristotle in his

Politics wrote that "in all states there are three elements; one class is very rich, another very poor, and a third is a mean . . . it will clearly be best to possess the gifts of fortune in moderation; for in that condition of life men are most ready to listen to reason. But he who greatly excels in beauty, strength, birth or wealth, or on the other hand who is very poor, or very weak, or very much disgraced, finds it difficult to follow reason." These views are similar to the ones expressed in Chapter 1, but they are written in a more poetic language. Among economists, Marshall, in his *Industry and Trade,* made a similar observation, stating that "elasticity of mind and delight in hard work . . . are not often found among those who have inherited wealth" (p. 48), while among writers the Buddenbrooks syndrome (named after Thomas Mann's novel on the decline of a rich family) has been frequently exploited. Also, the similarities with some of Schumpeter's (1927) views should be noted again. He wrote not only on the success of the entrepreneurs coming from the lower classes, as this quote suggests:

Family and social history show that, in addition to the elements of chance . . . the method of rising into a higher class . . . [is] the method of striking out along unconventional paths. This has always been the case, but never so much as in the world of capitalism. True, many industrial families, especially in the middle brackets, have risen from small beginnings to considerable or even great wealth by dint of hard work and unremitting attention to detail over several generations; but most of them have come up from the working and craftman class . . . because one of their members has *done something novel,* typically the founding of a new enterprise, something that meant getting out of the conventional rut. (p. 174)

but also on the eventual decline of either the successful, lucky entrepreneurs or their heirs. He believed that the success of capitalism, in general, destroys the risk-taking entrepreneurs who are responsible for economic progress: They just live off the wealth accumulated in the past. He applied his views to explain shifts in families' positions in the class structure and stated that their relative positions undergo changes not in such a way that the "big" ones grow bigger and the small ones smaller, but typically the other way around, and summarized the evidence in the lines of the American saying: "Three generations from shirtsleeves to shirtsleeves" [pp. 159–69; but see Brenner (1983, 1985) to explain why this description fits some societies and not others, and the evidence]. Veblen also argued that the success of technological entrepreneurs is followed by a decline, since financial entrepreneurs, who build on the other entrepreneurs' ideas, only try to insure themselves by preserving the organizations built around the technological entrepreneurs' lucky hits.

Gigot's (1983) article provides a detailed description of the decline of entrepreneurial activities in an article titled "The Smallest Nation Has a Rare Problem: Too Much Wealth." Nauru, a tiny island in the Pacific (5,000 inhabitants), has a $25,000 income per capita derived from its exports of phosphate, which suddenly brought much wealth. The reaction? Workers are imported: Filipinos build houses, Australians pilot their jets (the airline losing $30 million per year), Gilbert Islanders dig phosphate and catch fish, later selling them to Nauruans waiting in cars. Most Nauruans work as bureaucrats or not at all. Moreover, imitating others with similar incomes, they also started to import expensive new foods, which, since they are not accustomed to them, are making them sick and obese (but apparently they do not care – see Adam Smith's earlier-quoted view suggesting an explanation for this apathy). No wonder one Nauruan stated that instead of suggesting wealth, to him phospate suggested a graveyard.

3   Entrepreneurship – some broader perspectives

Bertrand Russell once said that the concept of "the gentleman" was invented in England by the aristocracy to keep the middle classes in order. This view should not be surprising: If the rest of the society bets on the idea (of "the gentleman"), it provides the aristocracy insurance and helps restore or maintain a somehow achieved order. According to Wiener's (1981) quite extensive documentation, Russell's guess may have been accurate. Wiener thus explains the change in English character (with all the related ideas that it involves: the negative attitude toward profits, toward ruthless ambition, etc.) and the decline of the British entrepreneurial spirit – recall Samuels's history in the previous section. His and the already summarized evidence suggests that whatever entrepreneurship persists, seems to be the doing of outsiders, either by direct investments or by inducing "a greater will to be efficient" among some British subordinates.

What features characterized English society before the Industrial Revolution, before England became the richest and strongest country? According to MacFarlane (1978) there was considerable social mobility, based on wealth rather than blood, and with relatively few permanent barriers between occupational groups, town and country, and social strata [see MacFarlane (1978), Chapter 7]. These features have been noted by both Englishmen and foreigners comparing their own nations to others. De Tocqueville in his *L'Ancien Régime* wrote:

Wherever the feudal system established itself on the continent of Europe it ended in caste; in England alone it returned to aristocracy. I have always been astonished that a fact, which distinguished England from all modern nations and which can alone explain the peculiarities of its laws, its spirit, and its history, has not attracted still more than it has done the attention of philosophers and statesmen, and that habit has finally made it as if it were invisible to the English themselves. . . . It was far less its Parliament, its liberty, its publicity, its jury, which in fact rendered the England of that date so unlike the rest of Europe than a feature still more exclusive and more powerful. England was the only country in which the system of caste had not been changed but effectively destroyed. The nobles and the middle classes in England followed together the same courses of business, entered the same professions, and what is much more significant, inter-married. (pp. 88–9)

The same observations had been made 300 years earlier, around 1500, in an Italian ambassador's account to his government. Although the report notes the considerable social mobility, describing at length how apprentices amass fortunes and later marry the mistresses of the house, it also notes some darker sides, which seemed necessary for the existence of such an entrepreneurial system:

The want of affection in the English is strongly manifested towards their children; for after having kept them at home till they arrive at the age of 7 or 9 years at the utmost, they put them out, both males and females, to hard service in the houses of other people, binding them generally for another 7 to 9 years. And these are called apprentices. [as quoted in MacFarlane (1978), p. 179]

The parents do not take them back when their apprenticeship is over, but they have to make their own way, assisted by their patrons, not by their fathers. According to the author, this system leads to insecurity and the desire for constant accumulation: "whence it proceeds that, having no hope of their paternal inheritance, they all become so greedy of gain . . ." (p. 175), and to lack of trust: "Sincere and solid friendships amongst [the English do not exist], insomuch that they do not trust each other to discuss either public or private affairs together, in the confidential manner we do in Italy" (p. 174). (Were these attitudes the source of Adam Smith's suspicious view of businessmen?) For a detailed discussion on the relationship between trust, family ties, and accumulation of wealth, and an examination of evidence see Brenner (1983, Chapter 2) and Brenner (1985, Chapters 3 and 4) on the Industrial Revolution and on inheritance laws.

Wiener's outlook on the relationship between lack of entrepreneurship and belief in some "caste" system is not unique: Landes (1949) explained in a similar fashion the relatively smaller amount of French entrepreneurship not only before the revolutions of 1789 and 1830, but even after them:

In the French social structure, the businessman had always held an inferior place. Three major forces conducted to this result. In the present place, he was detested from the start by the nobility, which rightly saw in him a subversive element. The aristocracy, its military and administrative functions slowly . . . ossifying in a new world of gunpowder and mercenaries, centralization and bureaucracy, turned at bay on its bourgeois adversaries and wreaked revenge with the strongest weapon it had left, prestige. Unable to compete with the driving spirit of their ambitious newcomers, unable to defeat them on their chosen ground of business with their chosen weapon, money, the nobility . . . turned its back and tilted its nose. Against the practical, materialistic values of the businessman it set the . . . impractical, unmaterialistic values of the gentleman. Against the restless ambition of the parvenu, it placed the prestige of birth; against the mercurial efficacy of money, the solid stability of land, against the virtues of diligence and austerity, the dignity of leisure and the splendor of pomp and circumstance. (pp. 54–5)

Not all threatened elites reacted in this fashion: In a study of 52 medium-scale firms in India, Berna's (1960) interviews with Brahmin entrepreneurs reveal that their setting up of enterprises was linked with the perception that their community was discriminated against in its traditional intellectual and governmental roles because of their previous favored social position under the British.[22] It appears that they turned to entrepreneurship because of perceptions of discrimination *and* inability to gather political power to maintain the traditionally caste-related occupation. Geertz in a study on the Tabanan aristocrats in Bali after the independence, noted this, somewhat similar reaction:

Trade and industry, in so far as they can be profitably pursued, become in such cases an attractive means to maintain one's threatened status, wealth and power. So it is perhaps not entirely surprising to discover that it is this group of obsolete princelings, which is, in the main, behind Tabanan's recent economic expansion.[23]

However, these new entrepreneurs appeared less driven than their Brahmin counterparts. This less forceful reaction seems not so surprising since Geertz notes that although some traditional and political patterns were broken, the Balinese noblemen have still maintained many of the traditional ties with the commoners.

Still others reacted differently: Hoselitz (1963) summarizes evidence from Europe and notes that while in some countries the threatened aristocrats either became entrepreneurs or clung to some traditional patterns of social actions, others (in Central Europe) used "their political power, . . . their capacity to monopolize some crucial economic sections in order to maintain a socio-political system and a relative income position in which they remained unquestioned leaders and which preserved them a privileged, protected economic position" (p. 47).[24] These politics, although maintaining domestic stability, have long-run consequences (since they diminish domestic innovations and entrepreneurship). Their effect will be discussed together with additional evidence in the last two chapters within broader historical perspectives.

4   Conclusions

Since only people's *inventive faculty* can increase the wealth of nations, the theory presented in Chapter 1 examined this issue, and this chapter examined some of the predictions derived there. The fact that the verifications are done in contexts so different from the ones associated with the traditional literature on the behavior of firms should not be surprising. The view of human behavior presented in Chapter 1 deals with change, with the creation of new ideas (implemented in the form of new ways of organizing the business, new technologies, etc.), and not with either structure or an allocational problem of a given amount of resources. That is why entrepreneurs play a central role here, and no role, in fact, in the alternative approach.

But it should be noted that the examinations in this chapter fit only a model where the entrepreneur is defined as an individual who bets on new ideas and implements them.[25] There are other definitions of the word "'entrepreneur" that lead to different examinations. But they seem either vague or irrelevant. Some use the term "entrepreneurship" as synonymous with "small business." This use seems inappropriate for several reasons. First, one can create a "small business" for tax purposes only – but does not do anything noncustomary. Second, and more important, as suggested in Chapter 1, individuals within large corporations can be subject to the same motivations as individuals outside them. Others use the term as synonymous with "owning a business." They then classify entrepreneurs as being "innovative" and "conservative," implying that some owners gamble on new ideas, whereas others just pursue the customary ways.[26] But such a definition leads to inconsistencies and confusion since the same authors who use this terminology also advocate entrepreneurship as the means for improving the situation in the economy. But in doing so, they certainly refer to the *innovative* entrepreneurs only, and not to the conservative ones – so why call the latter sometimes "entrepreneurs" and not at other times?

What is then entrepreneurship? As Bob Moore, once an IBM financial executive, said: "When it came right down to it . . . I was betting on people. That's what you're always really doing. . . . You can quantify all you want – and believe me people do. But you can never replace the need for a judgment call" . . . (and another executive said) "After all the quantification, I think acquisitions are made on the basis of vision, not numbers" (Solman and Friedman 1982, p. 115). This is what entrepreneurship is about: "judgment calls", "vision," and "a bet on people" rather than "ownership," "small business," "rational management," or imitations.

CHAPTER 3

Competition – the leapfrogging game

The reasonable man adapts himself to the world: the unreasonable one persists in trying to adapt the world to himself. Therefore all progress depends on the unreasonable
man.

George Bernard Shaw

"If you move from third to second in your area, John [Gutfreund, chairman
of Salomon Brothers, Inc.] says you're getting there. If you move from second to first, John says you're vulnerable." . . . "But that ethos has its draw-
backs: Big risks can mean big losses, and Salomon's approach has created a
high-pressure environment that alienates some employees" (McMurray 1984).
Frito-Lay, a Pepsi Co., Inc., subsidiary that takes in $2 billion on snack food
a year, keeps its lead by coming up with new products. What is inspiring the
workers to become innovative and look for the perfect snack? George Reynolds, the potato-chip marketing director, puts it bluntly: "I don't want it on
my tombstone that I created the first big potato chip since Ruffles. But I do
want to get promoted to president."[1]

These opinions exactly reflect the meaning of competition that emerges
from the views presented in Chapter 1: Some entrepreneurs' and managers'
conscious driving against both other business firms and against people who
work beside them by *innovations*. Recall, every business was viewed as being
organized for exploiting some ideas. The straightforward definition of competition follows: Entrepreneurs and managers compete among themselves by
either betting or by inducing their subordinates to bet on new ideas, trying to
provide something different and better. Pursuing these ideas, which may be
about either the reorganization of the enterprise, a new technology, or a new
pricing strategy, represents competition. As such, it means change and uncertainty and stands in sharp contrast with the static, stationary, neoclassical
view that examines the allocation of given resources and, peculiar as that may
sound, defines "competition" within such a world (never raising the simple
question of who cares about and raises questions on the allocation of resources
in "stationary worlds"). But this view reminds us of Schumpeter's (1942)

well-known one: "In capitalist reality as distinguished from its textbook picture, it is not that kind of competition that counts but the competition from the new commodity, the new technology, the new source of supply, the new type of organization . . . – competition which commands a decisive cost or quality advantage and which strikes not at the margins of the profits and the outputs of the existing firms but at their foundation and their very lives" (p. 84).[2]

Numerous economists, whose research was based on the neoclassical approach, paid lip service to the idea that competition and innovations must be linked, but found excuses not to confront the problem. Stigler (1957), for example, wrote:

The way in which the competitive concept [as the neoclassical view defines it] loses precision when historically changing conditions are taken into account is apparent. It is also easily explained: the competitive concept can be no better than the economic theory with which it is used, and until we have a much better theory of economic development we shall not have a much better theory of competition under conditions of non-repetitive change. (p. 16)[3]

Much earlier Marshall wrote in his *Principles* that "the Mecca of the economist lies in economic biology rather than in economic dynamics. But biological conceptions are more complex than those of mechanics; a volume on *Foundations* must therefore [?] give a relatively large place to mechanical analogies; and frequent use is made of the term equilibrium, which suggests something of statical analogy." Although this reasoning is inconsistent, he justly warns that "fragmentary statical hypotheses are used as temporary auxiliaries to dynamical [ones] . . . the central idea of economics, even when its foundations alone are under discussion, must be that of living force and movement . . . Its limitations [of statical theory of equilibrium] are so constantly overlooked, especially by those who approach it from an abstract point of view, that there is a danger in throwing it into definite form at all."[4] The heavy dose of static theory that most economists seem to be buried in suggests that the warning was either forgotten, neglected, or that economists seemed unable to come to grips with the idea of "innovation" and with that of "change" in general, and thus decided to concentrate on "structure," use second-hand mathematics, and redefine well-known concepts of everyday life within such models (a more important reason for this operation is given in Chapter 5). The word "competition" turned out to be one unfortunate victim of this process. Let us see how.

1 "Competition" defined

For Adam Smith and for businessmen competition means a conscious striving against other business firms for patronage of buyers on price *or* nonprice grounds, inventions in particular. This simple concept is defined as "rivalry" by economists (but they rarely write about it), while "competition" means something entirely different. In the neoclassical approach, an industry is said to be competitive only when the number of firms selling a homogeneous product is so large, and each individual firm's share of the market is so small, that no individual firm finds itself able to influence significantly the commodity's price by varying the output it sells. Thus, the distance between this static concept and Smith's is very great: in *The Wealth of Nations* competition and economic growth were two aspects of the same process, whereas in the neoclassical economic approach competition and lack of growth became two sides of the same picture.

How did this semantic change occur? The conclusion that competition is through prices only was an inevitable logical conclusion: Since the neoclassical approach assumes stationary conditions (thus all innovations being eliminated from it), how can firms compete if not by price? Of course, one can argue that the idea of cutting price *is* an innovation too. The neoclassical approach disposes of this comment by assuming that prices are given for every firm. The rest of the definition follows from this reasoning: Realizing that a few traders might collude, a vast number seemed necessary to guarantee that collusion would not be feasible (neglecting the possibility that "vast" numbers may collude through a political process). When it was realized that even a thousand sellers and buyers were not enough if each pair dealt in ignorance of the others, "perfect knowledge" was assumed (neglecting the problem that human behavior in a world of "perfect knowledge" cannot even be defined – what do people do when they know everything?). The condition on the homogeneity of product came from the fact that even minor differences might lead some people to pay a slightly higher price. The dominance of this view of competition may have been due not only to most economists' inability to understand change, entrepreneurship, and creativity but also to the fact that price changes and price differences were measurable, whereas the notions associated with entrepreneurship and creativity were not. The static theory and measurability became the false bases for asserting the powerful primacy of the "price system." On them an enormous structure has been built (consisting, to a large extent, of mathematical and verbal fantasies), and perceptions of how weak the foundations were, have been lost – more on this point later in this chapter.

It would be unfair to leave the impression that some economists did not apologize for the lack of realism of these views. They did so by saying either that economics, unlike the physical sciences, is still in its youth – so, first, some simple models must be built and the world looked at through their lenses – or that the data are too complex and simplifications are first necessary. Unfortunately both answers seem inaccurate: Economics is *not* in its youth. Its history goes back to the Greeks, just as do the histories of the physical sciences. As to complexity of data: Is there any field of knowledge in the twentieth century that is not complex?[5] The apologies seem thus inaccurate and self-serving. The truth may be elsewhere and it will be discussed in Chapter 5.

Briefly, back to uncertainty and the definition of competition: The views presented in Chapter 1 provide a model of human behavior within which competition is defined exactly in the way businessmen seem to perceive it. The definition is simple: *Businessmen pursue strategies to discover a combination of customers and services with respect to which they have an advantage over those whom they perceive as their competitors.*[6] Some theoretical and empirical implications of this definition are examined next.

2   Prices and sizes of enterprises

Pricing new products

How are prices set in the world where competition is done through innovations? Since people introduce new products and bet on numerous new competitive strategies in either marketing, the internal organization of the firm, or advertising practices, there are no standards to which one can just adapt. The answer is that pricing just becomes one particular competitive strategy, a bet, an art. In particular, the prices of *new* products may have little link with *observable* costs (the link being with the expected ones in the decision makers' mind, which outsiders, of course, cannot observe). Before examining the implications of these statements, let us illustrate them by a few case studies. Once these implications are discussed, the role of prices will be examined within a broader perspective.

In his work on a lighting system, Edison took as given the price of the electrical illumination that he sought to supply: He *believed* that the price of a unit of electric light had to be that of a comparable amount of the currently used gas light, and he *felt* that he had to be prepared to lower his price to meet the price cuts he expected the gas companies to make as electricity began to supplant gas as a source of light. Later, as he turned his thoughts to the electric-traction field (which he envisioned as consisting of the feeder lines to the steam railroads), he believed that in order to succeed the cost per ton-mile by electric traction must be less than that of the steam railroad. Ford believed that the price of a car must be low enough to allow an industrious American worker to buy it. Evans (1959), who presents these and numerous other examples, reaches the conclusion that new products are priced with regard to articles, substitutes, to be displaced. But as already pointed out in the previous chapters, perceptions of what articles are substitutes, at what cost they may be produced, and what will be the demand for them, differ: What Edison thought, nobody else did. Thus, there is little wonder that the pricing of new products will have little relationship to observed costs – the cases described below further illustrate this view.

Texas Instruments was a small company making semiconductor chips. It *expected* that costs per chip could go down significantly when chips were produced on a large scale (but nobody then had yet produced them at such scales). They also knew that many other entrepreneurs were entering this market. What did Texas Instruments do? Its managers priced the chips as if they already produced millions of them. With the low price they captured a large share of the market, knocking out competitors (and probably changing the minds of a few potential ones), and eventually the production costs per chip were lower than the low price charged. (Note that, as emphasized in Chapter 1, demand was "discovered," although not "created."[7])

Recently, Texas Instruments made another coup: Less than a week after it had unveiled a new computer for artificial-intelligence applications, it had MIT as a customer for it, buying up to 400. The price? MIT's acquisition consists of a Texas Instruments donation of up to 200 computers and a sale at discount prices of up to another 200. As N.J. Watson, vice-president for data systems at Texas Instruments said: The deal is a "combination donation and sale," or "you can think of the whole deal as selling 400 computers at a discount." Will this pricing bet pay off? Maybe, since the computer will now also have the reputation of MIT behind it.

Military electronics is a $5.6 billion market in the United States (for 1984–85).[8] About 50 companies are vying for shares in it, and their first job is to try to guess the intentions of one customer – the government – which keeps its intentions classified. The managers must guess which particular Russian electronic gadget worries some government officials, which technologies they may decide to buy as countermeasures, and what their rivals' guesses are. So the companies spend time hobnobbing with defense officials, read Pentagon planning documents, line up champions for their product, and bid some contracts at a loss, hoping to find out more information on the procurement trends. Wayne Hawk, a chairman of Comptek Research, Inc., who previously worked for Moog, Inc. (an aerospace-component maker), says that Moog did not charge the government for some development work (which cost $100,000) because Moog gained access to classified data that it hoped to use in later bids. Jack Bowers, chairman of Sanders Associates, Inc., and a former assistant-secretary of the Navy, said that his company bids some development contracts at a loss because "it gives us a 'need-to-know' classified information which helps prepare a bid." But there is no guarantee that it will get it. Others in the business admit that projects without a "champion" die. Although a "champion" (frequently a politician or a bureaucrat) can't deliver a contract because of the lengthy military review process, he may influence a project so that one company's technology is at the heart of it. Looking for such champions is a costly bet (because of the time the executives of the company spend looking for them and trying to convince them of the relative attractiveness of their project), and the return on it quite uncertain.

The previous discussion and examples referred to the discovery of demands and the introduction of new products. Unless these products are patented, one may expect that some individuals may try their luck too and produce the same product. What features will characterize such a process? Another facet of Texas Instruments' strategy of producing a large quantity of chips enables one to infer an answer. As noted, its managers undertake a bet by guessing future demands and costs. Simultaneously they make another bet: that their competitors will not imitate them. If the competitors did, Texas Instruments would suffer a loss. For if Texas Instruments' actual or potential competitors think that they too can produce millions of chips at a cost that Texas Instruments can, they may lower their price at the same level that Texas Instruments did. If the buyers are indifferent between the products of the various companies, the sales will be split between them. In this case all firms lose, since each firm calculates its price by *hoping* for more sales and lower costs. The outcome is "cutthroat competition," characterized by price wars that will last until one or all the firms revise their strategies. What determines the final size distribution of firms and the stable price? This question is dealt with in the following section.

Competition and the size distribution of firms

There are numerous possibilities concerning the size distribution of firms, so let us describe the two extreme ones. If one company's managers are more driven (in the terminology of management literature they are "hawks"), whereas eventually all the others just adjust passively (they are "doves" in the management terminology), the risk-taking company becomes either the biggest producer or the only one. This dominant position is obtained because of the greater entrepreneurial skill (risk taking included) of some individuals. But if at least two companies have hawks at their helm, both must eventually revise their initial strategies (which were based on the assumption that each of them will be the only one dominating the production of a good) and raise their prices. In any intermediary case, therefore, the varying degrees of entrepreneurial skills or risk-taking ability will determine the number of firms and their relative share in any particular industry. This conclusion should not surprise social scientists since their particular "industry" is characterized by this feature too: There are a few social scientists whose ideas dominate the field (Smith, Marx, Weber, and Freud). They, and their ideas, provide employment to most of the others who seem to adopt them and adapt to them.

The conclusion should not be surprising for the additional reason that the evidence on the size of enterprises producing similar products seems consistent with the prediction of the previous arguments. For if entrepreneurs play central roles in determining the sizes of enterprises, an outsider will find that their size distribution at any point in time is consistent with the prediction of a model that views this size as determined by chance. Scherer (1980) presents the following numerical example: Suppose an industry comes into being with 50 firms, each with 2 percent share of sales and $100,000 of sales. Each firm may have the same average growth every year, but with a variation around the trend: In any year some may be luckier, growing more rapidly than the average, whereas others are unlucky, growing less than the average. Let the probability distribution of growth rates confronting each firm be normal, with a mean of 6 percent and a standard deviation of 16 percent. (Scherer chose these parameters to reflect the average year-to-year growth actually experienced between 1954 and 1960 by 369 companies on *Fortune*'s list of the 500 largest industrial corporations for 1955.) If each firm's growth in each period is determined through a random sampling from the aforementioned distribution of growth rates, one of the results obtained is that after 100 periods, the four-firm concentration ratios ranged between 33.5 and 64.4 percent, with a mean of 46.7 percent, a distribution that seems to often fit real-world industries. Scherer's view that stochastic factors – which he interprets as being due to one form or other of entrepreneurial, innovative skill and chance – seem to determine the size distribution of enterprises is not novel. He admits that his numerical example conforms to Gibrat's "law of proportionate growth;" since the number of firms was fixed, the distribution of growth rates confronting each firm was the same, being independent of both firm size and the firm's past growth history. Such growth processes generate a lognormal size distribution of firms, and statistical studies reveal that such distributions often fit the data. But one may object that if the entrepreneurial talent is interpreted as the central force in the process, then there is a contradiction with the assumptions of growth being independent of firm size and past history. Thus, it may be useful to note that in other simulation studies, Ijiri and Simon (1964) have shown that size distributions similar to those generated by Gibrat's models can also be obtained when there is serial correlation in firms' year-to-year growth rates.

Simon and Bonini (1958), reasoning backward from observation to hypothesis, concluded that some form of stochastic processes must thus explain size distributions since they show such a regular and docile conformity (p. 608). The reasoning in the studies presented here is different: It goes from hypothesis to observations. Moreover, the prediction is grounded in a view of human behavior rather than on a statistical model that fits mindless objects. (Recall that within my model concepts of probabilities, luck, *and* entrepreneurship are *inseparable.*)[9]

Prices and competition

And now back from the issue of size to prices: It is unclear whether or not prices may be higher when one entrepreneur is a "hawk" and the rest of the competitors "doves" or if all are hawks. For, in the first case, although the hawk could sell at relatively low prices, he may also be aware of the fact that the rest are doves. Thus he may try to keep prices relatively high. If at least two firms have hawks at their helm, each produces at smaller scales than the dominant hawk in the previous case (and probably at higher costs), but each must continuously worry about the other's reaction, a worry that did not exist in the previous case (although in both cases the hawks may still worry about new entrants). Although such a vague conclusion on prices may worry economists, one should have expected to reach it. Prices play a secondary role within the viewpoint pursued here since they reflect just one facet of the deeper entrepreneurial process that takes place. Let us show how and why; the next chapters, on advertising and innovations, will illustrate the arguments in further detail.

It would be misleading to reach the conclusion that the analysis of price formation in this chapter applies to "technologically" new products only. A novel way of marketing an already existing product makes it "new" too. A Lark airplane carry-on bag sells at Bloomingdale's for $210, while a few blocks from there at Lexington Luggage it sells for $129. Of course, the latter has low overhead, less advertising, no slick, fancy catalogs. Elliot Saks, its owner, thinks that at $210 he could sell three per month, while at $129 he sells 100. A Stanley Blacker's blue blazer goes for $140 at Gimbels and for $104 at Gold Leaf Co. down on Orchard Street. A Wamsutta Beacon Hill sheet that Macy's and Bloomingdale's sell at $18–$20, Ezra Cohen Corp. near Orchard Street sells for $13.50. The lower prices are based on the same principle: less advertising, but greater turnover than the department stores.

How do the standard approaches deal with these persisting differences? They provide the following answers: People have less information on the smaller stores, it may be more time consuming to shop there since not all sizes and variety of styles may be available, shopping at the bigger store is more entertaining and relaxing than shopping on clogged Orchard Street, the message delivered by a gift wrapped in Bloomingdale's paper is different from the one wrapped in another paper (did you buy a birthday present for your spouse on Orchard Street?) and so on. An alternative way of looking at the differences would be to say that these enterprises are not in the same market, but each is in a different one selling the same "physical" product with different perceived characteristics. Thus different enterprises can charge different prices. This structure is called "monopolistic competition" and some economists attribute to it a negative connotation since according to them the quoted price does not equal minimum average costs (implying that outsiders could somehow know what the latter are – an erroneous implication as explained in Chapter 1).

But let us look at these answers through the lenses of the views presented until now. The various methods of selling the same product can simply be perceived as competing strategies that entrepreneurs came up with to satisfy different segments of the population. Mr. Saks thought that at $129 he could sell 100 pieces of luggage per month, and this combination of price and turnover (and allocation of space in the store) may make the greatest contribution to his wealth. But first the Bloomingdale's managers gambled on another strategy, one that Mr. Saks took into account when gambling on his. These decision makers succeeded in finding a combination of customers, services, and prices with respect to which they had an advantage over those that they perceived as their competitors – these combinations exactly represent the competitive process [also see Carlton (1978)].

The concentration on observed prices is most peculiar since not only are they not the only variables by which firms compete but also they are not always the ones that concern customers most. The "price" one pays for a commodity involves characteristics such as search, time, quality, and location, among others [see Becker (1976)]. Consumers do not just buy, let's say, gasoline: They buy it at convenient locations (saving time and thus lowering the "full price" they pay for it), at places where they are relatively sure of the quality of gasoline sold, where their oil is checked at the pump, where their windows are cleaned and their cars washed, or where they carry out credit transactions rather than pay cash. All these characteristics determine "the full price" that consumers perceive paying when filling their tanks. Since entrepreneurs realize that demands depend on this "full price," rather than just the quoted one (of gasoline in this example), they will correctly perceive competition as a process that lowers it. But, of course, lowering the full price implies something radically different than cutting observed prices. Firms can compete with numerous strategies (fighting for better location for the gas stations, introducing automatic "car-wash" machines, etc.) and still keep the quoted price unchanged. After all, a better location and greater density of stations save more money to a group of customers (as measured by the opportunity cost of their time) than a drop of a cent or two in the price of gasoline. Thus, one should not be surprised if, in this particular market (or, in general, for commodities whose quoted prices are small relative to the full one), the quoted prices by different companies would be the same, there would be relatively few price changes, but there would be intense competition through nonprice strategies.

This argument should be taken into account not only when making superficial accusations of "price fixing" and "conscious parallelism" but also when the legislation refers to delivered prices and freight costs [see Brenner and Courville (1982), Brenner and Brenner (1986)]. For, if either freight costs are small relative to the price of the final products or the customers one serves are not swayed by tiny variations in prices, then it may be advantageous to both firms and customers to charge the same freight costs, and compete with other strategies. Indeed computations in Carlton (1984) show that, on average, freight costs of Neiman Marcus and L. L. Bean (both prestigious houses, certainly facing intense competition from Saks Fifth Avenue, Magnin, Bloomingdale's, Lord & Taylor, etc.), both using a uniform delivered price system in their catalog orders, are 5 to 10 percent of the price of the product.

Two conclusions follow: First, even within some traditional frameworks, quoted prices cannot provide much information on whether or not competition prevails.[10] Examining quoted prices only when looking at the behavior of enterprises is inconsistent with the analysis of potential customers' behavior when the notion of full prices is thought to be pertinent.

But if observations on quoted prices do not provide information on competition, what observations may? The answer to this question is the second conclusion that can be drawn from the analysis done until now: Unless customs or laws exist that can be enforced to prevent entry, competition exists and innovations will be observed – whatever the dispersion of quoted prices may be and however they may move. Their dispersion and their movements reflect, in part, some entrepreneurs' bets, at times good and at times erroneous, and these bets are the signals of a competitive process.

The role of prices: theory and facts

As can be inferred from the discussion and evidence presented so far, prices play a very different role within this approach than within the neoclassical one. Let us reemphasize their exact role: Suppose that the price of a commodity or service has increased. If the increase was either expected or is perceived to be of a short duration, nothing of much interest will happen since the change was either discounted or can be neglected. Suppose, however, that a significant, unexpected alteration takes place, which is perceived to be of a permanent nature. Then some people's wealth is diminished, their position in the distribution of wealth altered, and the relative attractiveness of implementing some ideas is altered too. The unexpected, significant change in relative prices has therefore two effects: Both alter some people's position in the distribution of wealth and the relative costs and benefits of implementing some new ideas.

The change in relative prices is linked with perceptions of changes in relative demands: People will try to *discover* by how much the demand for substitutes for the product whose price rose has increased, and will redirect the innovative effort to fit the changed perception. (In what circumstances can one speak about a situation where the demand everywhere is perceived to be rising? This particular situation will be mentioned later, linking it with anticipated increases in population, domestic or international, with whom one expects to interact, and the resulting, expected innovations.) Thus, changes in prices provide both the signal toward the redirection of the innovative, entrepreneurial effort *and,* for those who fell behind, the motivation for making such efforts. The role of the entrepreneur is therefore the one that Stigler (1956) once described, namely, that in dynamic circumstances "the competitive entrepreneur who in a stationary condition had only the task of allocating resources now has also the task of predicting – and possibly shaping – the future conditions of supply and demand" (p. 273).

This type of entrepreneurial reaction reflects, however, only part of the picture. The sudden, significant alteration in relative prices may also bring social and political upheaval: The confusion, the instability of the transition provide opportunities for some and, at the same time, are viewed as a sign of breakdown of customs, of the established order by others. Thus, perceived changes in relative prices play within this view of human nature a role that can be associated with conflicts and resolution through them, and not only with harmony, sympathy, and resolution through such utopian, peaceful human sentiments (as implied by Smith and the neoclassical view).

It is useful to emphasize this implication since it is the idea that significant meaning of the economy (of the ordered chaos) can be found by examining prices only, that, if it were accurate, could justify the economists' effort. But the idea is *not* accurate. Stability of prices is only one of the visible, measurable signs of the fact that a somehow achieved order is maintained, whereas the formation of prices is only one of the visible, measurable signs of some entrepreneurial effort and the reaction to it. The views and facts presented here suggest that this static, number-based mentality impoverished the economists' understanding of the world since the nonquantifiable facts of life, creativity among them, were screened out.[11]

Although the evidence presented in the previous chapters illustrated clearly this interpretation, recall some additional ones in order to reemphasize it. For half a century, between 1880 and 1930, the Chilean nitrate industry was the backbone of Chile's national revenue. The export tax on it provided, on average, 42.8 percent of the government's revenue during this period. But between 1920 and 1933, a revolution took place in the nitrogen industry (many Western governments subsidized domestic nitrogen production for military reasons). The price tumbled, Chile's foreign trade declined, unemployment increased, government revenues fell off, and political and social unrest intensified: Between July 1931 and January 1933 Chile changed presidents seven times, usually without the formality of an election.[12] The social and political instability that was the consequence of drastic changes in other relative prices (of wheat, or due to inventions, before and during the Industrial Revolution in particular), is amply documented.[13] But it would be misleading to jump to the conclusion that such reactions characterize only very specialized economies – agrarian or other. Although in milder forms, the aforementioned reactions characterize Western economies too (the United States in particular).

During the twenties, the American bituminous coal industry had excess capacity, not only because of the unanticipated declining demand (due to inventions of substitutes) but also because of expansions during the war. The altered demands and innovations in the coal industry resulted in widespread unemployment among the coal miners, bankruptcy for some mine owners, and deep distress in coal-producing communities. Other reactions were a joint selling agency, Appalachian Coals, Inc. (which received the blessing of the Supreme Court, in spite of apparent conflict with antitrust laws), and price and wage controls imposed by the 1935 Bituminous Coal Conservation Act (and, after a major section of this act had been declared unconstitutional, by the Bituminous Coal Act of 1937).[14] Similar reactions later characterized the copper industry, today the car industry (with "voluntary" import quotas being requested from the Japanese), and numerous others, all intended to soften the impact of some drastic alterations in relative prices on long-term unemployment and dislocation. More evidence on the nature of some reactions will be presented and discussed in the last two chapters.

The lessons from the evidence are clear: Changes in prices have more than just "economic" consequences, and no significant meaning can be given to them, unless one puts them in a broader perspective.

3   Monopolies and oligopolies

If competition implies innovations, a *secured* monopolistic position implies their absence.

Recall, "monopoly" means one seller. If one interpreted the term literally, everybody would be a monopolist since people are not alike: There are no two grocers, no two singers, or not even two McDonalds alike (the latters' locations are different). Of course, this is not what Cournot, Marshall, and before them, Adam Smith seemed to have in mind when writing about and condemning "monopolies." Rather, they referred to situations where the *entry* of would-be producers of close substitutes was severely limited (in Smith's case by regulations inherited from the past).

"Severely limited" – why? And how severely? Who is imposing the limitation?

Today there seem to be two approaches that try to answer these questions.

One perceives monopoly power as being obtained and then protected by the decision makers' own actions without any aid from government, whereas a second perceives it as being due to various forms of government intervention.[15] Both viewpoints imply that having such power has negative consequences. Of course, their policy recommendations differ. According to the first view antitrust legislation, regulation, and so forth may be needed to prevent firms from getting and using monopoly power. According to the second, if the government did not make some interventions, there would be no monopolies.

When attributing negative connotations to the fact that there is only one seller, the advocates of both viewpoints have in mind a situation where this position was *not* secured either by a patented innovation (since patent laws are viewed as a necessary form of government intervention for promoting innovations and long-range planning) or by superior entrepreneurial and managerial talents. The negative connotation is given only when the one-seller position was secured either by chance (a landowner discovered that he has the only gold mine, although, in fact, he bought the land for agricultural purposes), by collusion, or by government intervention. In these circumstances, the negative economic impact of monopoly is attributed to the misallocation of resources because of the tendency of monopoly profits to be converted into social costs, while the negative political impact is attributed to the facts that monopolies transfer wealth from the relatively poor to the relatively rich, and that they may manipulate the political process.[16]

The approach pursued here suggests that the negative impact of having a secured monopoly power is associated with *the lack of innovations whether managerial or technological.* Indeed, the model gives a literal interpretation to Hicks's phrase: "The best of all monopoly profits is a quiet life": When people do not perceive threats, they do not deviate from their customary behavior, in business in particular. Note, however, that this negative impact occurs *only* if the one seller either knows or perceives that entry is blocked. If the one-seller position was obtained because of superior entrepreneurial talent, this conclusion is incorrect. For the entrepreneur may realize that there might be others too, who, perceiving his success, may try their luck. Thus, fearing entry, he perceives competition and may continue to innovate or induce innovations within his firm (recall, however, the evidence in the previous chapter, which shows that the reaction depends on the specific historical background, the length of time one was accustomed to having a "quiet life" in particular). Indeed, as frequently emphasized until now, only perceptions of *change* and not *structures* (in this case being "one seller") play explanatory roles in the discussion.[17]

It would be too easy to jump to the conclusion that one seller can persist only if there are either legal restrictions to entry or an entrepreneur is more talented. This is not exact: Lags in entry may be a consequence of the sellers' actions, their effects on the outsiders' perceptions, and just chance. Let us show how – the next section illustrates the arguments with some case studies.

Suppose that the sales of a product, which has one producer, increase. The price is raised and measured profits increase. Outsiders perceive the alterations and try to enter. They do so because they perceive that the decision makers in the existing firm either do not want, cannot, or have no relative advantage in expanding capacity. If the insider did not increase capacity because he perceived the increased demand to be temporary, the fact that others try to enter may change his mind and lead to the perception that the increased sales are of a more permanent nature. What will the insider do? In order to gain time, he may lower the price, even below current average costs (but not the expected one, once capacity is enlarged). Thus, he induces customers to buy enough of his product so that until he expands his capacity, the demand for the intruders' product drops so significantly that they may abandon their plans of entry. Once this happens, and the insider enlarges capacity, he may increase his price to a competitive level (i.e., a level that takes into account the now perceived possibility of entry). Yet he may stay the only seller. This is an example of a process where one seller persists without legal aid and eliminates his competitors – some illustrations of this process appear in the next section.

Was the insider more talented? Not necessarily – he may have been luckier rather than being more talented. After all, he made an error at the beginning of not perceiving that the increased sales were of a more permanent nature, whereas the new entrant misinterpreted the insider's dangerous game. If the intruder reacted in a way to suggest that he is determined to stay, the insider would have changed his strategy.

In terms of the views presented in Chapter 1, the more formal translation of these arguments would be the following: When the one seller reacts by lowering his price in response to one's entry, he alters the perceived costs and benefits for the new entrants (if the entrants did not discount this response). One cannot say by how much they are altered since the change depends on how the new entrants perceive the response, whether of a more or of a less permanent nature. If previously the entry to this field was perceived to be attractive, the insider's reaction turns out to be less so and discourages further attempts. At the same time, the response also lowers some people's wealth unexpectedly (again, if they did not expect the insider's response), who may then turn their entrepreneurial drive to other directions. Thus, outsiders will now perceive that one seller persists and there are no attempts to enter. Essentially, this process is not different from the one discussed in Chapter 1 when a successful company's president was quoted as saying that inside the corporation one must invariably kill a program at least once in order to get down to the fanatics. The difference is only that sometimes this strategy is used *within* a corporation, at other times outside it: In the latter case the insider tries to learn something about just how fanatic the new entrant is. Let's illustrate how the aforementioned strategies have been used.

Case studies

Solman and Friedman (1982) describe the following case: Wilson Harrell, an Englishman, comes to America in the 1960s and purchases a small company producing a cleaning spray liquid (Formula 409). By 1967, he had a 5 percent share of all U.S. cleaning products and 50 percent of the spray-cleaning segment. "It was a comfortable franchise, a comfortable living. Harrell didn't have to worry about stockholders [his company was closely held] or big competitors . . ." [p. 24, maybe this unexpected comfort led Harrell to complacency]. But then Procter & Gamble entered fresh from a recent victory over a new liquid cleaner [p. 24; a victory that, in terms of the views presented in Chapter 1, may explain their subsequent conservative behavior] and it began test marketing a spray liquid cleaner called Cinch. Instead of a national launch, which the Procter & Gamble managers perceived as too risky, they decided to test market it only in Denver. What did Harrell do? He withdrew his Formula 409 from Denver, stopping advertising and discouraging sales people from refilling the shelves. Cinch, of course, did extraordinarily well in the test market. When Procter & Gamble began the national launch, Harrell slashed the price of Formula 409 below cost in order to "load up the typical spray-cleaner consumer with what [he] figured would be about six months' worth of product. . . . The only customers left [for Procter & Gamble] were new users, and there weren't nearly enough of them to justify Procter & Gamble's expenditures on Cinch" (pp. 26–7). Within a year Procter & Gamble withdrew the product.

Although this episode was never celebrated, another, somewhat similar one, was. Posner (1976) summarizes the district-court decision in *Telex Corp.* v. *International Bus. Mach. Corp.* in these words:

IBM had made drastic price reduction in equipment that was "plug-compatible" with its main-frame computer equipment in order to repel the competitive inroads made by Telex, another producer of equipment plug compatible with IBM computers. In holding that the price reductions were evidence of unlawful monopoly, the district court emphasized that (1) IBM was the dominant firm in the relevant market (oddly and inaccurately defined as the sale of equipment plug-compatible with IBM computers); (2) the price reductions reduced IBM's net revenue from sales of the products in question; (3) the reductions were not cost justified; and (4) IBM's purpose was to weaken Telex. (p. 194)

Note how perfectly the court's emphasis would fit Harrell too. Posner criticizes the court's view by pointing out that IBM's reaction fits a competitive response to sudden entry. The same interpretation is given by Fisher et al. (1983), who document the IBM case within a broader perspective. According to them, the government's economists' error was not only the totally irrelevant definition of "markets" but also that they examined the facts through the lenses of irrelevant "long-run equilibrium theories," thus mistaking price and product changes forced by rivalry for restrictive behavior of monopoly.

In January 1985, American Airlines announced its Ultimate Super Saver program, which cut fares by as much as 70 percent on a fraction of places on most flights. American's main targets were not its big competitors but the new entrants and discounters, People Express and Continental. The major airlines, United, Delta, Pan Am, TWA, Northwest, said that they would match American's strategy. What's the point of Crandall's (American's new chairman, recognized as one of the best airline managers) strategy? As in the previous case the goal seemed to be the same: To weaken the competition sufficiently, preventing them from expanding capacity until their own is expanded. Indeed, the strategy cannot be viewed in isolation from the fact that, in 1984, American placed an order for 67 new M.D.-80 jets from McDonnell Douglas, which are more fuel efficient and are expected to lower variable costs in the future. Another aspect of Crandall's strategy further illustrates the skepticism toward models attributing central roles to observed, quoted prices, for either inferring competitive behavior or for measuring welfare. Although the new price charged by American was significantly lower than the regular one, there were two constraints: a 25 percent cancellation charge and the traveler must spend at least one Saturday night before returning. The strategy enabled American to compete for two different segments of the air travel clientele. (By the way, what is thus "the price" that each traveler perceived?)[18]

Recently, Alfred E. Kahn, who as head of the Civil Aeronautics Board in the late 1970s deregulated the airline industry, expressed concern over the rivalry between People Express and Northwest Airlines, accusing the latter of predatory behavior. What happened? In June 1984, People Express initiated service between Newark, N.J., and Minneapolis at one-way rates of $99 peak, $79 nonpeak. Immediately, Northwest dropped its fares to $95 and $75 to all New York airports, advertised services that People Express was not providing (free meals, wider seating, luggage handling, easy transfers, etc.), and increased the number of flights. Mr. Kahn suggested that Northwest's behavior constituted predation and was illegal because Northwest "substantially undercut" the People Express fare (?! $4 is "substantial"?) and increased the number of its flights. By August, things settled: People Express was running four flights at $99 and $129, whereas Northwest had 13 flights with a standard coach at $298, discount fares of $99 and $159 into La Guardia and Kennedy, and a special first-class rate of $155 into Newark. As in the previous case, Northwest's reaction can be perceived as a competitive one to a rival's behavior.

All these cases illustrate how companies who suddenly fear falling behind compete with new strategies, that the changes in prices represent just one facet of the more complex entrepreneurial decision, and that it is misleading to attribute to these changes a negative connotation *even* if one seller may dominate a large segment of the sales of a product or service.[19] This domination is due to entrepreneurship, innovations, *and* luck.

4   Innovations or prices? A criterion for competitive behavior

If pricing does not provide information on noncompetitive behavior, how can outsiders infer (in the absence of obvious legal restriction on entry) the possession of *secured* monopoly power? The answer is simple: A necessary, but not sufficient, condition is to observe *lack of innovations*. Neither information on the sizes of firms, on concentration ratios, on pricing strategies, nor on profits can shed light on this question. For, as has been pointed out, *any* size distribution, and thus any concentration ratio, can be generated by a distribution of entrepreneurial talent and chance. Also, pricing behavior where innovations occur or are expected to occur can be interpreted in numerous ways [also see detailed discussions in Posner (1976), Bork (1978), Fisher (1979) on "predatory" pricing in particular][20] – looking at prices leads to unambiguous interpretations only in static worlds. As to relatively high rates of profits, as argued in Chapter 1, they can be attributed to superior performance, noncustomary insights of managers, *and* luck.[21]

However, it must be admitted that the criterion of "lack of innovations" is not always an easy one to use. Yet the criterion is of more than just theoretical interest, and in some antitrust cases, it could have provided a clear answer. In one of the most celebrated ones, the IBM case, it provides the following insight: Since in 1979, 80 percent of the revenues of its data processing divisions came from products manufactured since 1974, one can infer that this company's decision makers were not sitting on their laurels.[22] By comparing this fraction with that of other firms, one is provided with a criterion of whether or not a company's decision makers have used various pricing strategies in order to just maintain its position *without* changes in its production facilities or the changes in pricing strategies occurred simultaneously with innovations.

What is this fraction for other industries? Choffray and Lilien (1980, pp. 4–5) present this evidence: In the scientific instruments area, the Office of Economic and Cultural Development reported that many American firms have 60 to 80 percent of their sales from products that were not in existence five years earlier. In the same industry, according to Utterback (1969, p. 30), 17 percent of its 1960 sales were of products not in existence in 1956, and even this relatively low fraction ranked the industry second (on this measure) to the aircraft industry. For 223 manufacturers, the percentage of 1966 sales attributable to the sale of products first marketed by the company within the past five years was 20 percent. At the less aggregated level, the evidence is this: According to Pearson (1982, p. 22) 3M Corporation has a record of introducing new products at such a rate that between 20 and 25 percent of any year's sales are from products introduced within the immediate past five years. At Hewlett-Packard in 1981, 75 percent of the sales were in products that had been introduced during the preceding five-year period (Hammond 1982, p. 124).[23] Relative to these numbers, IBM's performance seems outstanding and inconsistent with accusations of perceiving a secured monopoly power (i.e., that entry is blocked and they can *raise* prices of existing products). IBM was not the only company against which antitrust policy may have been perversely used. Gee and Tyler (1976, p. 5) criticize the suing for separation of the Bell System and Western Electric on similar grounds. They too emphasize that these companies were a major source of innovation: The discovery of the transistor, electronic switching, long-distance communications transmission systems, the solar cell, all took place in Bell Laboratories. They also note that since 1925 Bell scientists were awarded more than 600 awards and prizes, two Nobels among them, and that the availability of the lowest cost communication system in the world is a consequence of all the innovations being carried out within a single entity.

The perverse use of antitrust laws – accusing the *innovative* firm of anticompetitive behavior – may have its origin, according to Bork (1978), in the opinions expressed by the Supreme Court in 1911 in the *Standard Oil* and *American Tobacco* cases. For the Court seemed to adopt uncritically the idea that it was easy for a firm to injure others by means *other* than the use of superior talent and luck and seemed to agree with the idea that vertical integration, local price cutting, and so forth are strategies by which injuries are improperly inflicted.

The views presented here provide support to Bork's (1978) criticism and suggest a radically different criterion for guiding the courts in antitrust cases. Instead of pricing, concentration ratio, profitability, and other criteria used today to infer noncompetitive behavior, a measure of the accused firms' relative rate of innovation should be used. By taking into account this measure not only can one dismiss many accusations but one can also suggest a solution for the much debated point in antitrust law on the relevance of evidence on "intent." Whereas according to the pricing and structural criteria competitive and predatory intents are confused, the criterion concerning innovations distinguishes between them, and it shows something about the accused firm's perceptions of entry and about its intentions to compete – more on this point will be said below, when discussing the predictable perverse use of antitrust laws.

Competition, monopoly, and the law

One should not be surprised that with the inappropriate tools that the static, neoclassical theory has provided for perceiving a changing world, decisions in antitrust cases, where firms were accused of noncompetitive behavior, have frequently been inaccurate, inconsistent, and sharply criticized by among others, Posner (1976), Bork (1978), and Armentano (1982). Both Bork and Armentano remark that the four conditions under which a competitive market will rise (according to the traditional view) – perfect knowledge, large numbers, product homogeneity, and divisibility – may be a useful model for theorizing, but it is totally useless as a goal of law, as a criterion for antitrust laws in particular.

So how did judges, who recognized this inapplicability, decide? As the various decisions suggest – inconsistently. Each judge used his own interpretation of previous decisions as well as his own "common sense" for interpreting what is and what is not a competitive response. In the *United States v. Trans-Missouri Freight Association* (166 U.S. 290, 1897), Judge Peckham suggested that business combinations

. . . may even temporarily, or perhaps permanently, reduce the price of the article traded in or manufactured, by reducing the expense inseparable from the running of many different companies for the same purpose. Trade or commerce under those circumstances may nevertheless be badly and unfortunately restrained by driving out of business the small dealers and worthy men whose lives have been spent therein and who might be unable to readjust themselves to their altered surroundings. *Mere reduction in the price of the commodity dealt in might be clearly paid for by the ruin of such a class.* [as quoted in Bork (1978, p. 25), italics added]

Protection of a class as criterion for judging a price cut? Justice Tom Clark's dissent in *White Motor,* for example, seems to present the erroneous view that the elimination of all rivalry must always be illegal:

To admit, as does the petitioner, that competition is eliminated under its contracts is under our cases to admit a violation of the Sherman Act. No justification, no matter how beneficial, can save it from that interdiction. [as quoted in Bork (1978, p. 58)]

Although this statement is inaccurate (since it would not permit the elimination of firms even by more innovative ones), so is Bork's opinion that the identification of competition with rivalry will not do for antitrust purposes. As argued in this chapter, if properly defined, it may. Bork may have reached his erroneous conclusion because he did not have a precise view of what "rivalry" implies. Yet such a view was presented here: The perception of rivalry leads people to innovate. Since only innovations increase wealth, and since according to Bork creation of wealth should be the goal of antitrust (he calls such creation "productive efficiency," without, however, identifying it with innovations), the criterion for a judicial decree should be whether or not more or less innovation can be expected as a result of it.

Bork criticizes additional meanings of the term "competition" that have been given by judges in other decisions:

Competition may be read as the absence of restraint over one person's or firm's economic activities by any other person or firm. . . . This is not a useful definition, however, for the preservation of competition would then require the destruction of all commercial contracts and obligations. . . . [p. 59] "Competition" may be read . . . as the existence of "fragmented industries and markets preserved through the protection of viable, small, locally owned business." This was the meaning given the word by Chief Justice Warren in the Brown Shoe case. . . . There are a number of objections to this definition. . . . "Fragmented" is a word without much content. . . . Second, "competition" . . . has nothing to do with whether the business units are locally owned. Third, the definition would lead, and in fact very nearly has led, the court to say that all horizontal mergers are illegal. (p. 60)

To a large extent, Bork attributes the variety of inaccurate decisions to interpretations of opinions in the *Standard Oil* and *American Tobacco* cases. One, as already noted in the previous section, was that the Court adopted the idea that it was easy for firms to injure others by means other than superior efficiency. The other is Justice White's unclear prose, his inconsistent use of the phrase "rule of reason," as well as Justice Harlan's "demagogic and uncomprehending dissent." Fisher et al. (1983) attribute the confusion to opinions like Judge Hand's, who in the 1945 *Alcoa* case stated that a market share of 90 percent "is enough to constitute a monopoly; it is doubtful whether 60 or 64 percent would be enough; and certainly 33 percent is not" (p. 2). This opinion, relating market share and monopoly power, has been frequently quoted since, although the reservations he made when stating that "the successful competitor having been urged to compete must not be turned upon when he wins," and making "superior skill, foresight, and industry" a defense, seem to have been forgotten.

Bork reaches the conclusion that the only plausible definition of competition is one that designates a state of affairs where consumer welfare cannot be increased by moving to an alternative state of affairs through judicial decree. The problem with this definition is obvious: The notion of "consumer welfare" is well defined only in the static models (which Bork criticizes), but is much more complex within the dynamic model presented in Chapter 1. Moreover, although Bork emphasizes that antitrust is a subcategory of ideology and that it connects with the central political and social concerns, representing the struggle of ideas in the larger social order, he does not make it clear either how the goal of "consumer welfare" itself is related to these bigger concerns or what these "bigger" concerns might be. Although some of these broader issues have been touched upon in the previous chapters [and were also discussed in Brenner (1983, 1985)], they will be discussed in later chapters once some further, simpler, practical implications of my views are verified and more evidence is presented.

Dominant firms

Already the definition of monopoly as an only seller who perceives no intrusion (without the aid of government) should have suggested that such cases must be extremely rare and raise the question why then does one read about monopolies so much? Closer inspection reveals that, indeed, language was abused. The word was used as a synonym for *any* large-scale business, whether it competed and innovated or not. Once again "form" (i.e., language defining a particular form of structure) seemed to be interpreted as "substance" (i.e., implying a particular form of behavior).

Indeed, many studies have pointed out that monopolies are rare, but then they argued that the same theory applies for situations when one "dominant" firm coexists with numerous small ones. This inference is flawed, for the existence of small firms suggests that entry is *not* blocked. Thus, one must explain both why the smaller firms do not expand or others intrude, and why the dominant firm's decision makers don't take into account the threats of expansion and entry. The traditional answers to these questions are flawed too [see Posner (1976)].

Moreover, no convincing evidence was found to suggest that this type of structure indeed implies noncompetitive behavior. Scherer (1980) summarizing an extremely wide range of evidence concludes that: "Prices often hover closer to cost than one would predict from an analysis that takes into account only the fewness of sellers, ignoring coordination obstacles and long-run constraints. These more subtle structural and behavioral variables [threats of entry, as Scherer emphasizes] help explain why pricing performance in modern industrial markets has on the whole been fairly satisfactory despite significant departures from the structural ideal of pure economic theory" (p. 266). The unavoidable question is therefore: Why pay attention to either "ideals" or "pure economic theory" (by which Scherer seems to mean models where neither risks nor uncertainties are taken into account) since anyway they do not shed light on the facts?

The explanation for being either one seller or the dominant one based on the views presented in Chapter 1 is simple: Since entrepreneurial, managerial talents and chance play central roles, these facts are hardly surprising. There are only a few financial, industrial Napoleons – just as there are a few Adam Smiths, Darwins, Walt Disneys, and Picassos. Some firms' dominant position may have been obtained not only by securing a patented innovation but also because they happened to have the right men, at the right time, and at the right place at their helm, who implemented some ideas that others could not or dared not. Because of this combination of entrepreneurship and chance, they were able to sell a good either of a higher quality or at a lower price, eliminate or discourage their competitors from expanding, and indeed, by definition, possess some power due either to having such skills or the smile of Fortune.[24]

Oligopolies

Theories of oligopoly attempt to predict the behavior in markets where rivals are "few." As Bork (1978) has correctly noticed, "the lack of rigor in that theory may be suggested by the observation that there appear to be about as many oligopoly theories as there are economists who have written on the subject" (p. 102). This disorder should have been expected since the departure point − looking at numbers to infer behavior − was wrong.

For there is no way to determine on a priori grounds where oligopoly turns into a competitive structure. The key to the distinction is subjective − whether or not the decision makers at the helm of the "few" firms consider themselves rivals and/or perceive threats of entry. It is useful to note that although this reservation has been made [Scherer (1980), p. 11], it has not always been drawn to its logical conclusion. That conclusion had to be that on a priori grounds one cannot give a negative connotation even to the existence of one seller since the question is whether or not he takes into account threats of entry. If he does, the outcome *is* competitive and the number of firms outsiders may count does not matter at all in shedding light on this one seller's behavior. In order to infer whether or not decision makers within firms take into account competition, one should look first at the fraction of these firms' revenues generated by relatively recent innovations, as compared with other sectors perceived as competitive. Only if this fraction compares unfavorably should suspicions rise and further investigations be pursued.

The reason for assuming a positive relationship between the number of firms and noncompetitive behavior is that collusion among few is more likely since coordination is cheaper.[25] Markham (1951), for example, suggests that collusive price leadership is more likely where the following conditions co-exist: The number of sellers is small; the products are close substitutes; the cost curves are similar; and there are barriers to entry and demand for the industry's output at the current price is relatively inelastic (so that price raising pays). Translated in the simple language that the model in Chapter 1 permits using with precision, all these conditions are reduced to the older "meeting of the minds" term that was thought to best describe the necessary conditions for collusive behavior. Indeed, note that the decision makers in Markham's view of oligopoly must have the same attitudes toward risks, must be similarly driven, and must think in *exactly* the same way how to organize their production – otherwise their cost curves could *not* be the same. The possibility of entry is arbitrarily disposed of by assuming that there are barriers to entry – but as the evidence presented until now suggests, these barriers may be in the decision makers' minds. The conclusion is simple and similar to the one obtained before: No clear-cut behavior patterns can be derived by looking at the *number* of firms. Instead one must look at evidence on relative rates of innovations that indicates whether or not the decision makers take into account the risk of falling behind their perceived competitors.

But as argued in the previous chapters, when managers take into account this risk and perceive a firm jumping ahead, they may decide to imitate the leading firm and bet on that strategy too. Such imitative behavior, however, is not a symptom of collusion but simply a lack of imagination. The next case illustrates this argument.

In the 1960s and 1970s the seven big oil companies started to look for alternative sources of energy and they all found uranium.[26] Why did all bet on "uranium"? Why not on solar energy, energy generated by lightning, waves (of the ocean, as one company did in France), winds? Wesley Cohen in his Ph.D. thesis at Yale examined how this decision was made. Through a request under the Freedom of Information Act he got access to the corporate-planning documents of the seven sisters. He learned that Sohio (Standard Oil of Ohio) in its "Nuclear Energy Review" of July 1969 recommended that the company venture into the nuclear power business by referring not to the world's future energy demands but to the strategies of other oil companies. This report had its origins in an earlier study of the synthetic-fuels industry. "In that study," says the Sohio report, "a survey of the activities of (our) major domestic competitors indicated heavy involvement by many in one or more aspects of the nuclear industry." An internal document of Standard Oil of California dated February 11, 1974, states that the boom in uranium exploration was on the horizon. What were some of the signals? The document reads: "Increased activity by majors, Exxon in particular. Industry rumors indicate that Exxon Minerals has been proceeding since at least mid-1972 on the basis that uranium prices were going to increase drastically. Conoco, Mobil and Gulf are very active; increased hiring of geologists and expansion of staff, including Exxon's recruiting goal of 100 summer students for 1974 vs. 80 in 1973 for mineral field jobs." Cohen concludes that this resulting behavior is "somewhat akin to noticing that the Joneses next door seem to be putting up a fence, and then putting up your own." Such imitative behavior, however, should not be confused with collusion.

Other companies who perceived falling behind innovated rather than imitated. Recall the evidence discussed in Chapter 2 and consider the next cases as well.[27] Charles A. Coffin, of the Thomson-Houston Company, was afraid of losing out as a competitor in an industry. Coffin decided to get into new fields, bought up the Van Depoele railway equipment business, and proceeded to develop for use on large-scale electric railways the equipment that Van Depoele had been successful with in small-scale operations. The entrepreneur behind the Ball Engine Company in 1913 was afraid of being left behind in the general progress of American business. With the growth of central power stations and the abandonment of small electric-generating plants, the Ball Engine Company had a significant decline in its sales. A chance meeting of this worried entrepreneur with a disgruntled salesman of a small steam-shovel manufacturer (who was unwilling to adopt that salesman's recommended improvements) changed the future of the Ball Company, which now became a successful manufacturer of small steam shovels. More recently Freeman (1983) describes IBM's change of strategy from punchcard calculators and tabulators, which were profitable in the 1950s, to electronic computers.[28] He notes that many companies failed to make an innovation or left the punchcard technology too late. "What was remarkable about IBM," notes Freeman, "was the speed with which it recovered from a situation in which it was in danger of falling behind and embarked on the large-scale development and manufacture of the new products once their advantage had been demonstrated" (p. 85).[29]

The predictable perverse use of antitrust laws[30]

Once again a warning, made in the previous chapter, must be repeated. Recall that the view of human behavior assumed here suggests that when people fall behind they may not only innovate, or follow an innovator, but also may compete by a foul strategy. One possibility is to sue the more successful firm claiming that its competition is "unfair." How frequent such accusations were is hard to know. Yet the following extensive evidence from court judgments in antitrust cases suggests that they may have been not less frequent than entrepreneurial acts pursued in "fairer" directions.

In *Telex* v. *IBM* (1975), Telex accused IBM of predatory pricing. The sequence of events was the following: Telex started to sell computer equipment similar to what IBM was selling. IBM reacted by making changes in production and marketing strategies *and* by lowering prices. According to Bartkus (1976) Telex then "found itself unable to compete on a price basis and instead sought relief under the antitrust laws" (p. 285, note 3). Although a first judgment was made in favor of Telex, the Court of Appeal repealed the judgment since IBM's price was not found to be predatory: "After the price reductions by IBM, the trial court found it was nevertheless earning a reasonable profit'' [see Erickson et al. (1977), p. 115]. The court rejected claims in similar circumstances in *Cole* v. *Hughes Tool Co.* (1954) and *N.W. Controls Inc.* v. *Outboard Marine Corp.* (1971).

IBM was again accused by *California Computer Products* (1979) when IBM innovated and reduced prices. In this case the court defended IBM with these words:

Granted that IBM's technological innovations resulted in growth as a consequence of a superior product. . . . Where the opportunity exists to increase or protect market share profitability by offering equivalent or superior performance at a lower price, even a virtual monopolist may do so. [ABA (1984, p. 138), quoting the court]

The court then explicitly mentioned that Section 2 of the Sherman Act "was not intended to shield competitors from the rigors of price competition by a dominant firm" (McEntee and Kahrl 1980, p. 187).

In two additional cases IBM was sued by companies that were falling behind: In *Transamerica Computer Co.* v. *IBM* the court dismissed Transamerica's accusations on the ground that "the plaintiff failed to show that its economic misfortunes were more likely caused by IBM's conduct than by its own mismanagement" (McEntee and Kahrl 1980, p.194). In *Greyhound Computer Corp.* v. *IBM* (1977) the court stated that Greyhound "failed to show that IBM's action (referring to a long-term location strategy) was anything more than a reasonable response to competition" (ABA 1984, p. 138, note 192).

In 1972 Kodak introduced a new camera ("Pocket Instamatic") and a film (Kodacolor II) that was compatible with it. Berkey, in *Berkey Photos* v. *Eastman Kodak Company* (1979) accused Kodak of attempts to monopolize since (a) it did not reveal its intention to introduce these new products; and (b) the fact that only Kodacolor could be used reinforced Kodak's dominant position. Berkey argued that Kodak had to announce its innovative strategy in advance so that the competitors can come up with alternative products (!). Although a jury voted in favor of Berkey, the decision was later reversed. Commenting on the first decision, Keith I. Clearwaters (1978), previously with the Justice Department's Antitrust Division, wrote:

It may lead a company with monopoly power to hold back on the introduction of new products and processes because of fear that innovations, without advance disclosure, will lead to an antitrust suit by a competitor and the possible break-up of the company. (p. 4)

In a Court of Appeals, Judge Kaufman reversed the jury's decision, stating that "the sucessful competitor having been urged to compete must not be turned upon when he wins. . . . It would be inherently unfair to condemn success when the Sherman Act itself mandates competition. . . . We must always be mindful lest the Sherman Act be invoked perversely in favor of those who seek protection against the rigors of competition" [see Jentes (1980, pp. 937–8), quoting the judge].

McEntee and Kahrl (1980) make similar comments:

Berkey, which no longer sells cameras, does not advance its predisclosure as part of a demand for equitable relief. . . . Instead it asks us to condemn Kodak retrospectively, holding that it violated section 2 and so is liable for damages, because it did not decide on its own initiative to take unusual, self abnegatory actions as a corrective for unadjudicated prior offenses. This is without justification. (p. 176)

Kodak was accused by others too. The *Antitrust Law Journal* (1973) in "The Private Actions – the Corporate Manager's Heavy Artillery" notes that Bell and Howell "competitively frustrated in the camera market place, filed a private antitrust suit against Kodak" (p. 14) in January 1973, and GAF Corp, again in 1973, wanted a ban on Kodak's acquisition of patent rights and technology.

In *Purex Corp* v. *Procter & Gamble Company* (1976), Purex accused Clorox and Procter & Gamble (with whom it merged) for pursuing a large number of noncompetitive strategies. The court, however, refuted the accusations "implying they amounted to nothing more than the petulance of one competitor for being out-marketed by another" (McEntee and Kahrl 1980, p. 188). The verdict was based on these conclusions:

(1) Clorox did nothing after the merger that it could not readily have done before the merger.
(2) Pre-acquisition Clorox regularly did a better job in marketing liquid bleach than did Purex, and the same trend continued after the merger.
(3) Clorox, under Procter, was not anticompetitive to any actionable extent under the antitrust laws.
(4) The comparative inferiority of Purex in marketing liquid bleach stemmed principally from decisions of its management.
(5) The claim expansion plans were frustrated by fear of Clorox, is an afterthought, induced by the contemplation of this litigation (ABA 1977, pp. 12–13).

In *Lormar Inc.* v. *The Kroger Co.* (1979), the owner of a grocery store accused one of his competitors of selling a product below cost, *when* a new store was opened. The court rejected the argument stating that the practice of "loss leader product" is customary in this sector. The court's argument is accurate: Recall the discussion on full prices, where it was pointed out that "the price" customers take into account when going *shopping* is not just the price of one of the products they will buy but also the value of the time they will spend in the store. The owners of stores know that and realize that relatively few customers will waste time by buying just one product, and may therefore charge a few cents more on other products compensating for the "loss leader." This is simply a competitive strategy. Another store could compete by carrying a greater variety of products, fresher ones, use an advertising strategy, and so forth.

In *SCM Corporation* v. *Xerox Corporation* (1978), SCM argued that Xerox has a monopoly power because of several patents, but that these patents were used for blocking entry. SCM made the charge when it introduced two "plain paper copiers" (in the sixties it produced "coated paper copiers") that competed with Xerox's products. It is clear that if the court agreed, SCM would have weakened Xerox's position. But the court did not agree, and in a 1981 decision the Court of Appeals stated that

. . . where a corporation's acquisition of a patent was not violative of section 7, as was the case here, its subsequent holding of the patent could not later be seen violative of that section. (*Merger Case Digest* 1982, p. 653)

The fact that Xerox was holding 1,700 patents in the United States in 1973 suggests that in spite of its dominant position, it continued to innovate. As argued in this chapter, this should be a criterion that the courts must take into account.

In *Kobe Inc.* v. *Dempsey Pump Co.* (1952), Kobe accused Dempsey of infringement of patents that it was holding for some hydraulic pumps used to extract oil, without having any information on Dempsey's new pump. The court decided that Kobe "violated Section 2 of the Sherman Act by using litigation in furtherance of its monopolistic scheme. . . . The real purpose of the infringement action and the incidental activities of Kobe's representation was to further the existing monopoly and to eliminate Dempsey as a competitor" [see Hibner (1977, p. 725)].

The sequence of events behind *Brunswick Corp.* v. *Pueblo Bowl-O-Mat* (1977) was the following. At the end of the fifties pin-ball arcades were popular and the defendant, Brunswick, sold equipment to these centers. At the beginning of the sixties the trend changed and several centers found themselves in financial difficulty, unable to pay Brunswick their debts. The deal Brunswick made was that it bought the failing centers (220 across the United States), turning itself into the biggest owner (owning five times more than its closest competitor), but still controlling only 2 percent of these centers. Six of the centers competed with Pueblo's, who then argued that Brunswick was trying to create a monopoly and that if the centers that Brunswick bought were closed, Pueblo's profits could have been higher.

The jury accepted this faulty reasoning, but the Supreme Court reversed it arguing that:

. . . that respondent's claim was essentially that their injury was occasioned by the preservation of competition in that their damage claim was designed to provide them with the profits they would have realized had competition been reduced [see Calvani (1981, pp. 323–4)].

Kaplan v. *Burroughs Corp.* (1977) is a case where a similar decision has been made, and below one can find a list of others where a competitor who was falling behind charged the one getting ahead of anticompetitive behavior. The courts (or the Court of Appeals) in these cases realized what was going on and made the accurate decision of dismissing them. The cases are:

- *The New Grant-Patten Milk Company* v. *Happy Valley Farm Inc.* (1963)
- *Utah Gas Pipeline Corporation* v. *El Paso Natural Gas Co.* (1969)
- *Fargo Glass and Paint Company* v. *Globe American Corporation* (1951)
- *Castlegate Inc.* v. *National Tea Company* (1963)
- *GAF Corporation* v. *Circle Floor Company Inc.* (1971)
- *Smith-Victor Corporation* v. *Sylvania Electric Products Inc.* (1965)

Not every judge made an accurate decision in such cases: In *Briggs Manufacturing Company* v. *Crane Co.* (1980), for example, the decision stated that "there was a showing of probable irreparable injury to the competitor," a statement that is beside the point since the law's intention is to promote *competition* and not to protect a firm against a competitor who became more formidable.

In some merger cases one finds a similar pattern: The competitor sues the company intending to merge, but the judges dismiss the claims. The cases are:

1. In *E. L. Bruce Company* v. *Empire Millwork Corporation* (1958), the judgment stated that "the plaintiff failed to show that there was a reasonable probability that competition would be lessened or that a present danger of irreparable loss or damage existed" (*Merger Case Digest* 1982, p. 479).
2. In *Missouri Portland Cement Co.* v. *Cargill Inc.* (1974), the judgment stated that: "Missouri had not shown that it would suffer injury from the acquisition and, in fact, its claim of an antitrust violation was premised on the contention that it would become a more effective competitor" (*Merger Case Digest* 1982, p. 571).
3. In *American Medicorp Inc.* v. *Humana Inc.* (1977), the district court denied Medicorp's request "holding that Medicorp had failed to show irreparable harm and a reasonable probability of success on the merits with respect to the section 7 claim" (*Merger Case Digest* 1982, p. 668).
4. In *Crouse-Hinds* v. *Internorth Inc.* (1980), "the court held that Crouse-Hinds failed to demonstrate that it would suffer irreparable harm as a result of the merger" (*Merger Case Digest* 1982, p. 649).

A further regularity can be detected in the next cases: Not only was a company falling behind but the accusations of noncompetitive behavior (predatory pricing in particular) occurred when the demand for the particular commodity or service that this industry was supplying fell (also recall the evidence presented in the previous chapter). Part of the accusations seemed to be related to differences in perceptions of future demands (which resulted in different interpretations being given to the decreased prices), and part to trying to impose costs on a competitor whose advantage came to the fore in the worsened circumstances.

In *Kestenbaum* v. *Falstaff Brewing Corp.* (1978), Kestenbaum wanted to increase its price, whereas Falstaff, its previous distributor, anticipating less demand, was reluctant to allow it. But as it was argued, "the antitrust laws were not intended, and may not be used, to require business to price their products at unreasonably high prices (which penalize the consumer) so that less efficient competitors can stay in business. The Sherman Act is not a subsidy for inefficiency" (ABA 1984, p. 126, note 110).

The circumstances behind *Pacific Engineering Co. of Nevada* v. *Kerr-McGee Corp.* were the following: These two firms were the only ones producing a certain chemical substance, for which the demand was falling, leading toward intense competition and diminished prices. One company accused the other of "predatory pricing." In the final decision (after reversing a lower court's decision), the court stated that "in an industry plagued by falling demand and excess capacity, the sinking of a competitor may be an indicator of healthy competitive process" [Vawter and Zuch (1982), p. 407]. Although Kerr-McGee would then become the only firm, the decision stated that "that does not mean the survivor necessarily violated the antitrust laws" (Vawter and Zuch 1982, p. 129). A similar argument and decision was also, finally, made in *Hommel Co.* v. *Ferro Corp.* (1981).

Recently, Baumol and Ordover (1985) described some cases (although in a different context than used here). They note that "Chrysler and Ford, the horizontal competitors of the joint ventures, . . . have pressed the Federal Trade Commission to reject the [GM–Toyota] venture on the ground that it will restrain competition. . . . Recently the FTC approved the joint venture. Undeterred, Chrysler has been pressing a private antitrust action in an attempt to accomplish what it failed to do at the FTC" (p. 256). Baumol and Ordover note that the accusations must be false, for if the enterprise were in fact likely to acquire monopoly power and charge excessive prices, that could only benefit Chrysler and Ford. Their interest was to slow down a competitor who became more formidable. The next case they examine is MCI's use of antitrust litigation as a means to restrain AT&T's ability to respond to competitive incursions, when they conclude that "the staunchest advocates of full-cost pricing have been firms anxious to hobble their disquietingly effective rivals"

(p. 258). In the next chapter additional case studies are presented showing similar patterns of behavior, that is, of using the FTC or antitrust litigations as a means of slowing down competitors when suddenly falling behind.

This evidence strengthens the previously made recommendations concerning the suggested changes in antitrust laws. First the law should state clearly that the word "competition" in its legal sense should not be confused with the use of the word in textbook economics. Second, the law should make reference not to a firm's pricing strategy but to its other strategies as well (as reflected by its relative rate of innovation or whether or not changes in pricing strategies have occurred simultaneously with changes in production facilities). The law also should penalize anticompetitive behavior, and thus impose penalty on firms that, falling behind their more innovative competitors, try to slow them down by perversely using the existing antitrust legislation.

What are the other lessons from the arguments and evidence presented above? The behavior patterns are the same everywhere and perceptions of being left behind motivate them, initiating antitrust suits in particular. Neither the number of firms nor pricing strategies give us the slightest clue for understanding the behavior of enterprises, and there is no reason to invent theories based on these features. Recall that (a) high concentration ratios, which often fit observations, can be generated by models assuming scarce entrepreneurial talent and chance rather than noncompetitive behavior; (b) whatever was the structure of an industry, threats of entry did not permit significant departures from behavior perceived to be competitive; and (c) variations in entrepreneurial talents can lead to any distribution of firms and size within an industry. Thus, no justification can be given for building models based on some numerical features, whether concentration ratio, size, or any other number-based notion. The central issue is to infer whether or not firms compete. This can be inferred by looking at the relative rates of innovation (measured as suggested above). Of course, one would expect that pricing behavior depends, among numerous other factors (see next chapter), on the number of perceived competitors too. But such behavior represents only one facet – not the most interesting one – of the deeper, entrepreneurial and innovative process that takes place.

5   Conclusions

In conclusion, as already emphasized in this chapter, the reason for confusing pricing behavior with competition was that in the neoclassical economic models *all* innovative, entrepreneurial behavior has been eliminated, thus the only thing that firms could have competed with inside these models were prices and nothing else. The mistake was then to look at competition in the real world through the lenses of this quite irrelevant model. Indeed, Stigler (1956) suggested long ago that "it is necessary to contrive a definition of competition for the changing economy'' (p. 272). Although he wrote that "it is by no means obvious how such a definition should be formed; there is no long-run equilibrium under conditions of growth, and we have not yet devised normal patterns of development for industries, technologies and the like, from which we can derive a corresponding concept'' (p. 272). Such a concept has been contrived here.[31]

Once these realizations are made, it becomes obvious that not much can be learned in answering whether or not firms compete by looking at prices only.[32] More can be learned on this question by looking both at the firms' *relative rates of innovation* and their other strategies. One of them – advertising – is examined next.

CHAPTER 4

Advertising, memory, and custom

REUVEN BRENNER
AND GABRIELLE A. BRENNER

How to attract people's ears, eyes, and, eventually, their pockets? This is the question that preoccupies producers when considering advertising. Why, by what mechanism, advertising succeeds in achieving these outcomes is the question that many writers have raised. Both questions will be examined here from a somewhat new angle, which suggests that advertising can be viewed as one particular competitive strategy that, by reminding customers of a possibility (in numerous imaginative ways), lowers the full price of using a product.

Even those skeptical of advertising admit that it is necessary to use it in order to provide information on new products. But they make the accurate observation that most advertising is not of this type. Advertising is most intensive for products where many brands already exist and buyers are fickle (thus causing rapid shifts in shares of sales); but advertising does not have an impact on the sales of all brands taken together. Such repetitive advertising is mainly examined here.[1]

The views presented in this chapter are simple: In contrast to the unique advertising that announces the introduction of novel products, thus informing the public of a new way to spend their money, the role of intensive, repetitive advertising is either to shift uncommitted customers from one brand to another or to prevent the already existing customers from forgetting an option. Advertising achieves this outcome by reminding potential buyers of an option that they may not have had in mind. Since the word "reminding" is associated with that of "forgetting," and both are associated with people's memories, the departure point for looking at some features of advertising will be a view of individual behavior that gives these memories a central role.[2] Other features of advertising – the relationship with customary behavior and the association with status – will be examined through the lenses of the views presented in Chapter 1. How entrepreneurs, who recognize the limited capacity to memorize and the quest for status, respond is also examined.

1   Theory of memory and consumer behavior

The constraints introduced in the formal examination of individual behavior
when examining advertising were mainly two: income and time. In spite of
the fact that one finds reference to the fact that people forget things and advertising reminds them of some possibilities, no attempt was made to examine
systematically the effects of our limited memory capacity and to view features
of advertising in their light.[3] So let us do it here.

The formalization draws on Becker (1971). The consumer is perceived as
facing these constraints: one on his monetary income, the other on his time,
and a third on memory capacity. Subject to them he maximizes a utility function:

$$U = U(Z_i, \ldots, Z_n) \tag{1}$$

where Z_i are a set of basic commodities (a dinner, entertainment etc.), each
produced by the consumer.

$$Z_i = f_i(x_i, S_i, t_i, R) \tag{2}$$

where x_i is the input of purchased goods into the production of Z_i, S_i is the
input of memory space, t_i is the input of time, and R refers to all the other
environmental variables involved in the production of Z_i.

The reason memory space is an input in production is simple: Any learning,
an occupation in particular, involves memorizing. Consider an example: preparing a meal for instance. A housewife may either remember a recipe or look
for it in a book, a time-consuming and therefore costly activity, or buy a
prepared meal, costlier in money than preparing the meal from scratch. Also,
when buying the ingredients, she may either recall where she saw the lower
prices or search for them. Thus, the alternatives to memory are costly whether
in time or in money. Advertising lowers such costs.

The consumer maximizes equation (1) subject to three constraints:

$$\sum p_i x_i = \omega t_\omega + V \tag{3}$$

$$\sum t_i + t_\omega = T \tag{4}$$

$$\sum S_i = S \tag{5}$$

where p_i is the market price of x_i, ω is the wage rate, t_ω is the time worked, T
is the time endowment, S is the memory endowment, and V is his nonwage
endowment. Equations (3) and (4) are not independent constraints and may
be combined in one:

$$\sum p_i x_i + \sum \omega t_i = \omega T + V \tag{3'}$$

Thus, the consumer problem is to maximize equation (1) subject to (3') and
(5). The first-order condition of this maximization problem is of the form

$$\frac{\delta U}{\delta Z_i} = U_i = \lambda \left(p_i \frac{\delta x_i}{\delta Z_i} + \omega \frac{\delta t_i}{\delta Z_i} \right) + \mu \frac{\delta S_i}{\delta Z_i} \tag{6}$$

where λ is the marginal utility of money income, and μ is the marginal utility of memory. Equation (6) can be rewritten:

$$U_i = \lambda \left(p_i \frac{\delta x_i}{\delta Z_i} + \omega \frac{\delta t_i}{\delta Z_i} + \frac{\mu}{\lambda} \frac{\delta S_i}{\delta Z_i} \right) \tag{6'}$$

where μ/λ is the shadow price of memory. Note that $\Pi_i = p_i (\delta x_i/\delta Z_i) + \omega(\delta t_i/\delta Z_i) + (\mu/\lambda)(\delta S_i/\delta Z_i)$ is the "full price" of Z_i, which takes into consideration the cost of each factor of production.

From equation (6') we can see how an increase in wealth will affect memory use. First, let us consider what happens when V, the nonwage income, increases. Then, if we assume that all the Z_i are normal commodities, the demand for each Z_i will increase as all monetary income is spent; thus both the value of goods bought and the time spent in commodities production will increase, and, *ceteris paribus*, the marginal productivity of memory is raised; memory becomes more valuable. Thus, in household production there will be a shift from memory-intensive toward more goods- and time-intensive production methods. More books, data banks, and so forth will be used in order to economize on memory. At the same time producers will have greater incentives to advertise, lowering the full price of some commodities (and as argued in the previous chapter, lowering them is part of the competitive process).

A rise in the wage rate ω would essentially have the same effect, except that in this case time also becomes relatively more expensive. Whether time or memory will become the relatively more expensive factor of production depends on the specific form of the production function. Production will shift toward more goods-intensive methods of production. If one assumes that income itself (i.e., ω) is also generated by memorizing (when learning any customary production process some of the inputs are time and memory), an increased ω (because of an increased demand, formally a change in one of the environmental variables, R) induces allocating more memory toward this direction and less for others. This alteration too increases the incentives of producers to advertise, and thus lowers the full price of some commodities. This model thus sheds a clear light on a controversy in the economic literature. Some argue that advertising causes a movement along a demand curve, whereas others argue that the demand curve shifts, and thus elasticities are irrelevant for discussion on advertising.[4] Both statements may be correct – *depending on what is exactly the price we take into account* when we speak about the demand curve. It we speak about the "full price," which also includes the shadow price of the memory used, then advertising lowers this price and we move along the demand curve. In this case, elasticity is relevant to the discussion. But the discussion will only be theoretical since this price is not measurable. However, if one looks at the demand curve as a function of the quoted price, then advertising shifts the demand curve (since the individual's wealth has increased) and elasticity is irrelevant to the discussion.

Two clarifying notes before examining the evidence: After reading this section some readers may have asked the following question: How can I use here a variation on the standard, neoclassical model following all the previous, sometimes brutal criticism? The answer is simple: As emphasized in the introduction to this chapter, the situation examined here concerns *repetitive, routine* behavior in circumstances that are perceived to be stable – a situation that the neoclassical model was built to handle. The second note is related to the first: Since mainly repetitive advertising is examined here, the issue of fraudulent advertising is touched on only in passing.

2   Advertising facts, or why are you paying $2.99 for a widget?

It is frequently observed that quoted prices in department stores, TV advertising, catalogs, and so forth are of the form $2.99, $399, $1,098. Clearly, marginal cost pricing cannot explain these prices. The probability that most marginal costs in the physical production of goods are just 1¢ or $1.00 below a "round" dollar number is very small (isn't it surprising that this observation was never mentioned by those who tried to show that the marginal cost in production equals price?). Some alternative explanations can be given to this empirical observation:

1. Suppose that a 5 percent proportional excise tax exists on sales of a widget sold at 99¢ apiece. The amount paid by the buyer will be $1.04, because the tax due on the sale is 4.95¢, or 5 percent of the sale price. Thus, on each widget, the seller's profit is increased by 0.05¢. On 10,000 units sold, this would represent an added gain of $5.00 – the result of the practical indivisibility of the cent and of the assumption that each is sold separately. For, if the seller had sold 10,000 widgets to the same customer, this added gain would not have been made. But if the existence of a proportional excise tax were the explanation for the occurrence of prices 1¢ below a round number, we would not observe this type of price wherever the price is stated in integer dollar, for 5 percent of, say, $199 is $9.95. But prices like $199 are frequent. Thus, this is at best only an incomplete explanation of the phenomenon. Also, if the excise taxes were the explanation, then prices such as those would not occur when either there are no proportional excise taxes or when, as in European countries, the posted retail price includes all the taxes. But this type of price is also frequent there.

2. According to Scherer (1980), such pricing strategy serves as a "focal

point.'' By setting its price at such a level, a firm tacitly encourages its rivals
to follow suit without undercutting. He views it as a sign of noncompetitive
behavior that owes its acceptance to tradition. It is difficult to see the reasoning behind this argument: Why is $199.95 a focal point rather than $200?
Before defining it as such, Scherer quotes Schelling's (1960) example of a
focal point, but referring to a rendezvous at 12 o'clock *sharp* at Grand Central
Station in New York.[5] Second, traditions start somewhere, and as Aristotle
in his *Politics* pointed out long ago: ''He who considers things in their first
growth and origin, whether the state or anything else, will obtain the clearest
view of them.'' We try to pursue here Aristotle's suggestion.

Our explanation is based both on the arguments on the scarcity of our capacity to memorize presented above and the fact that once an advertising
strategy succeeds, others will imitate it, and it then becomes part of a tradition.[6] Being exposed to a continuous flow of information on prices, people
store in their memories the more valuable message, in this case the first digits
of a number. For instance, when a price is $398, the digit 3 is more significant
as information than 9, which in turn is more significant than 8. Thus the
consumer, perhaps unconsciously, will act so as to remember first that the
price is $300, then that it is $390. [Note that the discussion on ''conscious''
and ''unconscious'' decision is relevant here: The meaning of the formalization of a consumer's behavior in Becker's consumer-producer model (see Becker
1971, pp. 8–15) does not necessarily mean that one consciously decides at
each step what to remember and what to forget.]

The question that immediately arises is why do people not first round the
number (in our example, to $400) and then store it. The answer to this *critical*
question may be found both in the way information on prices is today transferred to the consumer and in the fact that rounding upward involves *one more*
decision than storing the integer part of the number (or rounding downward).
First, we read from left to right, and the first numbers have greater value.
Second, note the parallel with the way a computer works: Storing *the integer
part* of a number in the direct-access ferromagnetic memory is a very simple
operation that almost does not involve the attention of the operating system.
On the other hand, rounding a number upward involves a more complicated
procedure: A separate routine must exist that first must be fetched, then run
by, the operating system. If we compare the way our memories work with
this system, we may understand why rounding upward is a costlier operation
than merely storing the integer part of a number. Third, remember that information on prices is transferred to the individual by visual or written means.
Prices are advertised on TV, in newspapers, or at stores, and one may glance
at them there. But immediately after the message, one is exposed to additional
information: Either another TV advertisement follows or the program is re-
sumed and the criminal is caught, or an article in the newspaper page absorbs

one's attention. Thus, the information on the price must be stored in a very short interval, and a way to do so[7] is by storing the first digits.[8]

If this argument is correct, one would expect that the smaller the number of goods in the economy, the smaller the number of channels of communication, or the lower the wage rate (and these three are positively correlated), the smaller the probability of finding these types of prices in the economy, since people are less exposed to continuous information. When the value of one of these three variables increases, betting on an idea of a new type of advertising strategy (in the form of the odd $199.95 price, for example) will attract people's attention. This prediction is supported by the following casual empirical evidence: The occurrence of this type of price in the 1900 Sears catalog (1970), when the number of goods available and the number of communication channels were smaller and the wage rate lower than today, is very small. On the other hand, they are frequent in the 1980 Sears catalog. Another result is that goods that have fewer substitutes on the market, such as luxury goods on which the consumer will thus be subjected to less continuous price information, will be less likely to be priced in this pattern. Thus, a very expensive precious stone or an expensive fur coat or a Rolls Royce does not have a close substitute,[9] and the search for them will not involve as many communication channels as, say, the search for a regular coat.[10] Although it should be noted that once such an advertising campaign succeeds, many will imitate it, this pricing strategy becomes customary, and it will no longer attract much attention since it is no longer perceived as "odd."

3   Melodies and memories

Numerous other characteristics of advertising and strategies of firms can be associated with perceptions on the importance of memory in shaping people's behavior. Knowing that pictures, rhymes, rhythms, smells (remember Proust?), and repetitions facilitate the memorizing process, the next features are easy to understand.[11] At NameLab, Inc., near San Francisco, some people are experimenting with onomatopoeia, assonance, and mnemonic devices.[12] Their goal: To make a deodorant *sound* wholesome, lipstick sensual, and a frozen potato exciting. This firm does just one thing: It makes names for products (at about $15,000 apiece). Although the firm admits that a good name won't save a bad product (a statement that recalls the ad agency slogan that a "Good ad kills a bad product"), it contends that "the right" name can help *attract attention*. Ira Bachrach, the founder of the company, judges the names according to their memorability, unusualness, and "flicker perception" (i.e., the way a name is regarded as it is flashed across the TV screen). One of his company's creations was "Civic," the name of the popular Honda automobile, a name that according to Bachrach suggests that "the car is made for urban driving and that it's socially responsible – 'civic minded' – because it doesn't pollute too much or waste gasoline.'' This company is not a unique curiosity: Brand Group, Inc. is a 13-year-old Chicago "name" consultant, another is Inter Brand Corp. in New York (which came up with the name "Magnum" for Miller's malt liquor introduced in 1982). Perhaps the scarcity of words that can easily stick in people's minds explains some companies' strategy of storing trademarks too. In 1980, Seven-Up filed applications for 135 brand names, among them: Sunapple, Sunatural, Sunbay, Sunberry, Sunbelt, Sunbula, Suncap, Sunday, Sunpop, Sunshine, Sunspa, Sun Star, Sunswirl, Suntra, and Sunzest. In addition to the sun, association with academia seemed popular: Alumni, Cum Laude, Kappa, Phi Beta, and Phi Beta Kappa were some of the other words. In the same year, however, a federal judge's (Pierre Leval) decision seemed to put some constraints on the naming game. It ruled that companies cannot bank trademarks, unless they had good reasons. The decision was made when Procter & Gamble filed suit against Johnson & Johnson because the latter began test marketing "Assure! Natural Fit" tampons, claiming that the name violated P & G's "Sure" tampon trademark. J & J argued that its rival's claim was unjustified since the products weren't truly used commercially. Indeed, P & G had a "Minor Brand" program that consisted of shipping 50 cases of each registered name to a total of at least 10 states annually. Regardless of the product, the grocers were billed just $2 a case. In light of the discussions in Chapter 1 and here, this strategy can be perceived as an insurance in protecting an already owned "catchy" name.

Whereas the aforementioned entrepreneurs discovered the demand for such names, Greg Griswold hopes that he has discovered one for easily remembered phone numbers.[13] His company, Ciphrex Corp., already owns 500 (and would like 4,500 more). Among them 1-800-437-7439 (1-800-HERSHEY), 1-800-622-4726 (1-800-NABISCO), etc. For the moment he does not have many takers.

In the *Republic* Socrates explains that control over music is control over character and that rhythm and melody are more powerful than words. Although this may be an exaggeration, it may be useful to remember that the Church in the Middle Ages used music and painting to attract the illiterate, that Verdi was censored by the Austrians because of his stirring music (and words), as are composers today in the communist regimes, and that dances, hymns and bagpipes (for the Celts) stirred up the blood too.[14] The fact that even "light" music is potent in making associations and facilitating memorizing has been recognized by both firms and advertising agencies. A muchquoted dictum attributed to David Ogilvy (the founder of one of the biggest advertising agencies) was, "If you don't have anything to say, sing it." Probably remembering this advice, Brown & Williamson Tobacco Corp., makers of Kool and other cigarettes, sponsors Seattle's annual Jazz Festival.[15] A company marketing spokesman explained that the company wants to relate its brand to the world of music, *hoping* to associate Kool's name with something that isn't dangerous to health. Canada Dry hopes to turn ginger ale from a mixer into a fashionable soft drink by reaching more than one million young people on a 107-city tour by the rock-and-soul group Hall & Oates.[16] Local bottlers stage contests that award free tickets, and a six-pack purchase of Canada Dry knocks $1 off the price of their latest album (a tie-in arrangement, which represents a competitive advertising strategy and not much else). The bet may succeed. Tecate, a Mexican beer sold in 13 Western states, had a 25 percent sales increase as well as several new accounts after sponsoring a 55-city tour of Tom Petty and the Heartbreakers. The Rolling Stones were paid $500,000 to let Jovan, Inc. present their 1981 tour, Schlitz sponsored "The Who" at New York's Shea Stadium, and General Foods Corp. is sponsoring a 27-city tour featuring two country singers to introduce Maxwell House coffee's new vacuum-packed bags. A manager of the company stated that they "needed an event to build awareness of our new package."

Others try to attract our eyes instead of our ears by using famous faces rather than famous voices: from TV and movie stars to top models and from Geraldine Ferraro to some Olympic champions.[17] One purpose of all these features is to make associations, thus stirring people's memories, as a result of which they may decide to buy one brand rather than another.

The aforementioned advertising strategies are not always devised by the firms who produce the product but by advertising agencies. According to some books in marketing, there are three schools of thought in these agencies. One believes in seeking to identify the "unique selling proposition." Another, called the "visibility" school, believes that the main task is to get attention through all means: humor, bizarre visuals. The third, the "brand image" school, seeks to present an emotionally powerful image for a product. Note that the first two implicitly recognize the role of memory: Uniqueness grabs attention, as does visibility. The last uses a much broader criterion: Although memories can certainly stir one's emotions, so can many other pictures unrelated to one's memories, as will be discussed later in this chapter.[18]

4   Advertising and other sources of information

In the economic literature, there is controversy about whether advertising provides information or is a species of brainwashing (see Galbraith 1972).[19] The empirical evidence for the brainwashing hypothesis is alleged to be the existence of frequent advertising messages for, say, McDonald's, Coca-Cola, and so forth that do not seem to provide any information. However, our previous argument can help to emphasize what kind of information is provided by these messages: Our capacity to remember is limited, and knowledge stored in our memory, like any other capital, depreciates (we simply forget things). Thus, reminding us of names and products does provide "information." Indeed, this term does not necessarily refer to "new" information. What we once studied is also stored in textbooks and encyclopedias, but retrieving this knowledge is time and memory consuming. We use memos, reference cards, files and shopping lists, and even banks (for a fee) to remind us of relatives' birthdays – all this information which is not "new." Thus, consider the frequent messages in praise of McDonald's and their possible role. People who had already decided that McDonald's is a good alternative to having a meal at home will "file" this information. The advertising may only be a way of reminding one of the opportunity he did not necessarily have in mind. Without the message, the possibility that this option will not be considered, and people will order pizza, is higher (as a McDonald's representative has recently said: "We need to keep reminding people that we serve breakfast"). In this role too advertising provides information. According to this view the expenditures on advertising that lead to increased sales of a particular brand are of the type that lower the full price of commodities by "re-minding" the customers (literally speaking).

Other economists consider advertising as a "barrier to entry." Their argument is that massive advertising creates a consumer preference for existing brands that the new entrant can overcome only with even more massive advertising. The argument is *contrary* to evidence that shows that intensively advertised brands are associated with *unstable* brand preferences. Such advertising induces the customer to switch back and forth among brands rather than persist with a single one (the argument is made by those who believe that advertising creates a barrier to entry).[20]

Numerous other facts lead to the same conclusions: that is, advertising cannot be viewed as either brainwashing or as a barrier to entry. Advertising is *not* people's only source of information. It has numerous substitutes and faces strong competition from family and friends and the Better Business Bureau, and the key question is whether people continue to buy something *after* they or their friends and neighbors have used it. According to Prescott (1984) studies show that 80 percent of all consumer choices are rooted in someone else's *personal* recommendation. Katz and Lazarsfeld (1955) found that in opinion changes regarding brands of household products, 38 percent included some remembered personal influence, in 15 percent of the cases this influence being judged as the most important factor in decision making.[21] They also conclude that although mass media *exposure* was also very high, the effectiveness of this exposure was relatively low. The following extreme and curious events just confirm this picture and suggest something on the weight people give to word-of-mouth information relative to advertising (and remember: exceptions prove the rule). When the heavily advertised Bubble

Yum entered New York in 1977, the rumor spread that it contained spider eggs. The manufacturer, Life Savers, Inc., took out full-page newspaper ads to deny the rumor. General Foods took out full-page ads to combat the rumor that their candy "Pop Rocks" exploded in the stomach and caused cancer. In 1978 McDonald's sales in the Southeast were noticeably affected by rumors that McDonald's added red worms to its hamburgers to increase their protein content. Schudson (1984) describes one of the most curious episodes:

Rumors spread (in 1982), especially in the Bible Belt, that Procter & Gamble was linked with satanism. The Procter & Gamble symbol of a crescent moon with a man's face facing a group of thirteen stars was said to be a satanic symbol. The rumor began slowly, but after two years, in the spring of 1982, led to some twelve thousand telephone calls a month on Procter & Gamble's toll-free lines. Some shoppers threatened boycotts of stores carrying Procter & Gamble products. . . . Procter & Gamble would not say what effect the rumors had on sales but a spokesman acknowledged that the rumors are "a major distraction to conducting business." The company initiated lawsuits against several individuals identified as spreading the rumor. (p. 94)

The lawsuits did not help and Procter & Gamble recently dropped its trademark of 103 years.[22] Returning to more customary behavior: A 1983 Whirlpool Corp. study asked people what their most reliable source of product information was. Friends were cited most often (23 percent), then relatives (15 percent), and only 6 percent listed advertising, and according to a McNeil research, 80 percent of Tylenol users had *begun* taking it at a doctor's suggestion.[23]

In conclusion, advertising is just one source of information. It competes with numerous others, which seem to significantly diminish its power in influencing people's behavior. Its power seems to consist in reminding consumers, who *already* have bet on buying the product, that it is still available and attractive. In this role it diminishes the full price of some commodities.

5   Catchy phrases or fraudulent advertising? Policy implications[24]

Do statements such as "These second-hand tires are as good as new," or "This suit of clothes will wear like iron" constitute deceptive, fraudulent advertising? The courts have dismissed such statements and did not view them as such [*Warsen* v. *Walter Auto Co.,* 50 Misc. 605, 99 N.Y. Supp. 396 (Sup. Ct. 1906) and *Harburger* v. *Stern Bros.,* 189 N.Y. Supp. 74 (Sup. Ct. 1921), respectively], arguing that the customary behavior of most of us includes some bragging. Thus, exaggerated but catchy phrases are expected to be automatically discounted. Their goal seems to be just to attract attention so as to stick in people's minds, *reminding* them of a product. It may be useful to quote the court's decision in *Ostermoor* v. *Federal Trade Commission,* since it shows how the decision suggests that such discounting is part of our customary behavior. The case was the following: The petitioner was charged with misrepresenting in advertisements and labels the character of its mattresses. The misrepresentation consisted in showing a pictorial place of 35 inches where the mattress was partially ripped open, whereas the actual expansion of the cotton felt filling was about 3 to 6 inches. The court, in annulling the order, found that the commission had misinterpreted this pictorial presentation, and should not have taken it literally:

The pictures clearly assume to show the final stage in the construction of the mattress; the thickness and resiliency before compression and not afterwards; a mattress in process of manufacture, not one completed and, after some unknown time and unknown use, ripped open again. And there is no testimony that such a representation is a misrepresentation of the unfinished article. . . .

Concededly it is an exaggeration of the actual condition; indeed, petitioner asserts that it is not and was not intended to be descriptive, but fanciful. . . . *The time honoured custom of at least merely slight puffing, unlike the clear misrepresentation of the character of the goods, has not come under a legal ban.* [as quoted in Handler (1929) p. 44, italics added]

Yet, in more recent cases, the FTC (Federal Trade Commission) has frequently taken a literal interpretation of similar forms of advertising, as the following summary of cases suggests:

A seller of dime store jewelry [was forced] to disclose that its "turquoise" rings do not contain real turquoise, a toy manufacturer to disclose that its toy does not fire a projectile that actually explodes, a maker of "First Prize" bobby pins to change the name lest a consumer think that the purchase would make him eligible to enter a contest, and a manufacturer of shaving cream to cease representing that his product can shave sandpaper without first soaking the sandpaper for several hours. (Posner 1973, pp. 18–19)

How can one reconcile between the judges' decisions and the ones based on literal interpretations by the FTC? There are two possible explanations. If the majority of the population agrees that the judges' decisions reflect common sense (or customary behavior), then the logical conclusion is that the decision makers at the FTC lacked such sense. This explanation begs the question of how such people got appointed to start with – but we do not intend to dwell here on answering this question. There is an alternative explanation: Suppose that indeed the majority interprets the advertising text *literally* (and, a priori, this may not be such an outrageous assumption as it may seem at first sight: how many people still take various myths – religious, racist, or other – literally?).[25] Then the FTC regulators' literal interpretations may have been accurate and that of the judges not. According to this view, the judges may just be "too smart," and they interpret the advertising texts differently from the way the majority interprets them. If this is the case, the FTC regulators turn out to have common sense, that is, they understand the majority customary behavior.

Which explanation is accurate? This question can be answered by making the following investigation: Select a random sample from the population and ask whether or not they consider the types of advertising statements quoted here as either fraudulent or just reflecting exaggerated, but customary, patterns of speech or visual communication. Such investigations have been done and the conclusion seemed unequivocal: Exaggerated ads reduced the credibility of a product, and acceptance of statements judged deceptive by the FTC was quite low to start with, suggesting skepticism or discounting of claims [see Glassman and Pieper (1980) and a summary of evidence in Singer and Ferreira (1982)]. The evidence thus suggests that the first explanation seems to be the more accurate one, and the FTC's intervention and ruling in the aforementioned cases seems unnecessary. Most people seem to realize that the customary behavior of many of us includes some bragging and patterns of speech reflect both that and the use of some metaphors. But people are used to discounting both phenomena. Thus not all advertising statements are taken literally. They are "advertising" and not necessarily "false advertising." No wonder that in 1969 an American Bar Association Study charged that the FTC was mixed up in trivial matters.[26]

The cases mentioned until now were still relatively easy, and with an appropriate methodology used by social scientists, the right decisions could have been made by recognizing the role of memory (and thus of catchy phrases) in advertising. The next examples are more complex and raise further fundamental issues linked with the suggestion made here that the perception of customary behavior, of the language used in particular, must be the basis for deciding what constitutes fraudulent advertising.

6   Noncustomary behavior, innovations, and advertising

The Listerine case

The claim that Listerine prevents colds and reduces their severity had been used for *over 50 years* before the FTC started its case against the company's claims. The commission adopted a requirement that the producer, Warner-Lambert, spend a sum equal to the average yearly budget spent advertising Listerine between April 1962 and March 1972 (approximately $10 million a year) on corrective advertising that Listerine will not prevent or cure colds or sore throats.

This decision has been one of the most famous ones involving the FTC and is rather controversial from the legal viewpoint. However, we do not intend to discuss here the legal aspect of the case, but another issue. It is still unclear how the FTC, or anybody else, could decide that the advertising of Listerine was "deceptive." The discussion will be linked to the more general question of illnesses, beliefs, and cures.

Here is the text of the TV advertising for Listerine:

[It is raining. Two mothers start talking. One mother has just escorted her children to the school bus, the other (Muriel) is checking the mailbox.]

First Mother: Muriel, where are Dave and Sue?
Second Mother: Oh, down with a cold again.
First Mother: Again?
Second Mother: Oh, guess your family always seems fine.
First Mother: I got a theory.
Second Mother: A theory? Nothing can prevent colds.
First Mother: You can help. Let's get out of the rain.

[They go inside the house.]

First Mother: Muriel, I make sure they have plenty of rest, and I watch their diets.
Second Mother: Uh-huh.
First Mother: Then I have them gargle twice a day with Listerine.

Male Voice: During the cold-catching season, for fewer colds, milder colds, more people gargle with Listerine than any other oral antiseptic. Listerine. (Music)

Recall several things: (a) In various forms Listerine had been advertised for more than 50 years before the FTC intervened: (b) The first mother says that she "got a theory"; the second answers – what all of us know and what is an ancient joke on the medical profession – that nobody knows precisely how to prevent colds, neither physicians, nor anybody else. Although many of us have theories and customs on how to cure colds – for the Listerine mother it is "Listerine," for the Jewish mother it is "chicken soup" – in its customary use the word "theory" does *not* imply that the slightest evidence exists to support it (the Webster dictionary defines the word as "a proposed but unverified explanation"). The fact that the corrective message imposed by the FTC ran like this:

Hello, I am Walter Hughes [fictitious name], representing the FTC [or Warner-Lambert Company].

Contrary to prior advertising of Listerine, Listerine will not prevent or cure colds or sore throats, and Listerine will not be beneficial in the treatment of cold symptoms of sore throats.

Listerine is an antiseptic that kills germs on contact. It is effective for general oral hygiene, bad breath, minor cuts, scratches, insect bites, and infectious dandruff. But

it is not effective against colds and cold symptoms, because colds are caused by viruses and Listerine does not kill viruses.

does not clarify the issues involved. For the statement that "colds are caused
by viruses and Listerine does not kill viruses" is meaningless and irrelevant.
The question is the following: Why does one person fight off a virus, and
another succumb? To say that a disease is due to a "virus" does little to
explain it (if the FTC's "virus" statement was accurate, we all should have
colds). The facts are that for the majority the body's system of immune de-
fenses protects one from "colds," and the question remains why does a minority succumb to this virus, a question to which there is no satisfying answer.

The medical profession recognizes that "colds" and many other illnesses
also have a "mental component" (i.e., are psychosomatic), are related to one
form or other of stress (how many children get colds before exams?), and that
organically inactive agents frequently heal [see summaries of medical research in Totman (1979), Taylor (1979), and a more general framework linking economics and health in a broader context in Harvey Brenner (1973)].
Applying then a *customary,* pampering, treatment (that the patient believes
in) – be it Listerine (the mother may say "it worked for 50 years"), chicken
soup (the mother may say "it worked for 2000 years"), or hot tea with rum
(original date and source for this cure are unknown) – may have the desired
effects, and it is unclear on what grounds one can intervene and state that the
resulting beliefs are "inaccurate." One disturbing conclusion from this case
is that the subject of advertising belongs sometimes not only to the sphere of
the social sciences but of medicine too. Yet to the best of our knowledge no
study has been written on this famous case from the angle presented here. All
the studies found either assumed already that the Listerine case was "deceptive" or approached it from just the narrow, legal point of view, examining
its possible conflict with the First Amendment.[27]

Still, even the decision in the Listerine case may have been easy relative to
the ones that must be made in the circumstances next examined. What criteria
can one use in order to determine whether or not some ads are fraudulent or
not, when the words "ordinary behavior of decent people," which define
customs, customary use of words, in particular, are no longer well defined?
The next cases illustrate the difficulties and also show how the views presented in Chapter 1 shed light on some of them.

The Reynolds pen case[28]

On October 29, 1945, Gimbels, the New York department store, began selling Reynolds pens under the catchy phrase of "It writes underwater!" (it did
not). The success is well known: in six months, Reynolds turned a $26,000

investment into a $1,558,608 personal profit (after taxes, in *1945* dollars). Reynolds did not rely on this outrageous advertising only, but, to attract further attention, he filed suit in a federal court for $1 million (treble damages) against two major pen manufacturers, Eversharp and Eberhard-Faber, for antitrust violations. Reynolds claimed – completely unfoundedly – that the two firms had tried to prevent his entry and that they tried to produce a ballpoint of their own. The suit, of course, did not come to anything, but Reynolds got additional very cheap publicity in the newspaper headlines and turned his pens into a ''media event'' (economists estimating Cobb–Douglas advertising functions should keep this example in mind).

The burger battle[29]

In December 1982 Burger King Corp. agreed to stop showing TV commercials that said unkind things about McDonald's Corp. and Wendy's International, Inc. The commercials made the claim that customers prefer Burger King's broiled hamburgers over McDonald's fried ones by a wide margin. McDonald claimed that the whole claim was false since Burger King's hamburgers ''are often steamed and they are reheated and/or warmed in microwave ovens before sale to customers.'' In September, before the first ads were aired, McDonald already filed suit trying to prevent their airing, stating that ''for McDonald's to permit any competitor to falsely advertise, make inaccurate and incomplete product comparisons and mislead even one consumer is wrong. We take the hamburger more seriously than anyone else.'' McDonald's prompt reaction led to stories on all three American networks and in newspaper headlines. On October 29, the three fast-food chains met in Columbus, Ohio, and Burger King agreed to phase out its comparative ads. However, some damage was apparently done: Between October and January, Burger King's sales grew significantly faster than the sales of its competitors (whereas before they were *falling behind*). Burger King admitted that the publicity (over going to court) did for their product what commercials could not, and the other chains seemed to regret going to court. Indeed it was an advertising agency that helped turn Burger King's ''battle of the burgers'' campaign into a national news story. This substitution of traditional TV ads by a ''national news story'' may not be an isolated incident but may be due to the decline of mass TV audience, the swelling ranks of working women, and recent innovations (VCRs, cable TV, etc.).

The beer battle[30]

In the beer industry, too, competitors make frequent complaints against one another that are similar in nature to the ones the hamburger chains make.

When Miller Brewing Company quickly moved from seventh place to threaten Anheuser-Busch's number one position, the latter complained in 1977 to the FTC. They claimed that Miller's Löwenbrau had little resemblance to the German product and thus the advertising was fraudulent since it did not make it clear that the beer was made in the United States. [Note that this accusation, too, as in the Burger case, did not come randomly, but was related to the leapfrogging process discussed in Chapter 1. So Burger King's and Anheuser-Busch's managers' reaction of betting on a novel strategy either innovative or criminal (depending on one's perception) could have been predicted, and the accusations should have been viewed in this light and disregarded.] In 1979, Miller complained about Anheuser-Busch's advertising its beers as "natural," claiming both that additives are used and that the "beechwood aging" process the company used since 1933 "consists of dumping chemically treated lumber into a glass lined or stainless-steel beer-storage tank," and that consumers may misinterpret both words (i.e., "natural" and "beechwood-aging"). Anheuser-Busch countered by charging that Miller loads its beers with artificial foam stabilizer (saying that their product keeps its head naturally), and uses an industrial enzyme (instead of natural malt) to reduce the calories in its Miller Lite brand, and so forth.

What can one learn from these cases? Burger King and Anheuser-Busch started new strategies when their managers saw they were falling significantly behind their competitors. Reynolds's behavior may be understood, in part, by recalling his history (described in Chapter 2).

A perception of leapfrogging by either managers or entrepreneurs was not the only thing that these three cases had in common. In all three cases the existing legislation (on antitrust and fraudulent advertising) *and* the eagerness of the information channels (radio, TV, newspapers) to announce curiosities in their headlines (i.e., noncustomary acts) were *used* by the respective decision makers to advertise their product and obtain effects that not even a million-dollar advertising budget could buy (recall the criticism on well-defined "production functions" and "factors of production" that this evidence further justifies).[31]

Was Reynolds's, Burger King's, and Anheuser-Busch's behavior "fraudulent" or was their intention just to grab attention by a novel strategy? Reynolds did not do anything illegal, although his conduct was noncustomary. The public perceived the behavior as "innovative" rather than criminal or fraudulent. In the two other cases, it is not even clear whether or not one can prove that the advertising was fraudulent. In the Burger King case, their hamburger is produced differently (literally speaking). They call their steaming apparatus a "humidified holding cabinet" and use microwave ovens for just a few seconds to heat up the sandwiches. In the beer case, who knows how the public interprets the word "natural"? Few people expect the beer to come out of a spring. Also, the problem in these cases is related to the fact that while technology is changing, and goods are thus produced by new, non-customary methods, the vocabulary used is not. Most people still use the ancient words "broiling" and "frying" although their content is radically changed. Thus, it is hard to believe that any of the companies could reasonably expect to win their case. The motivation of the accusers was probably to slow down their competitors, and the competitors have used the existing legal and regulatory system as a cheap form of advertising.

This was not the only way enterprises adjusted to the constraints imposed on them by the government. Several ad agencies have pointed out that because of the federal officials' watchdog activities, advertising became heavily censored. Since it has become harder and harder to say meaningful, brief things (since they would imply generalizations, which, by definition, would be inaccurate) or use catchy phrases (as the previous evidence suggests), the substitutes found for grabbing people's attention are music or a "trusted" face.[32] But it should be pointed out that recently the FTC seems to require less proof to back advertising claims, perhaps because the former commissioner, Michael Pertschuk, finally concluded that "most consumer injury in advertising cases is small, and sometimes it seems the issues are not worth the trouble."[33]

This conclusion could have been reached earlier by considering the fact that fractions of evidence presented here were already available in the past and by realizing that, in a sense, advertising is also an art. Perhaps Kenneth Clark's words (in his book *Civilisation,* which was also a successful TV series) are worth recalling:

Writing for television is fundamentally different from writing a book, not only in style and presentation but in the whole approach to the subject. People who settle down to an evening's viewing expect to be entertained. If they are bored they switch off. . . . Their attention must be held by a carefully contrived series of images. . . . Generalizations are inevitable and, in order not to be boring, must be slightly risky. . . . There is nothing new in this. . . . , television should retain the character of the spoken word, with the rhythms of ordinary speech, and even some of the off-hand imprecise language that prevents conversation from becoming pompous. (p. XIII)

Indeed, as the evidence presented in this chapter suggests, advertising in general – TV ads, in particular, their catchy but imprecise phrases – seems to be interpreted exactly in this way rather than as being fraudulent.

7 Conclusions

This chapter has concentrated on one facet of competition: advertising. Its role is to remind people in numerous ways of possibilities that may have slipped from their minds. The reason for concentrating on this particular facet of advertising is simple: One of the main controversies surrounding the subject of advertising is its repetitiveness. There seems to be little disagreement on advertising that presents new products and their various features.

Yet one must be aware of the fact that the distinction between repetitive ads and ones that present new products is not always sharp: A "new" product is defined not only as one that is "technologically" novel but also as one whose use becomes different from the customary one. Schudson (1984) gives a detailed account of the history of cigarette smoking in the United States and the role of advertising in it. First, he shows how male attitudes toward cigarette smoking changed at the beginning of the century. The attitude was, at the beginning, negative: the act was perceived as "feminine" (it was banned in the army, even though tobacco smoking was permitted). After World War I, urbanization, the more crowded places where people worked and lived, the increased popularity of driving all seemed to make tobacco smoking more difficult, or even unfeasible, and cigarette smoking more attractive. The war contributed too since smoking cigarettes during it was easier, and later the ads appealed to memories of comradeship. Women's smoking is quite a different story: It started as a symbol of their liberation movement much before any producer of cigarettes dared to put a woman in his picture. Instead, the information on this new, noncustomary trend was frequently provided by the *New York Times* and other newspapers' *headlines*. Only slowly, and very cautiously, did the producers of cigarettes put pictures of women in their ads; first, the women were just looking from the background, passively, at men smoking, but did not have a cigarette either in their mouths or even in their hands. Thus, the advertising seemed to mirror trends rather than create them. In these circumstances "cigarette advertising," which may have seemed to some as repetitive, was, in fact, novel and provided images that reflected the tendency that cigarette smoking among women was becoming more and more popular, images that may have encouraged others to try. Indeed, some studies have found that people's reference groups influenced their choice of cigarettes, cars, and beer at both the product and the brand level. That is, the decision to consume the good at all and the decision on the brand of good to be considered were both made with some reference groups in mind.[34]

Pictures of women in ads that previously had a male-macho image are now taking place before our eyes. At first glance, a new Molson Golden beer ad looks like any other picture with a romantic association: It shows two tents, one illuminated, to reveal the silhouettes of a man and a woman sharing a beer. But note: For the time being this is the only brand appealing to female drinkers. The others still use horses, highways, trucks in the background, or make associations between beer drinking and male comradeship. But Alsop's (1985) survey indicates not only that other beer companies are now considering competing for this new public, but even that hard liquor producers (of scotch and whiskey) want to try their luck. The reason for the new trends? With greater participation of women in the labor force, they are drinking more at business lunches, meetings, and, like men, turn to alcohol in times of stress. But if previously women's drinking had a negative connotation, being associated with boredom in suburbia, now their drinking seems more acceptable and is perceived in a different light: the image of women pursuing high-paying careers. Again then, advertising seems to fit the discovered trends, but does not create them.

The conclusion that advertising seems to mirror trends rather than create them has been reached not only by those who have looked at the origins of some particular advertising patterns but also by those who have looked at some aggregates. Schmalensee (1972), for example, found that there was a closer correlation between consumption in a given quarter and advertising in the next one than between consumption in a given quarter and advertising in the previous one, and concludes that the total national advertising does not seem to affect total consumer spending; rather, total advertising expenditures lag changes in the sales of consumer goods. Gilligan (1977) found similar evidence: More than 75 percent of the 92 British companies surveyed calculated their ad budgets as a fixed percentage of either the previous year's sales or profits or the next year's expected sales or profits. In most cases the percentage taken had remained unaltered for at least four years.[35] This finding of passive adaptation leads Julian Simon (1970) to the conclusion that "those branches of advertising which are most in dispute – advertising for such products as beer, autos, soap and aspirin – do not seem to have much effect upon the economy in any way, direct or indirect, and hence from an economic point of view it is immaterial whether they are present or absent" (p. 284). But this conclusion is *erroneous*. Benham (1972) compared the prices of eyeglasses in states that completely restricted advertising with those where no such restrictions existed. He found that where advertising was completely banned, the price of eyeglasses averaged $37.48, whereas where there was no restriction, the price of eyeglasses averaged $17.98. Similar evidence was found by Steiner (1973): Although prior to the mid-1950s, a typical toy with a $5 list price tended to retail at $4.95 to $4.98, with occasional advertised sales at $4.49, after the mid-1950s when toy manufacturers began advertising on TV, the prices in cities where such advertising was undertaken dropped to $3.49 with sales at $2.99. Thus, advertising does seem to have a significant effect, at least for the price ranges examined in these studies. This effect should have been expected since the ads, by providing information, substitute for the time-consuming search that previously was incurred *and* lower the full price of these commodities.[36]

Last, but not least, a question must be raised: Since the wide range of evidence presented in this chapter suggests that advertising is essentially a competitive strategy and that customers seem most fickle for products that are most heavily advertised, how did the barrier view of advertising arise?[37] The view seems to originate from some economists in the 1930s, who, dissatisfied with models of perfect competition, tried to make them more "realistic." However, instead of realizing that in models where risks, uncertainty, and information costs (due to memorizing in particular) are absent, advertising could play no role, and then drawing the conclusion that perhaps the notion of competition should be revised by taking them into account (an approach pursued in this book), they decided that since advertising exists, the "real world" is noncompetitive (noncompetitive as defined in neoclassical economics). This *is* a logical approach, too, but it reminds one of the logic Alice encounters in Wonderland. How did it occur that many economists seemed to adopt this view? This is a broad question of how the particular world called "science" works. Some answers to it can be inferred from the evidence presented in the next chapter.

CHAPTER 5

Inventions and innovations
in business and science

Submit to pressure from peers and you move down to their level.
Speak up for your own beliefs and you invite them up to your level.
If you move with the crowd, you'll get no further than the crowd.
When 40 million people believe in a dumb idea, it's still a dumb
idea . . .
So if you believe in something that's good, honest and bright, stand
up for it.
Maybe your peers will get smart and drift your way.

Advertising by United Technologies, Inc., *The Wall Street Journal*

The view presented here, as well as in Brenner (1983, 1985), examines the conditions under which people bet on new ideas (in any domain) and the likelihood of others to adopt or reject them. The questions raised are simple: Since betting on new ideas represents, by definition, abandoning customary behavior, what induces some people to act in this way, and what determines the rest of the society's reaction toward them?

As shown in the previous chapters, the pressure of competition and the threat of rivals induce some people to abandon their customary ways of thinking and inspire inventions and innovations. However, it would be misleading to jump to the conclusion that only competition (as defined in Chapter 3) and no other incentives can make the sparks fly. There are numerous other forms of threat that can shock people out of their customary behavior and provide incentives for an innovative one. However, in order to keep the discussion manageable, this chapter concentrates on the emergence of some new ideas and the reactions to them within or close to the frame of reference chosen in this book.[1]

Modern stupidity means not ignorance, but the nonthought of received ideas.

Milan Kundera

1   Economics and creativity: words and facts

Words

In spite of the fact that *no* relationship between market structure and technological innovations is discernible [see summaries of a very extensive literature
in Johnson (1975), Scherer (1980),[2] Kamien and Schwartz (1982), and Freeman (1983)], as indeed one should expect from the approach pursued here,
many theoretical and empirical studies on innovations have investigated the
possibility of such relationships. However, although the words "innovation"
or "invention" appear in their titles, none of the theoretical models claiming
to deal with innovations and inventions does so, since all admit that they
cannot say anything about either people's creativity, their willingness to venture into noncustomary acts, or the notion of uncertainty. And, after all, what
is an "invention," and "innovation," or what is "technological change" if
not some people's new ideas and their ability to bring them to life?

The reason for avoiding this central question is simple and, as can already
be inferred from the previous chapters, it follows from the hard core of "microeconomics," where the assumption made is that technology is "given"
[in fact even in the so called macro-Keynesian models this assumption is
made, being based on Keynes's (1936) own statement that "we take as given
. . . the existing quality and quantity of available equipment, the existing
technique" (p. 245)]. Although this static character of neoclassical economics
has been frequently criticized, not much has been done to really change the
situation. In recent studies, Nelson (1984), Sylos-Labini (1984), Johnson (1975),
Loasby (1976), Freeman (1983), and Fisher et al. (1983) continue to point
out that neoclassical formalism does not and cannot encon.pass concepts
such as creativity, insight, genius, or entrepreneurship. Although Nelson and
Winter (1982) try to develop an "evolutionary" model, they too, as pointed
out in Chapter 1, do not deal with the issue of creativity, the emergence of
new ideas, and the gutsiness of some people in taking the plunge but offer
instead another mechanistic model. Freeman (1983) remarks that "innovation
is a coupling process and the coupling first takes place in the minds of imaginative people. An idea 'gels' or 'clicks' somewhere . . . [and] this begs the
question of creativity in generating the inventive idea" (p. 111), but then he
too no longer returns to this issue in his book.

The few economists who have touched on this issue have answered the
question, "What causes invention?" by saying that it is due to the random
inspiration, insight, and virtuosity of a small number of individuals and have
paid no attention to some features of society within which the inventions
could be brought to life [see Usher (1955), for example]. Others, influenced
by Ogburn and Gilfillan, took the opposite view and suggested that inventors

are merely tools of history. Gilfillan (1935) wrote that "there is no indication that any individual's genius has been necessary to any invention that has had any importance. To the historian and the social scientist the progress of invention appears impersonal" (p. 10).[3] Poor Beethoven! Poor Einstein! Poor Edison!

As noted in Chapter 2, the facts do not allow one to support either approach: not Usher's, since innovations in all domains, technological or other, appear in clusters and are *not* randomly distributed either across time or societies (thus, one cannot just pay attention to individuals), and neither Ogburn's nor Gilfillan's. Although evidence exists that at times similar innovations have been made just a few years apart (Leibnitz and Newton, Bolyai and Lobachevski, Darwin and Wallace), how can one state that if not Beethoven, Edison, Einstein, Napoleon (certainly a great innovator in law), and so forth, then somebody else would duplicate their inventions exactly *and* at the same time? Not even Marx can be accused of holding such an extreme viewpoint, as the next quote from one of his letters suggests:

World history would have a very mystical character if there were no room in it for chance. This chance itself naturally becomes part of the general trend of development and is compensated by other forms of chance. But acceleration and retardation depend on such "accidentals," which include the "chance" character of the individuals who are at the head of a movement at the outset. [as quoted in Carr (1982), p. 101]

Carr (1982) correctly points out that to say that individuals merely "accelerate" or "retard" but do not alter is just a play on words (accelerate or retard by how much? 10 years? 20? 100?), and the idea that one form of chance compensates for another is meaningless. In fact, both schools of thought seem to provide some comforting views of the world that *avoid* dealing with the central, disturbing questions of human creativity and uncertainty, and thus imply that one can deal even with inventions and innovations within some deterministic, impersonal framework.

This is a fundamental feature of the writings of most economists, who, for the last 200 years (until around the seventies) avoided discussions on risk and uncertainty. Instead, as already emphasized in previous chapters too, their major preoccupation was to look at human behavior through the lenses of models of certainty, creating vocabularies within them and forecasting. It may be illuminating to put this preoccupation within a broader perspective. Probably Mackay in his *Extraordinary Popular Delusions and the Madness of Crowds* (1841) provides good insights (and some evidence) into the rationale for this particular facet of human activity:

Dissatisfaction with his lot seems to be the characteristic of man in all ages and climates. So far, however, from being an evil, as at first might be supposed, it has been the great civiliser of our race; and has tended more that anything else, to raise us above the condition of the brutes. But the same discontent which has been the source of all

improvement, has been the source of no small progeny of follies and absurdities. . . .
Three causes especially have excited the discontent of mankind; and, by impelling us
to seek for remedies . . . have bewildered us in a wave of madness and error. These
are death, toil and ignorance of the future. . . . From the third [sprang] the false
sciences of astrology, divination, and their divisions of necromancy, chiromancy, au-
gury, with all their train of signs, portents and omens. (pp. 98–9)

Recall that for centuries astrology, for example, was used for forecasting,
promising diminished ignorance of the future, and was used by monarchs and
governments. In England, from the time of Elizabeth to that of William and
Mary, judicial astrology was in high repute. In the time of Charles I the most
learned, the most noble, and the most conspicuous characters did not hesitate
to openly consult astrologers. In every town and village astrologers were quite
busy casting nativities, prognosticating happy or unhappy marriages, predicting whether journeys would be prosperous, and suggesting lucky moments
for setting up enterprises, whether a cobbler's shop or the marching of an
army. Did the astrologers believe in the trade? Some probably did, whereas
others did not. Once a vocabulary is invented and is then passed on from one
generation to the other, form and substance can be confused: Some practitioners may have perceived themselves as being in the business of "astrological
explanations" rather than that of "explanations" of human behavior – just
like the managers of the movie industry regarded themselves as being in the
movie rather than the entertainment business, those in the dry-cleaning industry as being in the dry-cleaning rather than the cleaning business, or, perhaps,
like some economists, as being in the business of "economic explanations"
for human behavior rather than that of explanation for it. Other astrologers
did not believe in their trade, although they still practiced it. Kepler, while
writing a treatise on astrology, wrote in his correspondence that it was nothing
but worthless conjectures, but that he did it to avoid "starvation."

Many economists have harshly criticized the use of models of certainty, of
static models of competition in particular, and explained their persistence by
a reasoning similar to both Mackay's and the one that can be inferred from
the view of human nature presented in Chapter 1. Dobb (1937), for example,
remarked that "so long as mathematical technique retains its servitude to a
particular mode of thought the concepts which it fashions are calculated to
veil rather than to reveal reality" (p. 183). In a much broader context, concerning all the sciences, Kuhn (1970) too noted that "because they [the sci-
entists] can ordinarily take current theory for granted, exploiting rather than
criticizing it, the practitioners of mature sciences are freed to explore nature
to an esoteric depth and detail otherwise unimaginable" (p. 247), while Schackle
(1967) put it bluntly that indeed, the main service rendered by a theory is the
setting of minds *at rest*. A later section in this chapter shows what this statement implies. Meanwhile, I hope that the evidence on the long-run success

of astrology and the previous comments are sufficient, for the moment, to answer very briefly the question that some readers may have asked themselves (as some did when reading the book in manuscript form): How can people believe in and imagine things that could never be for very long periods of time? The answer is simple: In some circumstances, such beliefs maintain stability, maintain a somehow established order by putting our minds to rest, once again, literally speaking.

Facts

Most empirical studies done by economists who tried to explain innovations and technological change are not more convincing than the aforementioned theories. Since the inputs into the creative effort were not measured in any meaningful way (indeed they cannot be), it is not very surprising that the various indices built as indicators of this effort – expenditures on R & D, schooling of workers, number of employed scientists and engineers, having patent priority – failed to shed light on what ex-post turned out to be the successful innovations.[4] Johnson (1975), for example, remarks that although the advanced countries tend to have relatively higher R & D expenditures compared with those that are less developed, this does not necessarily imply a close link between such expenditures and growth, and notes that both the United Kingdom and the United States, with relatively high R & D expenditures, have grown much more slowly than Japan or West Germany. On a less aggregated level, Cooper (1983, p. 22) concludes from his study of 103 industrial firms that the relationship between R & D spending and innovations "is not as obvious and linear as might have been assumed. For example, in terms of new product effectiveness, there were no differences between high R & D and low R & D firms. . . . Indeed, the new product success, failure, and 'kill' rates vary little across R & D spending categories. Moreover, the rated success of firms' new product programs is *not related* to R & D spending" (p. 22).[5] Freeman (1983) too concludes that there "was no strong systematic evidence that larger or smaller firms or R & D departments were more or less successful" (p. 117), and that:

Perhaps surprisingly, for those who believe in the amenability of innovation to planning techniques, no relationship was found between success and the capacity to set and fulfil target dates for particular stages of the project plan, nor in the general approach to planning of the innovators.(p. 123)

The next remarks put this generalized conclusion in sharp focus. Peters and Austin (1985) write that:

After twenty-five years of studying American industrial innovation, Brian Quinn . . . said of IBM: "It was difficult to find any successful innovation that derived from formal product planning." After years of using Quinn's line with hundreds of audiences we've heard a demurring voice only once. It came from a senior AT&T executive: "Nonsense. I *know* it's not true for the Bell Labs." He pointed to a highly respected Labs vice president and said "You tell him." The Labs man . . . replied, "Well, I've only been at the Labs for a bit over thirty years, but I can't *think* of anything that ever came directly from the new product planning process." (p. 118)

Freeman (1983, p. 123) also points out that he found no relationship between success and the number of scientists and engineers on the main board of the innovating company, although this proportion varied considerably. This conclusion should not be surprising since similar ones have been obtained earlier when examining inventions and innovations from other angles. Schmookler (1957), in his study on "Inventors Past and Present," concluded that "what is surprising, in short, is not the large proportion of inventors who are college-trained, but the large proportion who are not . . . the conclusion seems inescapable that much modern invention could go forward without benefit of college training. Indeed, as has been shown, a lot of it in fact does" (p. 325). Earlier, Van Deusen (1954) concluded that "truly significant innovations generally are the work of outsiders, individuals far enough removed from an industry to have a fresh viewpoint on its problems" (p. 133). In order to give a feeling of what "outsiders" means recall that the electrical properties of metals were discovered by an anatomist, Galvani, while dissecting frogs, that Ohm (from electricity) was a "mere" Jesuit math teacher (and thus was at first not listened to). Mendel, the pioneer geneticist, was disregarded because he worked at a little experimental plot in a rural abbey – more evidence on scientists will be given later in this chapter. Chester Carlson, who conceived the idea of xerography (with the assistance of an *unemployed* physicist) was a patent attorney.[6] Canon, the great innovator in the photo industry, was started in 1937 by Chairman Takeshi Mitarai, a physician, while Kodachrome was invented by two musicians.[7] A watchmaker working with brass casting came up with the process for the continuous casting of steel, and dye-making chemists developed synthetic detergents, after soap-making chemists turned the project down as uninteresting. One of the top sellers among ulcer drugs is Smith Kline's Tagamet. But the team who invented it was almost stopped because the developer was "a disrespected, simple scientist from Glasgow." During the 1920s researchers at General Motors investigated synthetic rubber, and made several inventions. Du Pont's president (Du Pont and GM had at that time substantial joint ownership) reacted with skepticism, not because he looked at the inventions, but because they came from the GM labs rather than the ones from the chemical companies.[8] Rossman (1931) in a detailed study of the military provides the following information:

John Ericsson . . . who invented the screw propeller of the warship "Princeton" in 1841, was not a naval officer. This invention led to the installation of the engines and boilers below the water line, bringing about the development of modern naval construction. Hiram Maxim, the inventor of the machine gun, was not an army officer. Gatling, the inventor of the important machine gun bearing his name, was a real-estate dealer. Colt, who invented the Colt gun, was an American who worked in his father's textile mill. Dreyse, who invented the needle-gun which was so effectively used by the Prussians in the Franco-Prussian War, was a German locksmith and manufacturer of ironware. Fulton, Bushnell, Holland, and Lake, who made various submarine inventions, were outsiders to the navy. (p. 633)

– more evidence and discussion on outsiders in the next section.

Back to aggregated data: Hamberg's (1966) review of his own and others' findings led him to conclude that large industrial laboratories tend to produce mainly minor inventions. He claims that the fraction of total inventive output of these laboratories that can be classified as "important" is less than the comparable ratio for inventive output of other sources, independent inventors among them. Cooper and Schendel (1982) in their study on "Strategic Responses to Technological Threats" make similar observations, although they seem to be surprised by the fact that "the first commercial introduction of the new technology was, in four out of seven cases, made by a firm outside the traditional industry" (p. 327). Jewkes et al. (1969) too suggest that frequently innovations came from outsiders and from small companies rather than the established ones (also recall the examples discussed in the previous chapters: the oil industry, Bic and Gillette, Reynolds, the supermarkets, etc.). Scherer (1980) also emphasizes (as does Van Deusen) that outsiders and newcomers contributed "a disproportionately high share of all really revolutionary new industrial products and processes," among them: arc lighting (Brush), the incandescent lamp (Edison), alternating current (Westinghouse), radio telegraphy (Marconi), transistorized radio (Sony), self-developing photography (Polaroid), and so forth. Mansfield (1975) also notes that the laboratories of the major petroleum firms were not responsible for the radical inventions that occurred prior to World War II. The novel ideas – cracking by the application of heat and pressure, continuous processing, fractionation, catalysis, and so on – were introduced by independent inventors, and even recently, the bulk of the R & D done by the big oil companies is directed at minor improvements rather than radical advances. In the pharmaceutical industry too about one-half of the major innovations during 1935–62 were based on discoveries made outside the established laboratories (pp. 318–20). Kamien and Schwartz also recall that the innovations that led to the new wristwatches came from semiconductor manufacturers – Letronix, Hughes Aircraft, and Fairchild Camera – rather than the traditional watch manufacturers (Timex, Bulova, Longines, Seiko). *Revolution in Time,* David Landes's (1983) detailed history of this industry from ancient times, shows that the pattern is by no means novel. Although in the seventeenth century the British industry dominated the trade, during the eighteenth and nineteenth centuries it declined and was challenged by new entrants (the Swiss being the most prominent among them).

In addition to this regularity, on the insights of outsiders, an additional one was found that shed light on the emergence of inventions and innovations. From various case studies Sturmey (1958, p. 277) concluded that in the radio industry the major force leading to innovation is *not* any particular structural form but perceptions of entry. Where the entry of competitors, perceived to pose a threat, appeared to be impossible, innovations were slow to come. But where entry was perceived to be possible, innovations seemed to come faster. Stekler (1967) found that the U.S. aerospace industry became increasingly innovative when the federal government, its major customer, became less protective of the industry members. Comanor (1965) found that R & D is a major element of interfirm *rivalry* in the pharmaceutical industry, with profits largely dependent on a firm's continued innovative success. Scherer's (1980, p. 438) summary suggests that, in general, the threat of entry through innovations by newcomers stimulated existing enterprises to pursue innovations more agressively: IBM responding to the electronic computer innovations of Sperry Rand, Control Data Corporation, and Digital Equipment; the established aircraft makers pursuing basic research and systems engineering in 1955 when the U.S. Air Force chose the infant Ramo-Wooldridge Corporation to oversee its Atlas ICBM development program. Miller and Sawers (1968) make the same observation: Both Douglass and Lockheed entered jet production when the Comet and the 707 made their appearance, both aircraft being produced by relative outsiders who had little stake in the existing commercial market.

One conclusion from the examination of these facts is simple: Competition through innovations may come from any quarter, producers in similar lines of business as well as those in entirely different ones (a point important to recall when attempts are made to define markets). Thus, Schumpeter (1942) was right when he pointed out that such competition "acts not only when in being but also when it is merely an ever-present threat. It disciplines before it attacks. The businessman feels himself to be in a competitive situation even if he is alone in his field or if, though not alone, he holds a position such that investigating government experts fail to see any effective competition between him and any other firms in the same or neighboring field and in consequence conclude that his talk under examination, about his competitive sorrows, is all make-believe" (p. 85).[9]

The evidence and this conclusion reinforce those reached earlier concerning both the criterion to be used by antitrust laws for inferring competitive behavior (i.e., a measure of the accused firm's innovative effort) and the irrelevance of classifications of market structure based on numbers in existing markets for inferring behavior.

> People do not distinguish; without a test they take things
> from one another: even on things of their own day, not
> dulled by time, Hellenes are apt to be all wrong. So little
> pains will most men take in search for truth: so much more
> readily they turn to what comes first.
>
> Thucydides

2   Inventions and innovations: further implications for the theory of the firm

In light of the evidence presented here and in the previous chapters, one must unavoidably return to the subject discussed in Chapter 1 – the traditional theory of the firm – and raise further doubts about its relevance. Recall that economists categorize decisions within that theory in three groups: (1) those relevant for "the short run," when the quantity of some inputs cannot be varied; (2) the ones relevant for "the long run," when all inputs may be varied, but the technology of production is unchanged; and (3) the ones pertinent for "the very long run," when inventions and innovations are taken into account. As one can easily deduce from the discussions presented until now, most of the economic literature of the firm deals with the first two categories by using mathematical models developed to esoteric depth, and avoids dealing with the third. One can easily verify the accuracy of this assertion by taking a look at any of the now standard, graduate textbooks in microeconomic theory or the more classic ones – Henderson and Quandt (1971), Varian (1984), Malinvaud (1982), Samuelson (1971) – and see not only that inventions, innovations, and entrepreneurship are not discussed, they are hardly mentioned.

The question that must be raised is therefore simple: How pertinent are models describing some behavioral features of the firm, but which neglect inventions and innovations? Suppose that one finds that over a long period of time and across a wide range of industries a relatively large percentage of revenues is derived from nonroutine production, let us say, the sales of new products not in existence two or five years before. One can then quite safely be skeptical of the predictive ability of the so-called short-run and long-run models, and question their relevance.

Recall that these models can only make predictions concerning prices and quantities of existing products, *assuming* that neither are investments made to produce new ones nor is a threat perceived that new ones may be introduced. Predictions on prices and quantities would be radically different if the possibility of innovations that would make existing products obsolete was taken into account. The question is therefore empirical: If inventions and innovations are rarely made, and thus the sales of new products provide a relatively small percentage of revenues, the traditional short- and long-run models could still be useful for making useful predictions on prices and quantities. However, if evidence is found that this is not the case, one can quite safely dispose of these models. So let us look at the facts.

Du Pont started to produce synthetic dyes during World War I (when the United States was cut off from Germany). Sales of 1972 reveal that 25 percent of sales was in dyes introduced in the previous 5 years, 40 percent in the previous 10 years, and 75 percent in the previous 20 years. In 1973, the company produced three times as many pounds of nylon with only 20 percent more people as in 1963, selling them profitably at prices 35 percent below those in 1963 despite the general increase in prices during these years. For the company as a whole, Gee and Tyler (1976, p. 36) found that 25 percent of the 1973 sales were generated by products introduced in the previous 15 years, and the price index for Du Pont's entire output was 73 percent of that of 15 years earlier. Pegram and Bailey (1967, p. 39) found that for 223 manufacturers, the average (median) percentage of 1966 sales attributable to the sale of products first marketed by the company within the past 5 years was 20 percent. This average was approximately the same for both consumer and industrial goods companies. Choffray and Lilien (1980, p. 4) report the following facts: In the scientific instruments area, the Office of Economic and Cultural Development (1977) found that many American firms have 60 to 80 percent of their sales from products that were not in existence half a decade earlier. They note that although such figures are not available for non-U.S. firms, one Swedish instrument firm in 1966 reported that 60 percent of its sales were generated by half a dozen products with an average age of 14 months (!), and no product was older than 5 years, and one Japanese pharmaceutical company stated that 90 percent of its sales were associated with products that were less than 6 years old. Hopkins (1980) reports on industrial goods manufacturers' dependence on new products. Over 25 percent of the companies answered that more than 30 percent of their current sales were attributable to major new products first marketed by the company within the preceding 5 years. Pessemier (1977) presents detailed evidence on both the percentage of sales produced by "new products" (i.e., products less than four years old) in 1960 and the percentages estimated for 1970 (see Table 1). This information of the relatively high estimates suggests that pricing and production decisions already in 1960 must have reflected the various probabilities, and models that neglect taking them into account when making predictions can hardly be expected to be useful.[10]

Cooper (1983, p. 21), in his above-mentioned study of 103 industrial firms, found that in terms of quantity of output, a mean of 32 percent of current sales were from new products launched within the last five years. In 1960 Mansfield (1971, p. 6) found that 10 percent of the sales of all manufacturing firms

Table 1 *Percentage of sales produced by new products (products less than four years old)*

	1960 Actual[a]	1970 Estimated[b]
Iron and steel	5	8
Nonferrous metals	8	16
Machinery	14	25
Electrical machinery	12	26
Aerospace	—	49
Autos, trucks, and parts	10	
Transportation equipment		22
(aircraft, ships, and railroad equipment)	35	
Fabricated metals (including instruments)	17	18
Chemicals	16	20
Pulp and paper	9	10
Rubber	2	7
Stone, clay, and glass	9	20
Petroleum and coal products	2	7
Food and beverages	6	12
Textiles	9	21
Miscellaneous manufacturing	6	8
All manufacturing	10	17

Source: McGraw-Hill Department of Economics.
[a]*Business Week,* April 29, 1967, p. 34.
[b]*Business Week,* May 13, 1967, p. 73. As it appears in Pessemier (1977).

were accounted for by products developed since 1956. Roman (1968, p. 206) found that new products generate at times as much as 75 percent of the *growth* in volume sales. A 10-year study of 1,130 firms reveals that 7.4 percent of manufacturing businesses introduce new products at least every year, 14.2 percent every 1 to 3 years, 18.4 percent every 10 years, 23.9 percent every 5 to 10 years, and the great majority, 36.1 percent every 3 to 5 years (Hilton 1961, p. 5).

The conclusion from this quite extensive evidence is simple: By concentrating on the "short" and "long" terms and by defining competition, monopoly, and other words within them, many economists created a heaven and told their audience what angelic behavior (i.e., passive adaptation) is. In the process they just forgot to look at the world around them and realize that these heavens do not in fact exist.

The facts presented until now lead to additional insights: Recall one conclusion reached in Chapter 2 on the relative lack of importance of money in explaining entrepreneurial ventures ("entrepreneurial" as defined here, which, as noted, means something completely different from mere "ownership of

Table 2 *How long did it take?*

	Year of first conception	Year of first realization	Duration years
Heart pacemaker	1928	1960	32
Hybrid corn	1908	1933	25
Hybrid small grains	1937	1955	19
Green revolution wheat	1950	1966	16
Electrophotography	1937	1959	22
Input–output economic analysis	1936	1964	28
Organophosphorus insecticides	1934	1947	13
Oral contraceptive	1951	1960	9
Magnetic ferrites	1933	1955	22
Video tape recorder	1950	1956	6
Average duration			19.2

Source: Batelle Memorial Institute Study, 1973. As quoted by Dean (1974), p. 13).

business'') and the relative greater importance of coming up with truly new ideas[11] in some particular circumstances in explaining them.[12] The additional evidence presented here supports this conclusion: Larger R & D expenditures did not make people receiving them more creative. Rather, less well-endowed outsiders, whether as individuals or already as entrepreneurs behind small businesses, have thrown themselves into the swirl of innovations.

And ''thrown'' is the correct word *not* rational calculation (as, by the way, the view of human behavior presented in Chapter 1 suggests). Once again let us look at the facts: Chester Carlson, who had the patent on xerography, got the first image in October 1938. Although xerography became one of the great success stories of all times, it was not profitable until the early 1950s, 13 to 17 years after its conception. During this time, the man in charge of research reported: ''The members of our team were all gambling on the project. I even mortgaged my house. All I had left was my life insurance. . . . My feeling was that if it didn't work . . . [we] would be business failures'' (Goran 1974, p. 91).[13] Even for an innovation that seems as simple as the Post-it note pads, which is by now a staple in the American office and brings $200 million in revenues for 3M, it took 12 years between the germ of the idea and its commercial function. For, when first offered, major office-supply distributors thought that it was a silly idea (Peters and Austin 1985, p. 115). These data are not unusual: Dean (1976) raised the question of how long it takes for important innovations to mature from idea to product.[14] The answer he got was, on average, 19 years (see Table 2). What calculation, besides the vaguest hunch or one's gut feeling, can be relevant for understanding such decisions?[15] This calculation is linked, as shown in the previous chapters, not necessarily to the final outcome, but to one's perceptions of leapfrogging within a hierarchy.

Finally, let's clarify two further notions associated with the standard views of the firm: diversification and specialization. Diversification is frequently viewed with suspicion in the traditional economic literature, being a sign of either "monopolistic competition" or of creating barriers to entry, and both are given negative connotations. But the view of human nature explored here, with its emphasis on people's willingness to engage in innovations and, in turn, their attempt to insure themselves, provides a clear understanding for such a strategy. A dizzying array of variations on a product – whether laundry detergents, soaps, or cereals – insures the respective producers for two reasons. First, they reduce the possibility of any potential competitor developing a *truly novel,* and thus dangerous, rival product. The wide array captures most of the space within the attention span of consumers – whether on the shelves, TV screens, or newspaper advertising – slowing down potential competitors. Second, the proliferation provides additional insurance since if one venture fails, another may work. Thus, within the views presented here, diversification represents one facet of competition; it is linked to the continuous threat of inventions and innovations and cannot be viewed with suspicion. It represents the decision of managers within companies that have already succeeded to insure themselves. On what grounds can one condemn such acts? This is how people behave (scientists in particular, as shown in the next section).

As to specialization: There is little doubt that division of labor is a principle of any organization and not only of eighteenth-century pin factories, as in Adam Smith's famous example. Yet the evidence presented here, and in Chapter 2, concerning the insights of *outsiders,* suggests that carried "too far" such division seems to have substantial costs, and not only benefits, since it seems to block creativity. Indeed Schmookler remarked some 30 years ago: "What is surprising . . . is not the large proportion of inventors who are college-trained but the large proportion who are not . . . All that can be properly inferred from the evidence is that a respectable part of contemporary invention is not the product of those who have attended college. It may also be suggested that some of the invention produced by college men is not necessarily attributable to their college educations" (pp. 325–6) and notes that the reason for that may be that college training "often dulls creativity by emphasizing authority, memory and routine solutions" (p. 325).

In fact it seems strange that so much attention was paid to Smith's pin factory example, and relatively little to the fact that Smith himself chose to be anything but specialized. After all, in addition to his *Wealth of Nations,* he wrote a theory of moral sentiments, lectures on jurisprudence, a history of astronomy, of ancient physics, of ancient logics and metaphysics, not to speak about essays on music, dancing, and the affinity between certain English and Italian verses. This outpouring does not suggest that Smith had an unconditional belief in the benefits of division of labor and specialization (otherwise, why didn't he decide to become more specialized?). More evidence and discussion on this point later in this chapter.

> Men learn the elements of science from others; and every learner
> hath a deference more or less to authority, especially the young
> learners, few of that kind caring to dwell long upon principles, but
> inclining rather to take them upon trust: And things early admitted
> by repetition become familiar: And this familiarity at length passeth
> for evidence.
>
> Bishop Berkeley of Cloyne

3   The resistance to innovations in business and science

Scattered among the mathematical models and statistical analyses, some economists made brief statements on the relationship between wealth, status, hierarchies, and innovations. However, they did not try either to incorporate them with the rest of their analyses, to examine what assumptions on human behavior must be made in order to support such statements, or to see whether or not the same pattern can be found outside the world of business. Kamien and Schwartz (1982), for example, wrote:

The firm presently realizing monopoly profits may be less motivated to seek additional profits than the one earning only normal profits. It may, in other words, be less hungry for additional profits than the firm without a monopoly position. Several reasons for this are possible. First, it may begin to regard additional leisure as superior to additional profits. . . . Second, it may become more concerned with protecting its current monopoly position than acquiring a new one. (pp. 29–30)

These views suggest that somebody's utility must be taken into account when examining a firm's behavior, rather than profits. Elsewhere they write that there is also some evidence that success begets failure: "Either initial success leads to complacency or the successful firm is not as hungry as the newcomer or the behavior that led to the first success is maintained until it becomes obsolete in a changing environment" (pp. 74–5). . . . "The sluggishness of large firms in certain innovations has been explained by the desire to protect an investment in the then-current technology, satisfaction with the status-quo, underestimation of the potential demand for a new item, neglect of inventor, and misdirection of research, as well as by incompatibility of bureaucracy and creativity" (p. 68). These processes and reactions have been discussed in Chapters 1 and 2, and it has been shown both how they are related to the view of human nature presented here and how they can be integrated with a wide variety of additional patterns of business behavior.

In another context Scherer (1984) quotes Watt's letter in which the innovator expresses his anxious desire to stop innovating as soon as his engine's success is assured. In a letter to his collaborator, Boulton, he wrote:

On the whole I find it is now full time to cease attempting to invent new things, or to attempt anything which is attended with any risk of not succeeding, or of creating trouble in the execution. Let us go on executing the things we understand, and leave the rest to younger men, who have neither money nor character to lose. (p. 15)

Solman and Friedman (1982), commenting on the sources of innovation in general remark that:

Large American companies also seem to have this aversion to ideas from the outside. . . . They had these huge research-and-development departments and if they don't come up with better products than some guy from outside, then what's the rationale for their existence? It becomes a hard thing for people in a large company to accept the fact that they didn't come up with a given idea: it's a real blow to their pride and worse, a threat, so they turn it down. (pp. 165–6)

Briefly, although observations consistent with those made in the previous chapters can be found in the writings of some economists, they are not incorporated within a *unified* approach, linking features of the world of business either with chance and creativity or pointing out similarities in reactions with other, nonbusiness related, reactions.

Other social scientists observing the aforementioned patterns of behavior have done just that – Barnett (1953), with his *Innovation: The Basis of Cultural Change* being among the first. More recently McCaskey (1982), in *The Executive Challenge,* draws on a wide variety of sources to show that the problems executives and business managers face with innovations are similar to those that decision makers face in other domains as well. He starts his analysis by quoting Elting Morison's study concerning the adoption of continuous-aim firing in the United States Navy, which is worth summarizing since it reflects a typical pattern. William Sims, a U.S. Navy lieutenant stationed in China, learned about the innovation from its originator, Percy Scott of the *British* Royal Navy. Sims trained a crew, showed a remarkable increase in the accuracy of firing, and wrote 13 official reports presenting much data to naval officers in Washington on the merits of the innovation.

First there was no reply. Then the Washington officials said that the American equipment was as good as the British, only the crew were badly trained. When Sims objected, they conducted experiments on dry land (where, of course, deprived of the inertial movement, the system did not work) and accused Sims of falsifying the evidence. Only in 1902 when Sims wrote directly to Theodore Roosevelt was the change forced upon the Navy. Morison explains the resistance to innovation by the fact that the Navy's *social* system was organized around its major weapons, and that a change would significantly disrupt the existing hierarchy of status.

Similar patterns of behavior are repeated over and over whether one looks at some spectacular or some normal occurrences of resistance to innovation. The brief reminder below, based on Stern (1937), gives only a flavor of this reaction across fields of activity, across countries, and across time.

In the thirteenth century this reaction manifested itself when attempts were made to introduce carriages for various uses. Philip the Fair ordered the wives of the citizens of Paris not to ride in carriages in order to reserve the privilege for the ladies of the court. A similar law was introduced in Hungary in 1523. In 1588 Duke Julius of Brunswick made riding in coaches a crime punishable as a felony, on the grounds that it would diminish men's military skills, since they would forget how to ride horses (defending an outdated technology for military reasons seems widespread – see last chapter).

For centuries the textile industry has been the battleground of machine technology against hand tools. In 1397, the tailors of Cologne were forbidden to use a machine for pressing the heads of pins. Already in 1272 Borghesano's automatic machine for twisting silk thread was used in Bologna. Its secret was maintained through fear of the death penalty, and became known in Switzerland only in 1555 and in England in 1718. About 1579 the Council of Danzig had the inventor of a machine that would weave four to six pieces at once strangled, lest his invention reduce many workers to beggary. The reaction toward innovations in this industry during the Industrial Revolution is well known.

Turnpike companies profiting by tolls, owners of stagecoaches, tavernkeepers along roads, farmers who bred horses and sold hay, were all among the opponents of railroads. Since at that time steam carriages were also being considered as substitutes for stagecoaches, the choice was confined not only to fast horses, slow steamcoaches, and slow railroads, but also to tracks and highways. In the United States the "advocacy of 'people's road' as against monopolistic railroads became one of the political issues of the Jacksonian period. . . . [But] railroads emerged as victors in such a decisive fashion that extensive roadbuilding and the development of mechanical conveyances on those roads were checked for decades" (Stern 1937, p. 40). In England the resistance to railroads came from the landlord class, opposed to the aggressive industrial bourgeoisie, from the vested interests of canal owners, and from the legislators committed to the building of public canals, in which considerable investments had been made. In the United States too demands were made that railroad competition should not be permitted to affect the receipts of canals. According to the charter of the Utica and Schenectady Railroad, granted in 1833, the line was prohibited from carrying property except passengers' luggage, a regulation that stayed in effect until 1844. The general railroad incorporation act of 1848 levied canal tolls from railroads parallel to canals and within 30 miles, tolls that stayed in effect until 1851. Opposition to this innovative means of transportation did not come from those having vested interests only but also from "experts." In England, Nicholas Wood, a "railway expert," declared that claims that trains could reach a possible speed of 20 miles an hour were absurd. In Germany, the experts proved that if trains went at a speed of 15 miles an hour, blood would spurt from the travelers' noses, mouths, and ears and in tunnels the passengers would suffocate. Not only did many people oppose the introduction of railroads (some denouncing it as impious because they were not foreseen in the Bible – note below a similar reaction toward innovations in science) but later improvements got a similar reaction: Commodore Vanderbilt dismissed Westinghouse and his new air brakes, saying that he had no time to waste on fools, and when W. R. Sykes in 1874 presented the plan for automatic signaling in Britain, the railway companies rejected it out of hand stating that signalmen were better.

The precursors of modern cars encountered similar opposition. Although in the 1820s steam coaches already made regular trips between Cheltenham and Gloucester, and by the 1860s it appeared that this means of transportation was there to stay, the horse breeders and railroads succeeded in eliminating them. They secured passage of an act of Parliament in 1861, regulating horseless vehicles in the following way: The engines had to consume their own smoke, each vehicle had to have two drivers, and no vehicle was to exceed 10 miles an hour in the country and 5 in the city. In 1865 a more drastic act was passed requiring three drivers, one of whom had to precede the carriage carrying a red flag during day and a red lantern by night, and reducing speed limits to 4 miles in the country and 2 in the city. No wonder that with such regulations (repealed only in 1896), the steam carriage was derailed (one should say "pro-railed" and "de-steamed"). It would be misleading, however, to attribute the passage of such regulations only to interest groups: The public's attitude toward this innovation and toward the early automobiles was not only apathetic, but scornful, enabling the passage of such regulations [see Stern (1937, p. 44)].

The same attitudes characterized people's reaction toward the steamboat. John Fitch, whose steamboat was doing technically successful trips on the Delaware River in 1790, was reviled, harassed, and perceived as a deranged and suspicious character. So was Robert Fulton, who is acclaimed today for making steamboats a commercial success. A letter from 1807 shows the reactions he first encountered:

When I was building my first steamboat, the project was viewed by the public either with indifference, or with contempt. . . . I have often loitered unknown near the idle groups of strangers, gathering in little circles and heard various inquiries as to the object of this new vehicle. The language was uniformly that of scorn, sneer or ridicule. The loud laugh often rose at my expense; . . . the full but endless repetition of "Fulton's folly." Never did a single encouraging remark, a bright hope, a warm wish, cross my path. Silence itself was but politeness, veiling its doubts, or hiding its reproaches. [as quoted in Stern (1937, p. 46)]

Recently, Franklin (1986) has pointed out that although the submarine eventually came into its own, it happened despite the best efforts of the Navy to ignore it. Franklin's book clearly shows a long history of shortsightedness in American military procurement, a conclusion also reached by Hadley (1986), who attributes the failures in America's Armed Forces to two main reasons. One he calls "the Great Divorce": the separation of the military from the financial, business, and intellectual elites (one can identify this condition as one of too much protected, isolated specialization), which diminishes the ability to assess risks. The other involves rivalries among and within the services. According to Hadley, the Army, Navy, and Air Force are each more interested in preserving their privileges than in defending the public. On the day of landing in Inchon, a crucial moment during the Korean War, the Joint Chiefs were arguing about the number of Pentagon parking places to be allocated to the Marines, while during the Cuban missile crisis there were no spy flights over Cuba for five days because the Air Force and the CIA couldn't agree on who would fly the planes. More recently, because of the Navy's internal rivalry between its carrier and submarine fleets, money allocated for submarine nuclear missiles was diverted to aircraft carriers because carrier admirals happened to be in charge.

Before examining the similarities in both the reactions toward innovations in science and the expressions rivalries took in that domain, two notes. First, although the opposition to innovations described above had each its uniqueness, the regularities in reactions (trying to maintain some group's status and attempts to coerce individuals to conform) are evident. The same reactions come to the fore over and over when one reads the history of airplanes, printing, textile machinery, metals and building materials, the introduction of typewriters, of the telegraph and telephone (recall: The telephone, cable, and telegraph companies did not invent the wireless telegraph; on the contrary they first refused to buy it and later wanted to suppress it), the use of gas for lighting (recall: Scientists led the opposition by ridiculing the plan to store gas in reservoirs, and other groups objected that the use of gas would diminish England's military strength, because by eliminating the whale oil lamps, it would destroy the whale oil industry, wherefrom England took the personnel for its fighting ships), or Edison's invention of the incandescent lamp [recall: Some scientists declared in the *New York Times* (December 28, 1879), that Edison's experiments in electric lighting were not a wonderful success as claimed, but a conspicuous failure, others that Edison should not discredit his name by pursuing profits, and still others simply denied the possibility that he could use carbon for filaments].

Finally, the second note: The reader may have noted the reference in previous sections to "major innovations," "truly new ideas," and may have asked how can one define them? As the aforementioned evidence suggests, the definition will *always* be a long after-the-fact construct.

Inventions and hierarchies in science

Murray's (1925), Trattner's (1938), Polanyi's (1974), Cohen's (1985), and Ben-Yehuda's (1985) detailed and systematic studies of scientists reveal the same pattern: In spite of evidence, innovations were frequently greeted with disdain and incredulity by members of the profession where the innovations were to be applied, professions where hierarchies depended on preserving the paradigms. The reaction to Mesmer's hypnotic cures, Jenner's *An Inquiring into the Cause and Effects of the Varioloe Vaccinae* (1798), to Simpson's discovery of chloroform (1847), to Lyell's publication of *Principles of Geology* (1830–33), to Helmholtz's discovery of the conservation of energy (1847), to Joule's discovery of the mechanical equivalent of heat (1843), to Darwin's, Pasteur's, Lister's, or most recently Barbara McClintock's and Benoit Mandelbrot's[16] and others' discoveries and innovations shows the same patterns that Morison described in the military and the ones described in this book concerning the world of business. First, the innovations came frequently from outsiders: Pasteur was a chemist; Helmholtz's training was in medicine; Darwin started with medicine, arts, then wanted to become a clergyman; Huxley turned from physiology to paleontology; Lamarche from botany to zoology[17]; Robert Mayer was a physician (he came up with the idea of conservation of energy, and Helmholtz was annoyed that this idea was conceived by an "unknown physician"[18]); as was Thomas Young, a Quaker too; Barbara McClintock, a woman working at a small research institute; and so on.[19] The German sociologist Dahrendorf chooses the word "envy" when explaining why the American sociologist, C. Wright Mills, a prominent writer, was mercilessly criticized, and says that "much more can be read between the lines. They betray the intense mixture of anger, hatred and envy characteristic of the attitude of the profession towards its successful outsiders."[20] Being outsiders to the fields to which they turned their interest, they frequently did their early studies without the benefit (?) of university associations and well-endowed research facilities.[21]

Just as established managements in business refused sometimes even to consider new ideas and look at innovations, so did the establishment in science: Some refused to consider them, to look at the facts, while others declared them "false."[22] Galileo's telescope was denounced as an instrument of the devil, who sought to delude mankind. Orthodox astronomers refused to look through the glass arguing that in order to see any moons near Jupiter, man invented an instrument that created them. During discussions on the images of the eye, physiologists told Helmholtz that they had nothing to do with experiments, and when he built the ophthalmoscope, they refused to look through it stating that it was too dangerous to admit light into the diseased eye and that the mirror might be of service to oculists with defective eyesight. "Scientific" commissions investigating the facts on hypnotic cures produced by Friedrich Anton Mesmer either denied them or explained them away. Mesmer was broken, his art discredited, and he was stigmatized as an impostor. Another pioneer of hypnotism, Elliotson, a professor of medicine at the University of London, was ordered by his university to discontinue his experiments. At the same time a surgeon in the service of the government of India, Esdaile, performed major operations under hypnotic anesthesia, but medical journals refused to publish his account of these cases. Polanyi (1974, p. 54), who examines these and additional cases, concludes that the hatred against the discoverers of facts that threatened the cherished beliefs of science was as bitter as that of religious persecutors two centuries before and was of the same character. In 1879, Marquis de Sautuola walked through the cave of Altamira in the Cantabrian Mountains of Northern Spain and found the first prehistoric cave paintings. The professors who came to examine the pictures accused the discoverer of being a faker; some of them said that he had probably hired an artist in Madrid in order to be acclaimed as an archaeologist.[23] Ignaz Semmelweis, the father of modern surgical sterilization techniques, committed suicide in 1865, two weeks after being duped into entering a mental sanatorium. Seventeen years earlier, in 1848, while working in a clinic, he found that having a physician wash his hands in a chlorine solution prior to the delivery of a baby reduced immediately the maternal death rate in the clinic from 18 to 1 percent. One would have thought that such spectacular evidence should have led to an overnight change in medical practices. Nothing could be further from what happened: in 1860, in the same clinic, still 35 out of 101 mothers died. Semmelweis was perceived as an outsider, and since physicians did not take him seriously, his lonely voice was lost in spite of the evidence. It took 20 years until Lister and Pasteur came along, and were finally listened to – after exhausting public debates. Indeed, as one could expect, envy, malice, and hatred raised their heads (in the shape of, among others, Doctor Colin and Rossignol, the editor of *Veterinary Press,* who called for public trials against Pasteur, a "mere chemist"). Valley-Radot in the *Life of Pasteur* wrote that his "discoveries on ferments, on the generation of the infinitesimally small, on microbes, the cause of contagious diseases, and on the vaccination of those disease, have been for biological chemistry, for the veterinary art and for medicine, not a regular process, but a complete revolution. Now, revolutions, even those imposed by a scientific demonstration, ever leave behind them vanquished ones who do not easily forgive. M. Pasteur has therefore many adversaries in the world, without counting those Athenian French who do not like to see one man always right, or always fortunate."[24] When tired of all the attacks by physicians, Pasteur once replied:

Sir, your language is not very intelligible to me. I am not a physician and do not desire to be one. Never speak to me of your dogma of morbid spontaneity. I am a chemist; I carry out experiments and I try to understand what they teach me. [as quoted in Murray (1925, p. 31)]

The animosity between physicians and "outsiders" has a long history in France. Eugène Raiga in a book titled *L'Envie* (1932) emphasizes leapfrogging as a cause for the envious reaction of those who fall suddenly behind and documents his case with, among others, description of the fight between surgeons and physicians in the eighteenth century. What exactly was the source of the trouble? During the Middle Ages surgery was considered a "manual art," and the surgeon a mere "artisan." In contrast, "medicine" was viewed as a "liberal art," and the physician perceived as belonging to the "nobility." The surgeons served the physicians and were completely under their authority. But at the end of the seventeenth century, Louis XIV not only chose a surgeon to operate on him, but paid him three times more than the honorarium he paid his court physician. The result was a big scandal and great confusion among the physicians and the public: Who was one now supposed to trust and pay more, the surgeon or the physician? In 1724, Louis XV endowed five chairs for teaching surgery, to which the Faculty of Medicine reacted violently, trying to close the classrooms to prevent the surgeons from teaching their trade. They were unsuccessful in their attempt, but they continued to put up a fight. In 1748, Diderot still remarked that one should put an end to these quarrels, which the Revolution finally did.

The reluctance to consider new evidence, or the insights to which new theories have led, was based on the existing dogma, paradigm, and the reference to "big names." Anaxagoras, a century after Pythagoras, had been cast into an Athenian jail for maintaining that the sun was not a heavenly chariot daily driven by the gods through the skies. A law was passed that demanded "the immediate prosecution of all those who disbelieved in the established religion or held theories of their own about certain divine things."[25] When Copernicus came up with his startling new story of the heavens, the critics asked: Who will place the authority of Copernicus above that of Holy Scripture? The geological findings in the seventeenth century had to fight with biblical ideas too, as interpreted, for example, by William Whiston. In his *New Theory of the Earth* (1696), he argued that Noah's flood was caused on November 18, 2399 B.C., when the tail of a comet passed over the equator (apparently every generation has its share of Velikovskys). In the nineteenth century too Jenner, Simpson, and Darwin had to fight with interpretations of biblical ideas. In other fields innovators had to fight not with holy reputations (and inquisitions that tried to maintain them) but worldly ones. Over the past generation, for example, there has been a growing willingness to settle issues in economics (and other social sciences as well) by an appeal to theories, without any pretense to a study of the evidence. Theoreticism – the recourse to unsubstantiated theory, serving not just as a tool, but an end, the feeling of nonobligation toward empirical scrutiny – has become customary. And with the custom a hierarchy came into existence. Like every hierarchy, it has some "big names" at the top, whose opinions carry weight because of custom, the resulting tunnel vision, and not much else, and their behavior is, of course, human rather than "scientific." Since in this activity the hierarchy is based on a paradigm, a new idea, *if* it is truly new, by threatening the paradigm threatens the hierarchy, the reputations, wealth, and status that scientists derived from its acceptance. When perceiving this threat, one can expect that – just as in the world of business – scientists will react by fair and foul strategies.[26] Thus, one should not be surprised to read in all the aforementioned cases about the "unreasonable" obstacles that the scientific community imposed on an innovator, relying on "big names" to discard and to ridicule the new idea rather than attempting to confront it with a "scientific argument." Indeed, this pattern is so well known that it needs no further elaboration.[27] The main thing to pay attention to is the regularity that one can detect in the emergence and adoption of truly new ideas, whatever field of activity one is discussing, business or science.[28]

Raiga (1932), in fact, turns to additional fields of activity too and his evidence complements the previous ones. He not only describes the fights among innovating competitors in the arts and literature (Michelangelo and Raphael, Corneille and Racine, Gluck and Piccinni, Victor Hugo and his adversaries, etc.) by all the methods one is familiar with in the world of business but also the envious reactions toward innovators. Among the numerous sources he quotes, one finds segments from Voltaire's correspondence and Molière's plays that will sound familiar. Voltaire, in a letter to Mlle. Quinault wrote: "What did I earn from twenty years of work? Only enemies. That's the prize one should expect when one is writing: much ridicule if one fails, much hate if one succeeds" (recall Watt's letter at the beginning of this section). One character in *L'Impromptu de Versailles* is reflecting Molière's views in these lines: "Why is he writing all these nasty plays that all Paris is running to see? . . . Why doesn't he write comedies like M. Lysidas? If he did, nobody would be against him and all the playwrights would have only words of praise for him." Schopenhauer shares their views. According to him envy has two favorite methods – to praise what is bad or, alternatively, to remain silent about what is good, "for everyone who gives praise to another, whether in his own field or in a related one, in principle deprives himself of it: he can praise only at the expense of his own reputation."[29]

These observations are made in numerous studies examining patterns of behavior not only across very different fields but also different countries and times. Anthropologists have frequently related the absence of innovations in some societies to the hostility, envy, and displeasure with which they are greeted. Schoeck (1969), who perceived this regularity, discusses, among numerous examples, the events surrounding attempts to introduce a specially prepared seed and a new fertilizer in tradition-bound Indian villages, attempts that were, for a while, unsuccessful. Why? The Indian's reply was: "Should the innovation, as promised, produce an especially good harvest, the man would go in fear of *nazar-lagna*. This is an Urdu word of Arabic origin . . . used . . . in relation to the malevolent, destructive, envious look of another person" (p. 60). This anticipated social reaction diminished the perceived benefits of success. But the Indians were also afraid of failure, a fear that seemed to be related to a loss of status, rather than a loss of wealth. The man who applied the innovation of an outsider feared the ridicule of his fellowmen if he failed to produce the results he expected. Belshaw (1955) describes how, among the Southern Massim, who live on an island in Melanesia, anticipations of envious reactions so restrict leaders that, in the interest of maintaining the somehow achieved social order, and in fear of being perceived as profiting themselves from an innovation, they refrain from undertakings that may even benefit the whole community.[30] In general, these types of studies [see extensive evidence in Brenner (1983), Chapters 1 and 2] reveal that in relative.y isolated, small communities individuals or families who lose something are viewed as a threat to the stability of the community, their fear and envy leading to aggression (and isn't the scientific community somewhat isolated, small and personal?). At the same time those who become wealthy are also viewed as a threat to the stability of the community. This regularity led Gluckman (1965) to conclude that:

For though a man gains prestige by his productive capacities, if he outdoes his fellows too much, they will suspect him of witchcraft. Richards reports of the Bemba, that to find one beehive with honey in the woods is luck, to find two is very good luck, to find three is witchcraft. Generally, she concludes, for a man to do much better than his fellows is dangerous. . . . Here accusations of witchcraft and sorcery maintain the egalitarian basis of the society in two ways: not only is the prosperous man in danger of accusations but he also fears the malice of witches and sorcerers among his envious fellows. (p. 88)

In addition to this broad regularity, it is worth noting to what additional observations in the field of science this view of human behavior leads. One may have reasonably raised this question: If the previous discussion concerning the relationship between facts and interpretation in the scientific world is close, why do many people still perceive that, in general, incentives exist in science to promote originality? A closer inspection reveals, of course, that this perception is not quite accurate. What one finds in science is incentives for originality, but within a *very* narrow range, channeled to that range *exactly* through the anticipated reactions so well described above by Voltaire, Molière, and Schopenhauer. Minor innovations are praised and provide the illusion of complete originality since praise magnifies the freedoms that are, in fact, constrained to extremely thin domains.[31] At the same time, truly new ideas are frequently greeted with ridicule and disdain. Such channeling of students toward minor innovations reinforces the existing paradigm and the hierarchy and reputations built on it by maintaining stability. No wonder, therefore, that frequently one should expect to observe phenomena in science that Clark (1940) called "tragic." In his *Conditions of Economic Progress* he wrote:

It would be laughable, if it were not tragic, to watch the stream of books and articles, attempting to solve the exceptionally complex problems of present day economics by theoretical arguments, often without a single reference to observed facts. . . . The result is a vast output of literature of which, it is safe to say, scarcely a syllable will be read in fifty years time. But the discovery of new facts, and of generalization based on them is work for all time. (p. VII)

Although one may call this activity "tragic," it should be expected. For it is the discovery of new facts that threatens a paradigm and the hierarchy based on it. Rare are the scientists who encourage finding facts outside the established paradigm's field of vision.[32] Instead, valuing niceties and subtleties of reasoning, metaphysics and logic pose no threat at all – on the contrary, they provide insurance – and channeling thoughts in these directions is thus encouraged. Recall that "pure logic could never lead us to anything but tautologies. It could create nothing new; not from it alone can any science issue"[33] (as Henri Poincaré once put it), and that Kuhn (1962) defined "normal science" as one that "does not aim at novelties of fact or theory and, when successful, finds none" (p. 52).[34] No wonder that mathematics flourished and flourishes in dogmatic societies, which do not welcome innovations.

All my previous criticism of economic theory should be interpreted from this broader perspective – so, of course, I do not expect either much tolerance or "scientific" reactions only. To those readers who are reminded in this section of Escher's etching of the hand that draws itself, well, I admit it was consciously done. And if this statement will be perceived as courageous by some readers, and arrogant and immodest by others, I can have no objection. But it may just be useful to recall that the virtue of modesty itself may have been invented only to avert envy and maintain stability. At least this is one of the ideas in Raiga's, Schoeck's, Schopenhauer's, and some Chinese anthropologists' work. One of them, Hu Hsien-Chin (1944), explains with this insight the excessive modesty and diminished ambitions of the Chinese. According to him Western observers are wrong in attributing this characteristic to hypocrisy, humbug, or lack of self-confidence. Rather it is a case of a carefully institutionalized attitude invented to discourage envious reactions. Raiga, Schoeck, and Schopenhauer share this view, and they too argue that envy gives rise to only *one* virtue, that of modesty. How are envy and modesty related? Among others Schopenhauer illustrates the relationship with the following quote from a *London Times* article (October 9, 1858):

There is no vice, of which a man can be guilty, no meanness, no shabbiness, no unkindness, which excites so much indignation among his contemporaries, friends and neighbours, as his success. This is the one unpardonable crime, which reason cannot defend, nor humility mitigate. ''When heaven with such parts has blest him, have I not reason to detest him?'' is a genuine and natural expression of the vulgar human mind. The man who writes as we cannot write, who speaks as we cannot speak, labours as we cannot labour, thrives as we cannot thrive, has accumulated on his own person all the offences of which man can be guilty. Down with him! Why cumbereth he the ground? [as quoted in Schoeck (1969), p. 171]

If the successful man is, however, modest (and, as it frequently happens, circulates his ideas among his friends and postpones publication), he may diminish or delay these envious reactions. This virtue (in fact, a fear of envious reactions) may explain why, when the historian of science I. Bernard Cohen scoured the annals of discovery for scientists who announced that their own work was ''revolutionary,'' he could produce a list of only 16. The 16, who as one would expect, turn out to be visionaries *and* cranks, are: Symmer, Marat, Lavoisier, von Liebig, Hamilton, Darwin, Virchow, Cantor, Einstein, Minkowski, von Laue, Wegener, Compton, Just, Watson, and Benoit Mandelbrot (the mathematician who now reshapes applied geometry).[35] Since it is the most recent, features of Mandelbrot's career are worth noting. Gleick (1985) describes it: He was always an outsider, in more than one sense: A Polish immigrant in France, then a French immigrant in the United States. He missed chunks of basic schooling, and remained on the periphery of dogmas – at home nowhere. He explored disciplines in which he was not welcomed, ''hiding his grandest ideas to get his papers published – surviving mainly on the confidence of his colleagues at IBM's Thomas J. Watson Research Center'' (rather than an established university, of course). Gleick also notes that for decades, Mandelbrot had to couch original ideas in terms that would give no offense, pretending in the first version of his book, published in French in 1975, that it contained nothing startlingly new (only in a recent edition he dared to inform readers of what to expect), since he realized that he had to cope with the ''politics of science.'' Mandelbrot illustrates what he means by such ''politics'': ''There is a basic unlikelihood of what I have done having been done by one person, which makes people think it's unlikely so it's probably untrue. It's something which is very much part of everyday life in academia . . . where tempers are strong.'' But such tempers should be expected: It needs guts[36] and effort not to be pontifical, when one's work after a lifetime of dedication to the proof of some ideas and to finding facts within a narrow vision, is suddenly threatened with oblivion.

So, civilizations and fields of activity may be many, but men are the same.

4   Inventions and crises

The evidence illustrating the typical reaction to innovations shows that a discussion on the ''costs'' and ''benefits'' of their introduction cannot be separated from a discussion of features of society. Thus one cannot discuss ''the economics'' of innovations in any field of activity separately from its other dimensions. The regularity in reactions across countries, time, and fields of activity raises in fact another issue: With such regularity, can one explain in what circumstances innovations are, in any domain, more likely to be adopted? Just a brief answer to this question is given here; its elaboration can be found in Brenner (1983, 1985). Repeating it would take us, however, too far from the subjects examined in this book.

The reader may already have guessed the answer. Whereas creativity was linked above with some individual ''crises,'' the adoption of inventions is linked with collective ones, the frequency with which they occurred in particular. How? A society that can still remember the origins of some ideas that, for some, became part of habitual thinking, can be expected to adopt the new more quickly if it is realized that the circumstances that have led to the emergence of the habitual thinking have changed. In contrast, a society with a heavy burden of intractable habits is expected to adapt more slowly to some suddenly altered circumstances. What ideas should be discarded and why becomes a much more difficult choice to make. This explanation seems valid (i.e., leads to a close relationship between facts and interpretation) not only on the ''grand scales'' examined in the two previous books but also on the more minor ones examined in the second and this chapter, showing how inventions have been done by outsiders, by less specialized individuals, who made detours along their way, roaming from field to field, confronting confusion, rather than by others who had ''tunnel vision.''[37]

Upheavals (call them social, political, or economic if you wish), however, may not so much explain the *origins* of an idea: rather they provide the opportunity for its realization, due, in part to the collapse of hierarchies during such periods, in part to the fact that it points a way out of ''chaos,'' the suddenly destroyed customary associations, and, in part to the fact that in any upheaval there will be people who fear falling behind.[38] Thus, one should not wonder at the extensive evidence on forgotten scientists "ahead of their time." Thucydides observed 25 centuries ago that when times are "normal" people "do not distinguish; without a test they take things from one another: even on things of their own day, not dulled by time, Hellenes are apt to be all wrong. So little pains will most men take in search for truth: so much more readily they turn to what comes first." And in normal times, what comes first is reliance upon hierarchy and authority, science being no exception to this rule, frequently leading its practitioners to discard new ideas[39] or not even publish them.[40]

What role this view of innovations, and creativity in general, leaves to policymakers is discussed in the next chapters. In order to interpret such policy implications correctly, the next reminder may be useful. A pioneer explorer who suggested that there is a regularity in the way new ideas come to life was Giambattista Vico (1668–1744), the son of a poor bookseller.[41] He had an almost fatal accident as a child, when doctors predicted that he might become imbecile. He turned out not to be, and in the late eighteenth century his work was discovered and appreciated (his contemporaries ignored him), Goethe and later Marx being among those influenced by his thoughts. The novelty of his *Principles of New Science . . . Concerning the Common Nature of Nations* (1725) was that he viewed ideas and institutions (with the exception of Christianity) as symptoms of social experience. If he was almost correct ("almost," since one may ask why any idea, a faith in particular, should be excluded from a history of human inventions), one implication of his views is that nobody's ideas have absolute validity, but are a by-product of the particular societies within which one finds oneself. Although this conclusion implies that a bias is introduced in the interpretation of facts and in the policies one recommends, it should not disturb the reader. For, as Herbert Butterfield once wrote: "It is not a sin in a historian to introduce a personal bias that can be recognized and discounted. The sin in historical composition is the organization of the story in such a way that bias cannot be recognized." This sin is certainly not committed in this book. These arguments also imply that the policy recommendations derived in the next two chapters fit some particular circumstances, but not all.

CHAPTER 6

Origins of state-owned enterprises

To criticize is relatively easy. To provide an alternative approach toward explaining some facts is much more difficult. Still, I hope that once again the readers will have the patience first to become acquainted with some of the traditional approaches toward the subject of state-owned enterprises and criticism of them. For only then can one understand the alternative viewpoint pursued here. But I must immediately admit that the facts presented in this chapter cannot carry the weight of my arguments, which also draw support from a number of studies dealing with a wide variety of subjects, among them the role of the state in particular [see Brenner (1983, 1985)].[1]

There have been numerous studies written on the origins of state-owned enterprises, many of them with little, if any, appeal to the facts. What can one learn from such studies? Not much. Although some ideas may turn out to be just fine, in the absence of reliance on facts, one is quickly lost in, oy, again that pompous, technical vocabulary.[2]

Before surveying some of the traditional approaches, a few facts about state-owned enterprises across countries and time will be presented. This evidence will serve to cast doubt on a number of approaches that have been proposed to deal with the subject of state-owned enterprises, to narrow down both the possible departure points and the contexts in which the subject may be illuminated, and lead toward the approach suggested here. Next the approach pursued in the book is extended to examine both the role of the state and of state-owned enterprises within it. Finally the policy implications are discussed.

1 State-owned enterprises – in what context?

From ancient times some enterprises have been owned and managed by pharaohs, kings, and their entourages – the one dealing with ancient Egypt's stock of grain jumps immediately to one's mind.[3] Much later Adam Smith,

This chapter is a revised version of Brenner (1984b).

perceived today as an unqualified advocate of "free markets," clearly authorized publicly owned and operated enterprises (canals, post office, bridges, and highways) and intervention in the shipping industry for the requirement of defense.

Variations on these themes can be found in numerous articles written since then that justify public ownership.[4] But what facts should we look at, during this century in particular, if we want to get additional insights into this question? Should one draw conclusions by looking only at the Western countries and so-called capitalist regimes? Or should one also take note of the quite clear-cut evidence from the communist bloc and the developing countries? If one considers such a global, historical outlook, it becomes obvious that the subject of state-owned enterprises cannot be separated from a discussion either of the role of the state or of ideology. Indeed, the evidence and discussion presented next suggest that narrow approaches, which have avoided touching these central issues, have shed little, if any, light on the subject.

Let's start with a brief discussion of some economic, ahistorical arguments that have been put forward to justify why some enterprises are state rather than privately owned. The arguments can be broadly put into these two categories: (a) existence of economies of scales and (b) externalities. There have been numerous other arguments put forward by economists for justifying state intervention – on sovereignty, regional development, nationalism, and wealth distribution. The reason for discussing them apart is that traditional approaches in economics have nothing to say on these subjects. Thus, economists' opinions on these topics should not be interpreted as implying that they have a theoretical apparatus supporting them, and should be given no greater weight than the opinions of laymen.

Other studies have taken a different direction. They concentrated not on the question of state versus private ownership but state ownership versus other forms of state intervention. This topic too belongs to a different sphere. It already implicitly recognizes the role of the state and it can thus concentrate only on the question of various instruments that may be chosen to implement its goals. But, of course, it cannot illuminate the question of *why* state intervention is needed to start with.

2   Economies of scales and externalities – where are the facts?

It has been frequently argued that economies of scales, which manifest themselves in the so-called natural monopolies, can justify public ownership. This argument has been frequently put forward for utilities, communication, and transportation. But is the argument accurate? First, Demsetz (1968) found a flaw in it even on logical grounds. He asked: If indeed average costs fall so that the lowest dictates but one firm, why should that firm be publicly owned? In principle, the state can call for competitive bidding and grant the ownership and management of the firm to the lowest bidder. Thus, it is not enough to state that there might be economies of scale; one must explain, within this view of the world, why such bidding arrangements do not emerge.

The reason for the lack of emergence of such a process may be either that it is costly (a viewpoint that cannot be tested), or that, in fact, the whole approach may be discarded, that is, that the downward average cost argument, although theoretically appealing to some economists, may not be in fact the problem, and the emergence or lack of emergence of state ownership may be linked with an entirely different reasoning. Indeed, as it will be repeatedly shown in this study, the *emergence* of state-owned enterprises has never been associated with economies of scale (i.e., with the perception that one big enterprise can provide a good more cheaply than several smaller ones) but with completely different perceptions[5] (as noted in Chapter 4, whenever possible I try to examine the origins of an idea or an institution, since only such analysis can provide a clear insight).

In his 1976 article on public ownership, Pryor wrote that economies of scale "may be common in certain utilities (water, sewage, electricity, gas), in communication (postal and telephone), and in transportation (possibly railroads)" (p. 9). Yet later in the study he makes these observations: "It can be quite plausibly argued that the natural monopoly argument does not really fit electricity production and other arguments must be employed to examine this case" (p. 10). Indeed, at least in Canada, part of the reliance on Crown Corporations in electricity can be understood in terms of a number of features, none linked to the perception of economies of scale. The decision to nationalize the electric utilities in British Columbia and Quebec resulted from the goal of avoiding paying taxes to the federal government. Since a provincial Crown Corporation is immune from federal income tax, the provincial governments recognized that they would be able to lower costs by public ownership. The desire to change the distribution of wealth, not only on the federal but also on the provincial level, played a role in Quebec's nationalization plans. The goal was to deliver senior jobs in the industry to French-speaking rather than English-speaking Quebecers.[6] More on the Canadian experience with electricity appears in the next section.

In the United States, too, evidence that the idea of economies of scale can justify ownership for electric utilities is hard to find. The debate seems to be ideological. In the late twenties, President Herbert Hoover, vetoing a public power bill, proclaimed: "I hesitate to contemplate the future of our institutions, of our government, and of our country if the preoccupation of its officials is to be no longer the promotion of justice and equal opportunity but is to be devoted to barter in the markets. That is not liberalism; it is degeneration,'' and Walsh (1978) adds that:

President Dwight D. Eisenhower echoed Hoover's opinion when he branded the Tennessee Valley Authority as "creeping socialism." Again twenty years later, the Central Maine Power Company led a publicity campaign to defeat a proposal to establish a state power authority in Maine by stressing that free enterprise was the "American way." The company's chief executive described the proposed authority as "the most radical plan ever advanced in these United States." But, in fact, throughout the United States, 299 private power companies, 1,898 municipally owned electric utilities, 112 state and county power corporations and utility districts, 923 rural electric co-operatives, and 10 federal agencies were in the power business. (The 299 private companies, however, enjoyed 80 percent of the retail sales.) Despite a widespread dissatisfaction with electric service and despite prices that were among the highest in the nation, the voters of Maine *defeated* the public power proposal. (pp. 14–15, italics added)

Primeaux's (1985) description and conclusion of the attempt of the Alaska Public Utilities Commission to dismantle electric utility competition reinforces this point – that economies of scale do not justify ownership in this industry – from a different angle. He concludes that the reason regulators are hostile toward competition in this industry is that its very existence reflects serious flaws in the theory of "natural monopoly." Since much of the justification for the regulatory process rests upon that theory, anything that tends to indicate weakness in the theory automatically raises questions about the value and purpose of regulation (and about the regulators' jobs one should add – the similarity with the arguments and evidence presented in the previous chapter needs no comment).

Further, Pryor (1976) notes that:

Some industries involve economic power sufficiently great to compromise the independence of the political system. One prime example is weapons production. . . . Another (and perhaps better) example is the postal system which is nationalized in every country in the world [this statement was written only eight years ago!]. The type of power base it provides is shown in certain ancient despotic societies where the Postmaster General was also the head of the internal security apparatus. Similarly, defense is a vital aspect of political sovereignty; therefore most governmental leaders are loath to permit private armies in their territories or to allow the private accumulation of mortars, torpedos, and other instruments of war. Since rapid transportation of troops is often a vital necessity, certain transportation industries might also be nationalized. The energy and fuel industries might be viewed similarly. (p. 9)

Today the argument about postal services seems, in a sense, outdated: after all Federal Express, Purolator, and numerous other companies compete with postal services; the only thing keeping them from providing additional ones is government regulation. On the other hand, one must admit that although in the West postal services are no longer associated with the issue of security (except in case of war), in the communist bloc they clearly are and letters are censored. But other channels of communication are still associated even in the West with sovereignty and political power – this was the justification given for state ownership of the TV channels and radio stations in France, where, by the way, telephone conversations are tapped (consider the "Canard Enchaîné" episode not so long ago).

Pryor's discussion and evidence thus raise some uncomfortable thoughts: First, where is the evidence for economies of scale? The regularity he captures when looking at the prevalence of state ownership in the West and in communist countries, observing a higher percentage in utilities, transportation, communication, and services (defense and public administration) – although with enormous variations around the trend – may as well be attributed to the fact that the same sectors are perceived to be linked everywhere to security, sovereignty, and political power, a perception which is not so surprising. Moreover, the view that state ownership is linked to security (rather than economies of scales) would even shed light on some of the variations around the trend (that an economies-of-scale argument cannot): The smaller extent of state ownership in the United State relative to the Western European countries is linked with the fact that in historical memory loss of sovereignty was more frequently a palpable threat there than in the United States. Second, which sector in the economy cannot be associated in one way or another with the question of security? Even agriculture fits the bill in more than one way. Embargos on grain exports have been used as a political weapon. Should one then conclude that practically every sector is a candidate for state ownership? Third, economists' and statisticians' comparisons based on categories of industries across countries and time must be viewed with skepticism: Although the words used are the same – "postal," "telephone" services – the perceptions of their services differ significantly. Fourth, the discussion draws attention to the fact that one must distinguish between reasons that can justify the emergence of a state-owned enterprise and those that are given to justify its persistence. For only by looking at the circumstances that have led to its *emergence* can one check the accuracy of the economies-of-scale argument.[7]

Let us illustrate this last point with the example of the railroads, a sector where state ownership or government intervention is frequently attributed to the existence of economies of scale. Was it really this view that led to state ownership sometimes, to regulation, other times? Again, the facts suggest a negative answer. As Stevenson (1981) summarizes:

State ownership of railways has had a long and complex history in Canada and elsewhere. To some degree, the railway might be considered to have the characteristics of a natural monopoly. . . . Yet in practice it usually was not, particularly in the United States and the United Kingdom. . . . As late as 1933, it was estimated that only 38 per cent of the world's railway mileage was under state ownership. Private ownership predominated in North America, South America, and Africa, while state ownership predominated in Europe, Asia, and the South Pacific. (p. 320)

According to Middletown (1937) the main reason for Bismarck's nationalization of railways was of course political, with a frank realization of the importance of the railways in a military sense (p. 131), whereas in Italy soon after 1870 the government began to buy up the railway lines in the north because there was thought to be danger of Austrian interference with the new regime. The government decided to build the main trunk lines because it feared that if foreign capital was permitted to enter the field, it would constitute a threat to the nation's independence (pp. 204–5). The same arguments were put forward in Japan: war with Russia and the fear of foreign influence. In France the government purchased the country's private railroad companies in 1930 to rescue them from what was perceived to be an unprofitable field and organize a national network – more about the social and political climate within which this step was taken will be said later. In Canada, as Stevenson (1981) notes, state ownership at the federal level "began with Confederation, by which the new federal state assumed both the assets and liabilities that had arisen from the railway-building efforts of New Brunswick and Nova Scotia. The British North American Act also required the federal government to build the Intercolonial Railway connecting those two provinces with Central Canada" (p. 320). Later, for a variety of reasons, Canada found itself with "three transcontinental railways, just as the war dried up the supply of immigrant farmers and British portfolio investment on which at least two of them depended. The response of Sir Robert Borden's government to this unhappy situation led, in a series of steps, towards Canadian National Railways" (p. 321). In England the nationalization of railroads occurred in 1948 and was part of the Labour Party's comprehensive plan to restructure the economy, although it is also noted that the goal was "to shield the railways from financial disaster caused by competition from road vehicles" (p. 33). How can this view, which explicitly recognizes the existence of *competing* transport forms, be reconciled with one that still today perceives railroads as being a "natural monopoly," is hard to understand.[8]

Although in the United States railroads are not nationalized, it may be useful to note that their regulation stemmed *not* from the perception of the existence of economies of scale but of dishonest, discriminatory business practices. Davis et al. (1965) noted that "the common thread running through most of the anti-railroad charges is one not of monopoly but of inequity . . . of charging different prices to different people for the same service" (pp. 311–12). Although this argument still implies the existence of monopoly powers, the description of the process that eventually led to the intervention of, first the state, and then of the federal government illustrates that the interventions may have been obtained not necessarily through appeal to "cold facts" but rather through an emotional reaction set in motion by an unexpected change for the worse in a group's wealth:

> The first serious complaints [against the railroads] were voiced by the midwestern farmers who, finding their incomes falling and unable to understand the nature of the world commodity market over which they had no control, chose to blame the railroads for their problems. Although many of their particular complaints were probably unjustified. . . . For a time the railroads were able to ignore the farmers, but when they were joined by members of the business community, it was inevitable that the government would act against the roads. (p. 312)

A similar point was made by Hillhouse (1936), who wrote:

> Burdened with debt for that which they did not own or control, forced to deal with representatives of absentee owners, victimized by swindlers or oppressive freight rates, it is no wonder that the farmers and localities of the midwestern states were stirred to revolt. . . . Repudiation of railroad air bonds provided at least one way of retaliating against eastern capitalists and against the railroads upon whom the farmers blindly pinned all their agrarian troubles. (p. 157)

The view of human behavior presented in Chapter 1 predicts such reaction; the link with the role of the state will be discussed further in this chapter.[9]

Now let us consider the second economic argument: externalities. Although Pryor noted that examples of negative externalities leading to nationalization occur in industries in which pollution or destruction of collective resources cannot be easily controlled without government ownership, and examples of positive ones leading to nationalization occur in instances such as education, multipurpose river projects, and "production" of "high culture" in which the benefits cannot be sufficiently captured by private owners to encourage private production (p. 9), he emphasized that on externalities, one can use only intuition, not data. Thus, this particular causal factor underlying the nationalization pattern must go untested. According to Pryor's intuitive ranking along an externalities scale, the relationship between externalities and nationalization did not seem strong (p. 15). One may just add that not only are there no data showing any clear-cut trend but one can hardly expect any to be built, for the value of external effects is subjective (consider the attitudes toward the firearm industry in the United States or the military in general, and also note that in terms of the view of human behavior presented in Chapter 1, there is *no* activity by any one individual that does not effect others). Briefly: There is *no* factual support for the perception that there is a causal relationship between either economies of scale or externalities and the emergence of state ownership.

The regularity one can find when looking at the emergence of state-owned enterprises will be summarized next.

3   The emergence of state-owned enterprises – regularities

In spite of the enormous variations across countries and time in the patterns that have led to the emergence of state-owned enterprises, some regularities can be detected. Shepherd (1976), Pryor (1976), and Trebilcock and Prichard (1983) all agree that the principal influences that *may* lead to the establishment of public enterprise are: (a) nation building, (b) promotion of national security (among others by securing supplies), and (c) significant changes in people's position in the distribution of wealth.

If indeed the evidence enables detecting these regularities, the question is: What view of human behavior and of history can enable making the prediction that in these circumstances the intervention of state in various sectors is more likely? First, it is clear that if one speaks about "nations" and "national security," the role of the state is evident. Moreover, the context in which its intervention must be examined is *international*. Second, if significant changes in the distribution of wealth are linked with the role of the state, one must present some model of human behavior in which such changes play a significant, direct role. Such a model was presented in Chapter 1. Its extension links in a straightforward way individual and group behavior with significant changes in fluctuations in the distribution of wealth, whether on national or international levels. The model provides clear roles for the state, statesmen, politicians, *and* chance, when a significant change alters a somehow achieved social order, the role being that of restoring stability. The methods by which this goal can be achieved will be discussed later, once the principal features of the model are summarized. Since the model is a general one looking at motivations of human behavior, one cannot expect a precise prediction as to the nature of the state's intervention. But the model – if accurate – makes it clear that only by looking at the historical background can one understand the nature of this intervention – ahistorical theorizing will never do.

Before discussing these implications of the model, let us provide a sample of the interpretations that have been given to the emergence of state-owned enterprises. Sheahan's (1976, p. 124) observation on France was that public enterprise had a long tradition there, which was made much more important by a series of nationalizations immediately after World War II. These nationalizations followed directly from an agreement reached by the National Resistance Council in 1943, opposing any return to the version of "capitalism" France had known before the war. That kind of capitalism was one which relied on private enterprise, with very few exceptions, but which discouraged any active competition. Private agreements to restrain competition were not only accepted but backed up by legal regulations. Government intervention was oriented mainly to protecting existing positions of all social groups, from each other and above all from any external competitive pressures. The result was that the country lost its ability to keep up with the *outside* world in new fields of industry, and began to lose its earlier capacity for scientific leadership as well – more about this impact will be said later. Sheahan also notes that the 1943 agreement of the National Resistance Council in favor of public ownership of basic industries represented a consensus of dislike for the prewar economy but not one of purpose for the future. For some, the goal was to replace capitalism with gradually extended public ownership and centralized state control. Others wanted workers to take control of the public firms, independent of the state. A third interest was to use public enterprise, restricted to a few basic industries, as an instrument of planning to promote rapid modernization of the economy, and at the same time continuing private ownership for all sectors outside of energy, transport, finance, and communications (p. 125). The ideological vacuum following wars or other major disturbances is a common finding – again an insight into some implications of this problem will be given below.

Similar arguments can be found in Walsh (1978) in her detailed and massive examination of the public's business in the United States. She concludes that public ownership in the United States lacks an explicitly stated public policy, and that in the absence of a clear view of the role of public enterprise, politics has shaped public corporation haphazardly to fit specific, practical problems – the model will suggest a way to understand the order behind this apparent disorder. Coombes makes the same observation for the United Kingdom, noting that "state enterprise in Britain is normally identified with the undertakings called 'nationalized industries' set up mainly by Acts passed under the Labour Government of 1945–1950. It has never been clear what the objects of those Acts were" (p. 19).

Martinelli (1981) provides the following account of the Italian experience: During World War I, the demand for steel, metal, automobile equipment, and textiles led to the rapid expansion of the industrial sector and deepened the involvement of major banks in growing business. After the war, the major banks experienced a liquidity crisis. To prevent the larger corporations from going bankrupt, the state intervened. Again then, in response to domestic and international crises the government created a temporary state agency, IRI, to rescue the country's indebted firms (p. 87). Later, in 1953, the government established ENI under the aggressive leadership of Enrico Mattei, who was given considerable autonomy in developing the oil industry, in part because he was an experienced businessman, in part because he shared certain goals with the ruling party. Fanfani, the new secretary of the Christian Democrats, wanted to strengthen the party organization by penetrating the major decision-making centers (pp. 89–90), and Martinelli concludes that, increasingly, the ruling party has tried to use state ownership as an instrument to implement stabilization policy without significantly changing class or political relations (p. 92). Note again the reference to the goal of maintaining a somehow achieved status quo, the reference to international affairs, and the role individuals play.

In order to avoid any misinterpretation, it should be made clear that the notions of wealth distribution and classes that play roles in the model are *not* the "classical," dogmatic "capitalist" versus "labor," but any two classes.[10] The next episode, Vining's (1981) detailed account of the origins of Ontario Hydro, illuminates the difference:

Ontario Hydro was conceived more in the tradition of an older ideological struggle, the bourgeoisie versus the aristocracy. The conflict pitted the small industrialists of towns such as London, Berlin, and Hamilton against the "nobler barons" of Montreal, London, and New York. (p. 152)

Vining also notes that "fear of U.S. industrial competition and perceived over-reliance on U.S. coal supplies played an important role in generating momentum for public ownership" (p. 153) and concludes that this kind of division, with important variations, has played an important role in the development of each of the hydros: "The lines of pluralistic battle in Ontario were drawn on several dimensions: Toronto versus the hinterland, 'trust' entrepreneurial capital versus small, industrial entrepreneurs, 'foreign' versus 'native' interests being the most important" (p. 153). The threat of foreign influence seems also to be a factor in the origins of Air Canada. According to Langford (1981) there was by 1936 a strong pressure for the creation of a national intercity air service for passengers and mail. The pressure came from the expansionary tendencies of private American airlines, and the threat of foreign domination traditionally called for some form of nation-building or "community development" activity by the federal government (pp. 252–3). Langford also quotes Bothwell and Kilbourn, whose opinion was that in the depths of the Depression, the airway offered hope of dramatic future growth, a way out of despair. They also offered a potential new east–west link for a transcontinental nation, reinforcing that of the railways, and counterbalancing the north–south pull of the highways that first became an economic force in the 1920s (p. 252). Tupper and Doern (1981) also note that "the establishment of the Canadian Radio Broadcasting Commission in 1932 was a classic instance of defensive expansionism and the use of state enterprise to counteract the threats posed to Canadian identity by the American media. In this case the choice was clear – 'it was the state or the United States' " (p. 11).

The fear of falling behind other groups, not always necessarily "foreign" ones, seemed to have played a significant role in the emergence of state ownership. According to Tupper (1981):

The need to protect Alberta's economic interests from potentially hostile "external" forces was the dominant theme in the government's public explanations of the PWA acquisition. . . . the real threat, in the government's view was posed by the White Pass and Yukon take-over bid. That company's bid was particularly ominous, for as well as operating a railroad between Shagway and White Horse, White Pass and Yukon owned other transportation interests along the British Columbia Coast and in the Yukon. . . . Speaking of the possibility of a White Pass take-over, Don Getty remarked: "It was conceivable that such an acquisition would seriously threaten Alberta's position as the Gateway to the North through development of a traffic pattern from British Columbia to the Yukon, Northwest Territories, and Alaska, rather than through Alberta. (pp. 288–9)

Although the details of the story differ, one can identify similar arguments in the emergence of the Potash Corporation of Saskatchewan (Laux and Molot 1981, pp. 190–4, 210–11) and of the National Asbestos Corporation of Quebec (Fournier 1981). Rotstein (1984), in a detailed account of the history of the Canadian Wheat Board, highlights the roles of a number of critical events – two world wars and a depression – in its origins.[11]

The conclusion that *crises* (in the form of wars, threats, and prospects of prolonged, rising unemployment) have a major impact on the roles of governments is reinforced when one looks at other features of the European experience. According to Noreng (1981) after World War I several Western European governments took action to secure foreign oil supplies. The first oil nationalization of Western Europe began in the United Kingdom. In 1914, the British government became part owner of the Anglo-Persian Oil Company, now British Petroleum, to secure foreign oil supplies for military needs. Britain's willingness to enter into a position of ownership in an oil company stemmed from its desire to avoid reliance on foreign oil supplies in times of crisis. France participated in the redistribution of the old Turkish Petroleum Company, securing oil concessions in the Middle East for the first time, and in 1926, faced with the same concerns as France over dependence on foreign oil suppliers, Italy established Agip, a public company to explore and produce oil abroad (p. 133).

Whereas in Canada "nation building" seems to have been frequently put forward as an argument justifying state intervention, in form of ownership in particular, in Europe where "nations" already existed, the threat to their sovereignty has been more frequently used as an argument. However, the distinction between these two arguments is not always sharp. In more recent times statesmen in Europe seem to have struggled with the question of how to *rebuild,* rather than build, a "nation," when during wars fractions of the population collaborated with the enemies. There was no question but that the collaborators had to be punished – but how? In France and in Austria, the punishment took, at times, the form of confiscation – the transformation of Renault to a state-owned enterprise after World War II serves in French historical memory as a permanent, symbolical reminder of the type of punishment that may be inflicted on traitors (who are rich; the poor may either be executed or go to prison. The latter may not be perceived as sufficient punishment for the rich, who, once out of prison can still benefit from their unpatriotic behavior).

The summary of the evidence on the origins of state-owned enterprises in these two sections provides sufficient background for understanding that if one wants to shed light on the origins of state-owned enterprises, one needs a model of human behavior where the link between the role of the state and various "crises" can be clarified. The model presented in Chapter 1 enables such clarification. Once it is done, additional questions concerning state-owned enterprises will be examined.

> The great events of history are often due to secular changes in the
> growth of population and other fundamental economic causes,
> which, escaping by their gradual character the notice of contempo-
> rary observers, are attributed to the follies of statesmen or the fanati-
> cism of atheists.
> J. M. Keynes, *The Economic Consequences of the Peace*

4   Decision making and the role of the state

The previous sections described the origins of some new institutions. Any model that tries to shed light on such emergences must deal with these questions: In what circumstances are people more likely to deviate from the status quo, from the beaten path, and try new institutions? Why do people change their minds, on political strategies in particular? Why do they bet on new ideas and implement them? These are the same types of questions as raised in Chapter 1. The approach presented there suggested that bets on new ideas are triggered when customary behavior, failing significantly to produce the expected results, leads to the perception of a loss in one's relative standing in society. Implicitly, there are numerous important assumptions made that enable drawing this conclusion: The incentive to bet on new ideas appears when suddenly an individual's position in the wealth distribution has been (or is expected to be) significantly worsened. The incentives disappear if either customs or redistributive taxes exist that would lead to expectations that the individual will be compensated for his loss. In these circumstances the somehow achieved order (or status quo) is perpetuated. There are good reasons for such customs or such a system of taxation and redistribution to evolve (eventually) if these views of human behavior are accurate. For they predict that, when a person's situation becomes relatively worse, he may bet not only on an entrepreneurial act but also on a criminal one, which is costly for a society. Moreover, if a whole group's position in the wealth distribution is threatened, the probability increases that the persons affected will gamble on political, even revolutionary, ideas advocating redistribution of wealth in their own favor. Since such gambles too are also costly for society, redistributive policies or customs requiring redistribution of wealth may provide remedies that maintain the stability of the society, simultaneously, however, reducing its creativity. Nevertheless, if the standard of living in such a society happens to fluctuate (in spite of all insurances), and people become more creative, then they may be perceived in a negative light and may be discouraged from implementing their ideas. For their rise in the wealth distribution is expected to encourage those who fall behind to gamble both on additional entrepreneurial acts and on criminal ones. Both types of actions are viewed as costly since they are expected to lead to further fluctuations in people's positions in the wealth distribution.

What, then, is the role of the government within this model? Leapfrogging among groups (i.e., the process whereby some groups are outdone by their "fellows") increases the probability that those who fall behind will perform noncustomary acts whether criminal, revolutionary, or entrepreneurial. By promising to implement actual and future redistributive policies, statesmen and politicians try to restore stability, but in so doing walk a tightrope: Although expectations of such redistributions increase social and political stability, the higher expected tax rates and lowered aspirations may simultaneously diminish the incentives to engage in entrepreneurial acts in general. Yet some degree of stability is necessary to enable entrepreneurs both to make *any* calculations of risks and to expect their efforts to be rewarded. As the evidence already discussed, and that discussed later, suggests, state-owned enterprises have played these roles by indicating commitment to a particular direction. Not surprisingly, there is a wide variation in the specific nature of the ideas that have been pursued: Some individuals' ideas are followed in these circumstances, whose precise nature *cannot* be predicted. Also, state-owned enterprises have been used to maintain stability by policies that control the unemployment rate (thus protecting and insuring some groups' position in the wealth distribution). But in some circumstances when the perception is that the pendulum had swung "too far" in the direction of protection – the criterion being the performance of other societies, as shown in the next chapter – a tendency emerges to swing back and encourage more entrepreneurial attitudes. This has been done either by betting on ideas of "privatization" or by cutting customary benefits, funds, or subsidies (policies that in the light of this model may turn out to be successful).

With appropriate changes in terminology, the arguments on leapfrogging, extended from domestic to international relationships, result in similar predictions. Of course, the role of statesmen and politicians now becomes more complex. What will they advocate if they perceive that a "neighboring" nation ("neighboring" as defined by existing technology, military, and other) is suddenly outdoing them? Again, the model and the evidence suggest that nations and their leaders walk a tightrope. Such a leapfrogging process has a destabilizing effect, leading sometimes to wars and at other times to an entrepreneurial outburst in the nation that fell behind, an outburst initiated by statesmen's ideas and, frequently, through policies initiated by state-owned enterprises. (What other methods suggest to the population a commitment toward a new policy, forced upon one nation by external developments?)

Although at first sight it may seem surprising to link the role of the state with leapfrogging – the resulting disorder and sentiments of fear and envy that arise – it should be noted that this is not the first time that the link has been made. Although Tocqueville never made an extended analysis of resentment or envy, he seemed to view it as a driving force behind the "egalitarian impulse." Lakoff (1964) notes that:

He tried to separate the experience of violent hatred in the [French] revolutionary period from democracy itself, but he was not very successful. . . . Democracy was conceived out of envy and in Tocqueville's view it was to be forever tainted with the marks of its birth. From the standpoint of aristocratic ethics the revolution was justified; but, for the mobs which carried it out, the principal motivation was naked envy. . . . In attacking the holders of privileges . . . the populace sought not to protest an imbalance but to despoil the favored few; to gain for themselves the marks of privilege they professed to find intrinsically unjust. (p. 167)

Schoeck (1969), Foster (1972), North (1981), and Marina (1979) make similar points: They too try to understand the emergence of various institutions as a response either to the losers' reaction or other people's attempts to protect themselves against the possibility of such reactions [Schoeck's (1969) entire book is devoted to this subject – for a detailed discussion on these points see Brenner (1983, 1985)].

Yet at this point one may raise an additional question: Since forces exist within this model to restore and maintain stability, domestic and external, what can disturb the somehow achieved order and shed further light on the role of the state? The answer that innovations can be the cause is not satisfying within this model since, in a sense, they are endogenous. One answer given and verified in Brenner (1983, 1985) is that sudden, significant fluctuations in population (more correctly in the number of people with whom interactions can be expected) that were beyond control have frequently disturbed a somehow achieved order. As a result, governments have struggled with the question of how to relink an increasing number of people – a number of enterprises owned by the state can be viewed as attempts to deal with this question. This struggle is linked with the traditional roles attributed by both economists and political scientists to the state: to maintain law and order, to enforce contracts voluntarily entered into, and to define property rights. These roles are easier to describe than to carry out: Although sometimes having the same religion was perceived to diminish significantly contract uncertainty, at other times cheaper communication methods (postal, travel, etc.) were expected to achieve this goal. But few social scientists examined the practical question of how the state can achieve these goals when the population is growing and customs are weakened. Even if one accepts with reservation the next quoted generalization, it seems illuminating and saves on further theorizing (which, together with evidence, can be found elsewhere).[12] Lord Durham (1839) in his *Report on the Affairs of British North America* wrote:

I know of no difference in the machinery of government in the old and new world that strikes a European more forcibly than the apparently undue importance which the business of constructing public works appears to occupy in American legislation. . . . The provision which in Europe, the State makes for the protection of its citizens against foreign enemies, is in America required for . . . the "war with the wilderness." The defence of an important fortress, or the maintenance of a sufficient army or navy in exposed spots, is not more a matter of common concern to the European, than is the construction of the great communications to the American settler; and the State, very naturally, takes on itself the making of the works, which are a matter of concern to all alike. [as quoted by Aitken (1961, p. 183)][13]

The same point was made by Cochran (1950), who notes that the perceived benefits of land grants to railroads between the 1840s and the 1870s were linked with military protection and the provision of postal services. The federal charters frequently contained the explanatory clause: "by the construction of said railroad . . . to secure to the government at all times (but particularly in time of war) the use and benefits of the same, for postal, military and other purposes." Cochran also notes that: "By the ensuing Congressional session of 1856–1857 the principle of aid through land was so well accepted that the conflicts were over when the grants should be made. [The three major party platforms all favored aid to a Pacific railway.] Since politicians affirm what they as experts think their constituents want to hear, we may presume that from 1857 to about 1867 public opinion favored the land-grant policy." (p. 54) – as railroads were *then* linked with perceptions of providing security, this is not very surprising.

Although the approach summarized here is novel, the interpretation of the facts (on the role of the state in particular) and policy implications toward which it may sometimes lead have been given by some social scientists. A few of them will be referred to in the next section, but an elaborate discussion of theirs and others' views can be found elsewhere.[14]

5   State-owned enterprises – further evidence

Let us summarize both the model's predictions, which may illuminate the emergence of state-owned enterprises, and the facts:

1. The model suggests that such interventions will emerge following some

leapfrogging, that is, a perception of a "drastic" change in a group's position in the distribution of wealth, domestic or international. This observation has been made by almost all the studies written on the subject [see, in particular, Shepherd's (1976) summary, p. XIII]. Moreover, studies written on broader subjects – government intervention in general – have concluded that "crises" are their source, and politicians and statesmen struggle with the question of how to disperse the shocks [see Hughes (1977); or, in even broader historical perspective, some writers linked government intervention and changes in institutions to fluctuations in population, see North (1981), McNeill (1982), and others].[15] Indeed, Vernon (1981) concludes in a review of a conference on state-owned enterprises that there may be no reason to study state-owned enterprises as a separate subject; that a study of the relation of governments to *all forms* of intervention would be more fruitful (p. 15).

2. Individuals and their ideas play central roles in the model. Thus, although the model enables making a prediction on the general trends that will be advocated in some circumstances, it also shows that one cannot explain the particular case. Chance plays a role. Many writers have pointed out the apparent disorder in reactions and have suggested that because of it no "general approach" can be built. Yet the model summarized here suggests an explanation for both the perceived regularity and the apparent disordered reaction.

3. Following "crises" (as defined in the model), some people bet on new ideas. Thus a babel of voices is heard. The model suggests that the way out of the disorder is when a relatively large group finally bets on one individual's ideas, call him a statesman or a politician.[16] Indeed, all the case studies summarize the debates that took place, note the confusion, and emphasize the roles individuals played in the process.[17]

4. The changing goals from promoting entrepreneurship toward maintaining the status quo and redistributing wealth – and back – is not necessarily a sign of confusion, but a shift that can be expected, depending on changes in domestic and external circumstances. Such a change is related to the role of the state, as explained in the previous section.[18] The observation on the changing goals is made by Chandler (1983), Noreng (1981) (who, for example, shows that the enterprise created to support a branch of high technology finds itself diverted to maintain jobs, whereas an enterprise that emerged to support farm incomes is used to hold down urban food prices), and in a broader context by Hughes (1977).

5. Many studies concentrate on the issue of profitability of state-owned enterprises. It is not always clear what one can learn from an ahistorical interpretation of numbers. Suppose that an enterprise is set up to diminish a threat. Part of the measured "loss" of the state-owned enterprise can be interpreted in a similar way as expenditures on arms, army, and police. In what sense

can one say that the latter expenditures are "a loss"? True, just as sometimes total expenditures on the military can be perceived as being "excessive," so can people perceive subsidies to a state-owned enterprise. But that means that the examination of the numbers must be done in a historical context and raises, among others, the question of whether or not the circumstances that have led to the emergence of a state-owned enterprise have disappeared, or that the perception was erroneous to start with.[19] In the Canadian context where the building of a nation has been frequently put forward for justifying the emergence and persistence of some state-owned enterprise, those who just criticize their lack of profitability may be on the wrong track. For nobody can put a precise price tag on the goal of nation building. Instead the approach must raise the question of whether or not the enterprise can fulfill the goals for which it has been created, of whether or not time made both the goal and the enterprise obsolete, or whether or not there are alternatives for building a "nation."

6. Comparisons between profitability of state-owned enterprises in different countries cannot be always illuminating either. In some countries, national airlines seem to be perceived as a matter of pride (if one gives to their existence a positive connotation, "vanity" if one gives a negative one), of trying to raise the aspirations of the people (recall, an argument also given for Hydro-Quebec). In others they are perceived to be linked with the perception of security (in Israel with good reason, as the foreign airlines' reaction during crises have shown), whereas elsewhere they are just a rapid method of transportation and are privately owned. What can one learn from a comparison of measured profitability of the enterprises in the three types of countries?

7. The most frequent argument in the literature on state-owned enterprises concerns, implicity or explicitly, the redistribution of wealth by compensating groups who fall behind. Some authors put the argument bluntly, stating that workers expect to have higher wages and more protection when an enterprise is state-owned, although others put it in vague terms of "improving social relationships within an enterprise." Shepherd (1976) notes that the goals of state-owned enterprise include "some degree of improved equity by making output cheaper than it otherwise would be for needy citizens". . . , "an improvement in the regional and urban balance of enterprise activities" (p. XII) without ever clarifying according to which model of the world these changes can be perceived as "improvement," or what the implicit view of the state underlying such statements is.

Note, however, that according to the arguments presented here, it is *not* "the wealth distribution" that matters, whether or not it is more or less equal, but the perception of leapfrogging, of suddenly falling behind. A few studies on state-owned enterprises drew attention to this point explicitly. Nelson (1976) wrote that "if an industry becomes too profitable, and if its profitability cannot be controlled, or should not be controlled, or administratively cannot be controlled – then the public should have the right to acquire the industry. . . . This principle was written into French policy with the authorization for the first railway line" (p. 52), whereas Pryor (1976) suggests that "large un-earned income" (p. 9) may lead toward state ownership, noting that "certain production leads to large incomes which are considered unearned. This occurs in some mineral mining, as well as in natural monopolies" (p. 9). Although Pryor (1976) does not clarify with precision what view of human behavior justifies state intervention in this case, his observation seems accurate. If, by chance, a group's wealth increases, and others fall behind, one can predict some destabilizing effects, which governments will try to mitigate. But, as already emphasized, one *cannot* predict exactly what instrument governments will use: State ownership is one possibility, but there are others – a windfall tax, for example. Buchanan and Tideman (1974), examining the regulations in the gasoline market after 1973, suggest that the state intervenes when a market crisis wrecks the customary balance between producer interest and voter apathy, and, in a response to a large and sudden rise in relative price, it becomes a "broker" for a consumers' buying monopsony, rather than contin-uing as a broker for a producers' selling monopoly. The view underlying Buchanan's and Tideman's seems to be that of a politician facing choices, whose decision is dominated by the goal of maximizing votes. Yet some criticism must be drawn on this view of the world. Note that within it politi-cians (or individuals in general) don't seem to matter: Their ideas just mirror what they perceive to be the opinion of the majority. But those adopting this approach do not address the question: To start with, how did the majority form its opinion, in the new circumstances in which they suddenly found themselves? Whose ideas is the majority following? If the answer to this ques-tion is that the ideas of "leaders," "statesmen," are followed, then such individuals must play central roles in the argument explaining the political process, but in the model of vote maximization they don't.[20]

Borcherding (1983) comes close to my arguments [admitting that he lacks a theory, but he prefers dealing "imperfectly with what is important than to attain virtuoso skill in the treatment of that which does not matter" (p. 148)], summarizing the view of a number of scholars he concludes that the "excess" costs attributed to various forms of government intervention rep-resent the effects of redistributing wealth.[21] Aharoni (1983) makes the same point and goes one step further linking the notion of redistribution with "in-surance":

Whatever the original reasons for their creation, these enterprises have been used to shift risks to the public sector by protecting declining industries, by bailing out ailing firms, by guaranteeing input prices to the private sector, or by shielding workers against unemployment. Many of these enterprises have suffered heavy losses, partially at least as a result of their function as a protector and insurer. . . . In the 1960s and 1970s these enterprises were used to protect workers against the risk of unemployment and to save private entrepreneurs in declining industries from suffering losses. Dozens of private enterprises were acquired by governments in Germany, France, Italy, the Netherlands, Sweden, and the United Kingdom in order to prevent the collapse of their firms. Thus, the hard-coal industries in Britain, France, Italy, Spain, and West Germany were brought under state-ownership to avoid closure. . . . SOEs were created to assure guaranteed employment to thousands of workers. In many of these cases, the new plants suffered heavy losses, yet were not allowed to reduce their work force. (p. 167)

But the role played by the state as an "insurer," and using state-owned enterprises for this goal raises a further problem in interpreting their "lack of profitability." Costs being defined as forgone opportunities, the scholar interested in this question should look at the expenses the state (i.e., the taxpayers) would incur if the enterprise were let to go under. If the unemployment benefits, costs of dislocation, and so forth are perceived to cost, say $1 billion, whereas maintaining the state-owned enterprise to cost $750 millions, state ownership will be perceived as "profitable."[22]

Although state-owned enterprises have been used to deal with preventing a rise in unemployment rates in certain areas (consider Air France's and Renault's experiences in France or the numerous interventions in Italy to save textile factories in the Alps, near Rome, etc.), it would be misleading to interpret the policies as attempts to make "social reforms." The policies have dealt with localized fires in attempts to maintain stability.

8. As noted, the goal of building or maintaining a nation has led to the emergence of state-owned enterprises. But the goals have been frequently linked with the issue of the redistribution of wealth among regions too. The Italian case is revealing: The Italian south (the Mezzogiorno) was and is poorer than the north. It was poorer in the last third of the nineteenth century, and the situation did not seem to improve following national unification; according to Sheahan (1976) the region may even have been set back. In part, the setback was later attributed to regulations introduced by Mussolini, who designated the south as the agricultural base for his ideal of an autarchic, self-sufficient *national* system. How can an erroneous regulation be corrected? Either by canceling it (but such drastic, abrupt steps are not always easy to carry out if people have adapted themselves to the existing regulations) or by compensating for it. In 1957, a law was passed requiring state-owned enterprises to locate 40 percent of their existing investments and 60 percent of new ones in the south, while in 1971 these numbers were raised to 60 and 80 percent, respectively. Without explicitly relating nation building with the notion of wealth distribution and the perceptions of falling behind, implicitly this is what the next paragraph in Trebilcock and Prichard (1983) implies:

The notion of nation building is discussed throughout the literature on public enterprise. . . . The inhospitable [Canadian] environment refers to the difficulty of developing integrated communities, given the American presence to the South, significant regional identities. . . . Tupper notes that private enterprise may not be willing to extend transportation, message communication and power facilities to isolated areas with small populations, since the cost may exceed any reasonable revenue expectations. As a related concern, there is also the threat of economic and political domination by the United States if the Canadian government fails to act in those situations where domestic private investment is not forthcoming. If the only real alternative to public enterprise is a foreign owned private firm, the government in some sectors may perceive its options to be foreclosed. (pp. 53–4)

6 Policy implications

In the extensive literature on public enterprises, the authors frequently attribute their failure to the fact that ''no general theories of public enterprise or defined goals in the public interest [have been articulated], that might be reasonably imposed on government corporations. . . . The cure lies not in eliminating independent government corporations . . . but in defining, developing, and applying to them some long-range public goals'' [as Walsh (1978), p. 341, for example, puts it].

Sounds appealing? Maybe. But although in theory one can define and develop a ''public goal'' (implicitly the model presented here does so), one cannot recommend applying it in just *one* society. Such one-sided policy is dangerous. Instead one must turn back to John Stuart Mill's vague recommendation that the proper justification for the role of the state is the ''comprehensive one of general expediency'' – this recommendation will be further justified in the next chapter.

Some criteria for increasing the effectiveness of state-owned enterprises nevertheless emerge from this and the previous chapters.

1. The arguments and evidence suggest that their roles have been to diminish contract uncertainty (in a broad sense) and maintain social stability.[23] Thus their emergence and persistence should be viewed neither as a puzzle nor with suspicion. Their emergence is not simply a matter of politicians trying to maximize votes for their own private benefit (although their persistence may be, at times, related to such an argument).

2. The benefits of state-owned enterprises depend on specific historical circumstances. But since frequently no standards exist against which to test the effectiveness of this particular instrument (in contrast to a privately owned enterprise whose performance can be compared to its competitors') at regular intervals of time, one must reexamine whether or not the circumstances that led to their emergence still persist (today, obviously, the postal, telephone,

and the long overdue railway regulations or state ownership should be up for such reviews). If such reexaminations are not done, interest groups develop, and theories will be invented that will justify maintaining the somehow achieved order. There is nothing to wonder at in this, it is a well-known observation. As Schumpeter (1942) once put it: "Individuals and groups snatch at anything that will qualify as a discovery lending support to the political tendencies of the hour" (p. 95).

3. As noted, the "disappointing" financial performance of state-owned enterprises has been attributed to the roles they played in maintaining social stability. If frequently this was their goal – as the evidence suggests, and the model presented here suggests a rationale for such a role – a policy suggestion can be made to have a criterion for evaluating their performance. Vernon (1981) notes:

Great Britain, Sweden, Italy and France . . . have experimented at various times with a common approach. They have undertaken to identify the social tasks that they expected the state-owned enterprises to perform; to provide subsidies to such enterprises equal to the cost of these tasks; and thereafter to demand that, with the help of such subsidies, the enterprises should be financially self-sustaining. (p. 17)

Although the principle has not been consistently applied, it seems to be worth a try. At least it would force government officials to reexamine whether the goals still fit the circumstances, or whether they became obsolete either because of innovations or changes in international relationships.

4. As the views in Chapter 1 suggest, there is no reason to expect managers and employers within state-owned enterprises to be less interested in innovations and productivity than their counterparts in the private sector. They may be equally ambitious, may fear being fired, demoted, or humiliated, and may worry about their reputation. The state-owned enterprise's reputation for laxity puts them in a bad light, impairing future employment opportunities. Thus, if such enterprises are perceived as performing less well than private ones, that perception may be due to factors *other* than state ownership. If the government puts limits on salaries earned by executives in state-owned enterprises that are significantly lower than those earned in the private sector, that may lead to a process of self-selection. Those with superior business and managerial skills may turn to the private sector. If chairmen of state-owned enterprises are *not* threatened with being fired if they don't produce a satisfactory rate of return, one should expect an inferior performance (of course, if entry is blocked by government regulation, one should expect inferior performance too, as explained in Chapter 3). If, in general, job security exists at other levels of the staff too, and advance in the hierarchy is according to seniority rather than talent, one should also expect an inferior performance.

A distinction must be made between those factors causing measured inferior performance and others that are due to the fact that some goals other than monetary ones (military, maintaining employment in some regions) are im-. posed on state-owned enterprises. Whatever the other goals may be, performance *can* be improved by canceling the employment and hierarchical features mentioned above.

Indeed, in spite of slogans to the contrary, the French government under Mitterand did just that.[24] In 1982, it nationalized six major industrial concerns, employing 645,000 workers. In 1981, the six lost $69.9 millions. In 1984, they earned $337.7 millions. One of the concerns, Rhone-Poulenc, went from a $36.2 million loss in 1981 to a $215 million profit in 1984. Although the data are yet insufficient to distinguish between dumb luck (the effect of the upturn in the United States and elsewhere) and changed policy as determinants of this alteration, some of the changes within the nationalized firms should be noted. Although the original socialist promise was to use nationalization to create jobs and give workers a bigger role in running companies, now the government threatens chairmen of nationalized companies if they don't produce profits. The chairman of Rhone-Poulenc had thoroughly revamped executive pay, deemphasizing seniority. Executive pay raises used to hover within 1 or 2 percentage points of each other when the company was private; they range now from 12 percent down to nothing. The company also closed some operations, reducing the work force (in the case of one unit from 2,000 to fewer than 1,000). These changes were not easy to make. In 1983, chairmen of the state-owned enterprises demanded greater autonomy if they were to deliver the performance that President Mitterand wanted. Soon thereafter, the interventionist industry minister, Jean-Pierre Chevenement, lost his job. These are some of the simple facts hiding behind – do you remember? – the 1982 big words.

The lesson from this, and all the previous evidence, is simple (although implementing what one learned from it is not): A shift toward encouraging entrepreneurship and privatization requires not so much ideological commitment as the art of statesmanship. The state-owned enterprises, whatever their origins, have built up over the years dependent hierarchies, whose positions are threatened by the shift of goals. These groups must be carefully identified and credible promises made, giving them stakes in the new order. By disregarding these groups, one courts instability; by maintaining the established order, statesmen risk their nation falling behind. This conclusion is reinforced by the discussion and evidence presented in the next chapter.

CHAPTER 7

Restoring the wealth of nations

"Well, in *our* country," said Alice, still panting a little,
"you'd generally get to somewhere else – if you ran very
fast for a long time, as we've been doing."

"A slow sort of country!" said the Queen. "Now *here,*
you see, it takes all the running you can do, to keep in the
same place. If you want to get somewhere else, you must
run at least twice as fast as that!"

Through the Looking-Glass
Lewis E. Carroll

Innovations and entrepreneurship have been some of the main subjects examined in the previous chapters, and, as pointed out in this concluding one, their promotion must be the focus of policies whose goal is to *restore* the wealth of nations.

One should not be surprised to learn that such policies, today called "industrial strategies" or "industrial policies," have *always* been nationalistic in character and were advocated by some social scientists and politicians when their nation started falling behind. The sudden relative prosperity of others (achieved through innovations) was perceived as a threat by those outdone. And with good reasons: Those who lost ground by being undersold could choose between lowering aspirations (and thus reducing wages and standards of living) *or* maintain aspirations and then make greater efforts, become more productive and innovative.[1]

As the discussion here will suggest, there seems to be little disagreement that, indeed, only entrepreneurship and innovations can restore a nation's wealth. The questions are: What are the roles one assigns policymakers in this process, and what incentives can turn people into being more entrepreneurial and innovative? These are the questions that have been examined in the previous chapters and will be reexamined in this chapter from a different angle.

146

1   Industrial policies – a brief historical perspective

What is an "industrial policy"? One generally accepted definition today is that whatever the government does vis-à-vis private industry to achieve a variety of objectives can be viewed as representing such policy or strategy [see Ozaki (1984, p. 48)]. But, of course, nothing can be done with such an all-encompassing definition since policymakers have always decided to do something (the decision to do nothing *is* a big decision too). The question is *what* to do and *what for*.[2]

In the thirteenth century Philip the Fair ordered the wives of citizens of Paris not to ride in carriages in order to preserve the prerogatives of the ladies of the court. A similar law likewise sought to prevent the use of coaches in Hungary in 1523. In 1588 Duke Julius of Brunswick made riding in coaches by his vassals a crime punishable as a felony, on the grounds that it would interfere with military preparedness, for men would lose their equestrian skill.[3] Japan's shoguns closed their country for three and a half centuries to outside trade. In the United States interventions have included the encouragement of exports and relief from import competition, construction of highways, subsidized water for the West, price supports for farmers, the space program, and others. All these interventions constitute industrial policies – these are some of the things that governments have done – but what for?

In spite of such variety of continuous interventions from ancient to modern times, it is possible to get a clearer picture why new strategies were sought, once one distinguishes the trends from the noise. The "what for" question seems to have two answers: One is implicitly given below in Johnson's (1984) definition, and the second will be discussed later.

By industrial policy I mean the government's explicit attempt to coordinate its own multifarious activities and expenditures and to reform them using as a basic criterion the achievement of *dynamic comparative advantage for the American economy*. (p. 11, italics added)

Indeed, the idea of implementing a new industrial policy has been frequently connected with nationalism, more precisely, with the idea of *restoring* a nation's competitive edge.[4] The term "nationalism" should be broadly interpreted: Policies toward industry have been used to further national unification (Germany in the late nineteenth century, Canada in the late nineteenth and this century, Israel and numerous Third World countries today), and the political consolidation of new regimes (USSR), to restore and guarantee national security and prestige (Kemal Ataturk felt the need to bring Turkey into the orbit of Western Europe in order to maintain its life as a nation), and to maintain a unitary system challenged by linguistics and political divisions (Belgium, Canada).[5]

The idea of "infant industry protection" was nurtured in underdeveloped Germany of the beginning of the nineteenth century, concerned about the threat posed by the superior English manufacturers. The thought of protecting fragile domestic industries for similar reasons was strong then in France and the United States too.[6] Later the actors change but the reasoning stays the same. Young (1973) points out that the Englishman feared the loss of his superiority:

[A]bove . . . the Federation of British Industries loomed the shadow of the clever foreigner. . . . At the beginning of the last century the fear was of Germany; in the middle years, of American and, even more, of Russian competition; at the end, of Chinese. At each stage the threat of the other country's armaments, the other country's science, was used to batter down resistance to change. . . . The other countries had chosen better raw material and, by better training, had produced from it better aeronauts, better physicists, better administrators, and above all, better applied scientists. If Britain did not do likewise she was inviting defeat either in war or in trade; the recurring crises in the balance of payments made the second seem almost as deadly a threat as the first. . . . Britain survived so long because it had repeated blood-transfusions from Australia, New Zealand, South Africa, and Canada, countries less handicapped by inheritance, who sent their talent to their mother-country. (pp. 33–4)

By replacing the words "Englishman" by "Canadian" or "American" and "Chinese" by "American" or "Japanese" (depending on the context), one can see that these same arguments are repeated over and over today. Britton and Gilmour (1978) make these points in the Canadian context; Coutu (1983) notes that Europeans fret over mounting losses of scientists to the United States, attributing the U.S. scientific performance in part to these immigrants, in part to the U.S. success in training applied scientists, while in the United States numerous writers resent Japan's performance.[7]

The Russian advances in the field of rocketry and their launching of the first Sputnik in 1957 led to the perception that the United States was falling behind, and that education and national defense are closely related. The Congress responded by passing the National Defense Education Act in 1958 providing funds for the improvement of the teaching of science, mathematics, and foreign languages. The idea that governments must intervene in such circumstances is not novel. Mr. Forster introduced the Education Bill (later extended by Churchill) in England on the seventeenth of February 1870 in these words:

"We must not delay. Upon the speedy provision of elementary education depends our industrial prosperity . . . if we leave our workfolk any longer unskilled, notwithstanding their strong sinews and determined energy, they will become over-matched in the competition of the world. . . . If we are to hold our position among men of our own race or among the nations of the world we must make up the smallness of our numbers by increasing the intellectual force of the individual." Nearly a century later, Forster was echoed by . . . Sir Winston Churchill [who said that] "The Soviet higher technical education for mechanical engineering has been developed both in numbers and quality to an extent which far exceeds anything we have achieved. This is a matter which needs the immediate attention of Her Majesty's Government . . . if we are – not to keep abreast – but even to maintain our proportionate place in the world.'' (Young (1973), pp. 34–5)

According to Ozaki (1984), the industrial policy of late-nineteenth-century Japan was motivated by the fear of being colonized by Western powers (the covetous empires of Russia and Great Britain had already set their eyes on China), and the slogan of the day was "prosperous nation, strong military.'' And with good reasons: It was an American, Commodore Matthew C. Perry, who introduced the Japanese to the Western style of gunboat salesmanship in 1853, with an undisguised threat to bombard the shoguns' capital unless they opened their ports to trade. (Thus, increased expenditures on the military, and increased military strength being correlated with expectations of business expansion is not exactly a recent invention). Later, according to the treaties imposed by the Western powers, Japan was allowed a 5 percent maximum permissible tariff rate. Instead of conforming with the prediction of the static Ricardian doctrine of exporting labor-intensive goods (people being the only abundant resource they had), and producing toys, textiles, and matches (since its people's technical skills were far behind the West's), the government built and managed the first generation of pilot factories, later sold to private firms at considerable discounts, encouraged higher education, thus diversifying its economy behind such protective walls.

Herbert Stein (1983), a former chairman of the Council of Economic Advisors in the United States also seemed to note this regularity – of demands for formulating industrial strategies being linked with the idea of staying on top – but was skeptical of government's ability to achieve this goal. Joan Robinson (1962) noted this preoccupation with comparisons and suggested that the growth of statistics has provided much food for nationalistic ideology:

Several "League tables'' are published . . . of average National Income, rate of growth, percentage of saving, productivity . . . and we look anxiously at our placing. When the poor old United Kingdom, as often happens, appears rather low, we are filled with chagrin; or else we set about picking holes in the statistics to show that the placing is wrong; or we point to all sorts of unfair advantages that the wretched foreigners have, which make the comparisons misleading. . . . [T]he main appeal of the League tables is much more simply and directly to an instinct for keeping up with the Joneses projected on to the international plane. (p. 119)

Although Robinson is critical of such human response, and suggests that somehow this behavior can be avoided, the conclusion reached here is that it cannot be. This is how people always reacted and still do. The question is *what to do,* realizing that people suffer and may impose suffering on others when outdone by fellows on local, national, or international levels.[8]

There are two possible answers: One is to try to pursue policies to *prevent* such leapfrogging in the future. This option and its various implications have been discussed from what one would call a "universalist" viewpoint in Brenner (1985). But since there is little chance today that governments would agree to pursue the policy suggested there (of controlling population growth), I examine here the alternative option of living with such leapfrogging. One could call it a "nationalistic'" viewpoint since it examines policies that each government may pursue to restore the wealth of its nation (but policies already discussed in previous chapters, like changing antitrust laws, avoiding too much specialization – like Nauru on phosphate, Saudi Arabia on oil, Chile on nitrates – will not be repeated below).

2   Free trade, R & D, and politics: myths and facts

Since so much is written on and expected from practicing free trade and increased spending on R & D as the means of restoring some nations' wealth, it is important to examine the relationship between such practices and the incentives to promote innovations and entrepreneurship in the light of the arguments and evidence presented in the previous chapters. The conclusion will be simple: In spite of the fact that "free trade" was not much more than a slogan, never taken literally (indeed, it should not be), a step toward *freer* trade can, in some circumstances, provide greater incentives for innovations and entrepreneurship. As to R & D, the additional evidence and discussion in this section only reinforce the conclusions reached in Chapter 5.

One does not have to conduct very rigorous research to realize that even countries that advocate free trade do not practice it. This statement is not meant to be critical – it just sets some facts straight. The United States imposes stiff quotas and tariffs on sugar, steel, textiles, ceramic tiles, peanuts, rubber shoes, motorcycles, trucks, ethanol produced in Brazil, and so on.[9] The U.S. book printing industry is largely shielded from foreign competition. To be eligible for U.S. copyright protection, virtually all books and periodicals published there must also be printed and bound in the United States. The Jones Act, dating back to the 1920s, bars foreign ships from carrying passengers or freight between any two U.S. ports. In addition, the United States has negotiated "voluntary" export restraints with Japanese auto suppliers, and similar negotiations have been under way since September 1984 with some steel suppliers. There are also less publicized programs that help companies threatened by imports, like the Trade Adjustment Assistance Program administered by the Commerce Department.[10] Aid is given through 13 centers to businesses that can satisfy the government that they have been hurt by imports. They then may borrow up to $1 million directly from the government, or $3 million from a bank with a federal guarantee against default. The government will also pay up to 75 percent of the cost of technical assistance to make a company more competitive. Should such evidence surprise anybody? No.

First recall that although Adam Smith (1976) argued for the international division of labor, saying that "if a foreign country can supply a commodity cheaper than we ourselves can make it, better buy it from them with some part of the produce of our own industry employed in a way in which we have some advantages," he also approved of government interventions in the shipping industry, attributing the discriminatory and protectionist policies to the requirements of defense (recall that the Navigation Act did not permit shipment to be made to and from England in third-country vessels), and government intervention for building canals, highways, and providing postal services for other reasons. Moreover, he also argued that:

The undertaker of a great manufacture, who, by the home markets being suddenly laid open to the competition of foreigners, should be obliged to abandon his trade, would no doubt suffer very considerably. . . . The equitable regard, therefore, to his interest requires that changes of this kind should never be introduced suddenly, but slowly, gradually, and after a very long warning. The legislature, were it possible that its deliberations could be always directed, not by the clamorous importunity of partial interests, but by an extensive view of the general good, ought upon this very account, perhaps, to be particularly careful neither to establish any new monopolies of this kind, nor to extend further those which are already established. Every such regulation introduces some degree of real disorder into the constitution of the state, which it will be difficult afterwards to cure without occasioning another disorder. (pp. 494–5).

This is not only an argument against both the establishment of new monopolies and the rigid maintenance of old ones, but can also be interpreted as one for freer trade, but not a free one. Smith's view may be used to justify temporary protection with a guaranteed gradual elimination – but protection nevertheless.

Not only Smith but everybody else viewed defense as an industry apart, not to be included with others to which the idea of "free trade" applied.[11] The question is: What industry can totally be separated from "defense"? The United States uses agriculture as a military weapon: Embargo is imposed on the Russians, and, when some countries are given agricultural aid, it is not always because we care whether their people suffer and starve, but because we hope to keep the Russians out and the West in. The aircraft, nuclear, oil, computer industries, education (as pointed out in the previous section), and expenditures on R & D have all been linked with defense and the turbulent international politics (also recall the discussion in the previous chapter). The perception of this relationship has shaped constraints on trade. The restrictions on selling all sorts of hardware and software to the Soviets, not only those produced in the United States but also in Europe, in order to prevent the Russians from beefing up the military are common today.[12] Also, according to *Defense Week,* the United States blocked an Israel–Argentina deal of $100 million (the sale of aging A-4 Skyhawk jets), following British intervention, who feared that Argentina might use them in the Falklands.[13] Recall too that during most of the nineteenth century, free trade was denounced by Germans and Americans as a British plot to dominate the world.[14] Freeman (1983, Chapter 9) argues and presents evidence that in the United States, USSR, France, and Britain the public policies toward innovations were largely determined by the Cold War, the governments' support for aircraft, nuclear, and electronics R & D being massive. In the United States, the United Kingdom, and France the aircraft industry accounted for more than a quarter of total industry R & D expenditure during much of the postwar period, financed by public money. Then, as now, underneath the ''free trade'' controversy was the question of maintaining relative positions in the world.

But although there is little doubt that numerous industries can be justly linked with nationalist goals and defense, one must also remind oneself of Dr. Johnson's saying that ''Patriotism is the last refuge of a scoundrel.'' Beware of businessmen who try to link their product with requirements of defense in order to obtain some form of protection, and do not be surprised to find the next evidence. The recognition in the 1960s that it was no longer desirable to give such priority to new types of military aircraft was often followed by increased public expenditures on *civil* aircraft developments[15] (as one could have predicted from Adam Smith's argument on the impact of existing interest groups, of government bureaucracies in particular). Stocking and Watkins (1948, p. 169) note that after World War I producers of tin argued that the cartel they participated in promoted national security and thereby benefited the United States above all other countries and beyond all calculation, an argument that, according to Stocking and Watkins, was an afterthought. The Tin Committee's goal was to provide security to tin producers, rather than for a democratic society. More recently, with the appearance of the extremely efficient South Korean producers of steel, European steel executives, whose companies were falling behind, started to justify their existence in terms of national security rather than profitability (Tagliabue 1983). Agriculture in numerous countries is subsidized and protected in numerous ways, the justification frequently given being that of fear of isolation from world supplies in case of war and fear of loss of political power by becoming dependent on other countries for food.

When are such claims accurate, when do they serve the national interest (of defense), and when are they serving the producers' private interest? How can one make a distinction? As the next case study suggests, no general principles can be given, but each case must be examined apart.

There is no doubt that the provision of some products can be associated with defense and political power in the world: American farmers do not have to dig deep in the United States' historical memory when asking for protection on such grounds, since frequently the United States has used wheat for promoting such goals. But subsidizing one farm product does not imply that all should be subsidized. Consider the U.S. government's sugar price-support program, which began with the 1981 farm bill (a 4-kilogram bag of white cane sugar costing $1.50 in Canada, and $3.55 in the United States, just across the border).[16] Since close substitutes exist for sugar in case of emergency (artificial sweeteners, which may not be good for cakes, but in an emergency one can live without cakes), it would be hard to justify intervention by linking the production of sugar with defense. On the contrary, this intervention may have been harmful for the United States not so much because of the few more cents that American consumers must pay for sugar, but because it undercut the U.S. broader interest of maintaining economic and political stability in the Caribbean. According to Fauriol and Kopperl (1985), the U.S. sugar system alone imposed a loss of $250 million in 1985 on the already heavily indebted Caribbean countries. The U.S. share in their sugar exports dropped from 52 to 30 percent. At the same time exports of sugar to the Soviet Union (excluding those from Cuba) increased from 10 percent in 1981 to 25 percent in 1983. What is the cost of the U.S. intervention if this shift in trade and the American banks' increased risks are taken into account? Also recall that sugar was added to an already existing list of products (textiles, petroleum products, tuna, and leather) that had not fallen with the duty free provision of the U.S. Caribbean Basin Initiative. The Caribbean governments will not be erroneous in deciding that "free trade" is not much more than an empty term, that the United States is not really practicing it, and that they should not make their borrowing decisions by taking this principle seriously. Because of all these consequences, one may conclude that protecting the U.S. sugar producers was an erroneous decision.

In terms of the arguments presented in the previous chapters, there may be therefore two possible explanations for government interventions such as the introduction of tariffs, subsidies, price supports, and nationalization of companies. Either the interventions are obtained by special interests or they serve the public at large, and thus the national interest. The first view suggests that these interventions are the results of two factors: one – the relatively greater geographical concentration of some groups and the relatively greater number of people who belong to them and who appeal to politicians wanting future votes; two – the relative reluctance of the rest of the population to organize to prevent government intervention. The first factor was recently clearly expressed by Carol A. Campbell (the Republican representative of South Carolina in the U.S. Congress): "Anybody in the South who isn't supporting textiles is going to be in deep trouble."[17] The second factor, the rest of the population's reluctance to oppose such interventions, derives from the fact that if, for example, the effect of the intervention is to redistribute $100 million in one group's favor, that sum, when distributed among the rest of the public, constitutes, on average, a few dollars implicit tax. This sum may not provide sufficient incentives to those opposed to get organized and block the redistribution. This view implies that the intervention may have a harmful effect on entrepreneurship. For, in the absence of this protective policy, some members of the interest group whose position was threatened by, let's say, foreign competition, would have made greater efforts and pursued new strategies. Again, the textile industry in the U.S. provides a good example. With the recent furor over whether or not protective measures will continue, some companies who started to worry are already pursuing new strategies.[18] It is clear that wages in the United States cannot drop to the level they are in Third World countries that are now the source of the textile imports. But it is, of course, a mistake to think that only a drop in wages can make the United States competitive in this industry. Levi Strauss Co., Haggar International Co., Burlington Industries, Inc. all try to compete by drastically reducing the 66 weeks it now takes to turn a retailer's order into garments on the shelf. Only 11 weeks are spent actually working on the garment. The rest of the time is spent in transit, inventory, and warehouse shelves. Being in the United States gives manufacturers a time advantage since ocean shipping and complexities of doing business abroad prevent foreign manufacturers from significantly shortening this time.[19] This new strategy is expected to lower costs, in part by diminishing the probability of missed sales and forced markdowns. If the protective policy, however, were taken for granted, these innovative strategies may have never been pursued. Instead of easing adjustments to foreign competition, the certainty of protective policy maintains rigidity: It relaxes pressures both to restrain labor costs and to modify rigid work rules that hamper new technology.[20]

There is, however, an alternative interpretation of the same events. Suppose that the position of some groups is suddenly significantly worsened by innovation or foreign competition: Their wages are lowered and their jobs threatened. The rest of the population may be ready to transfer some payments (for protecting some jobs, retraining the unemployed, and hedging the bets against future shocks by greater diversification) in order to prevent social discontent from boiling over into civil strife, increased criminal activity, or, in some cases, separation. The few dollars, which according to the previous interpretation represent a tax, can be viewed here as a voluntary "social and national security payment." According to this view, the transfer benefits the public; politicians play a positive, entrepreneurial role rather than a harmful, cynical one, as in the previous interpretation; the state, instead of being seen as a predator, is viewed as an insurer. Also, entrepreneurship and innovations may be promoted in this case in spite of the intervention. For expectations of social instability in the *absence* of intervention may have diminished incentives to carry them out. Moreover, taking into account the international aspect of such disturbances (as pointed out in the previous chapter), the positive light within which such interventions can be viewed is strengthened.[21] (Would American businessmen expand their business by the same amount if the U.S. government had not reacted to the Russian Sputnik, trying to stay on top?)

Which viewpoint is accurate? Both: One mechanism may be at work in some circumstances and not in others. Only the examination of specific historical circumstances that give rise to one form or other of intervention can shed light on the subject, and a priori theorizing can shed no further light on it. However, these interpretations of events have two implications worth emphasizing. First, according to the "social or national security" interpretation of a protective measure, "free trade" should not be a principle: In some circumstances one form or other of protection is beneficial for a society. Second, even in theory one *must* make a distinction between "politicians" and others who make political decisions, whom one may call "statesmen." According to the first interpretation of the government's intervention, the "politician" is perceived as a man who uses the state's machinery to *his* own purposes, and who may even try to persuade the public that it is the public's interest that he promotes and not his own. But one could call a man a "statesman" if he has the courage to withstand this pressure, and prevent the political spirit from getting the upper hand (thus indeed becoming a man who may represent the state's interest). *If* he succeeds the process described in the first interpretation of events will not take place, and one can see the relationship between freer trade and entrepreneurship and innovations. When an industry is suddenly threatened by foreign competition and is falling behind, there will always be demands for protection in one form or another in an attempt to maintain the somehow achieved order. A statesman, by withstanding such pressures (among others by making credible promises – a stake in the future – to the groups that fell behind) maintains the society vulnerable between rigidity and change, a condition necessary for its creativity.

3   More on policy

There are some simple reasons for emphasizing this policy implication of the arguments and evidence presented in this book concerning people's creativity rather than "freer trade" or increased expenditures on R & D, two policies frequently recommended today. One reason is that this way of describing the policy shows not only that one cannot separate the economic, social, and political dimensions of the problem but also points to the clear-cut role leaders play in this process. The second is that it puts discussions on R & D expenditures in a proper perspective rather than an ahistorical one as is usually done.

Already the evidence presented in Chapter 5 suggested that *within* an industry no clear-cut correlation between R & D expenditures and innovations could have been detected. Of course, there is no doubt that more innovations will be done in directions where an increased demand is perceived for them (that is, the directions in which the government is expected to allocate more R & D funds). When this occurs, however, fewer innovations may occur and be brought to life in other fields. Thus the total number of innovations may *not* increase. This argument does not prevent one from recommending government's intervention for *directing* the innovative effort (it questions only the postulated positive relationship between total expenditures on R & D and the total number of innovations in society): If the goal is defense, such public policy should be expected. It may be useful to note that it was the success of the Manhattan Project (the development of the atomic bomb), the radar program, and military aircraft during World War II that convinced governments and some social scientists that an enormous investment in science and technology can produce not only payoffs in military terms during hot and cold wars but in *all* circumstances, in *any* domain. This extrapolation may well be inaccurate: people behave differently during wartime than during normal times [as indeed Viteles's (1953) summary of extensive evidence suggests]. Although I don't give the slightest confidence to the next numbers, for those who do and who make vague recommendations on increasing R & D expenditures, they should serve as a problematic reminder. According to Ozaki (1984), government's share of total R & D expenditures (excluding defense) is 28 percent in Japan, 32 percent in Great Britain, 33 percent for the United States, 41 percent for West Germany, and 47 percent for France – numbers that seem uncorrelated with these countries' innovative performances.

Some writers make a relationship between R & D expenditures and the government's role in a different way. Lester Thurow (1980), in an article titled "The Need to Work Smarter," states that "standards of living rise not because people work harder, but because they work smarter" (p. 80), and perceives the gap between warranted and actual performance of the U.S. economy as deriving from the fact that people are not creative enough: Either they do not come up with "smart" ideas or they do not dare to implement them. As remedy, Thurow suggests that the government, by subsidizing R & D, can achieve this goal:

From the point of view of the economy, cooperative, partially government-funded research projects are highly desirable. Partial government funding allows private firms to engage in projects with longer time horizons and more uncertainty than would normally be possible. Partial private funding ensures that the projects focus on potentially marketable products or useful new production processes. Being cooperative, money isn't wasted inventing the same wheel six times. And if the wheel is invented national productivity is enhanced by the fact that many firms get to use the new technology simultaneously. (p. 80)

While the title of Thurow's article is accurate, some of the statements and judgments made in this quote pose problems: First, why should the government subsidize greater uncertainty? Second, Thurow seems to assume that people working for the government can select and pick up winners when he states that "money isn't wasted inventing the same wheel six times." But the facts are that nobody knows who may make an invention or how long it will take. Many firms may spend money trying to develop new products, but only one, rather than all six, may make the lucky hit. Is there any guarantee that the person working in the subsidized firm will make the discovery? Thus, if the goal is to promote innovations, firm-specific government interventions should be avoided. Charles Schultze and Alfred Kahn criticized such policies on similar grounds, Kahn warning to "cast a skeptical eye on glib references to the alleged success of government interventions in other countries in picking and supporting industrial winners." The successes of such interventions in other countries, he declared, "have been greatly exaggerated" [as quoted by Stein (1983, p. 86)]. Indeed, as Krauss's (1984) data suggest, the European experience shows not only that the performance of high-technology industries receiving government support for R & D has not been any better than such industries not receiving this support but that frequently the subsidies went *not* to the "up and coming" industries, but to those falling behind: shipyards, the steel industry, mining, textile, and apparel industries. Last but not least, at the root of Thurow's guess there is the idea that in all circumstances people who are subsidized are more likely to become smarter and make inventions than others who are not. No evidence exists to support such a guess: The fact that in *some* circumstances industries linked to national defense were subsidized and innovated does not imply that all industries, if subsidized during calmer times, would do so. The evidence presented in this book suggests that one may expect the contrary.

Another recommendation frequently made today not only calls for increased R & D expenditures but also for promoting high technology. But what is, after all, high tech? In order to get a precise idea of what may be lurking behind this recommendation, it is useful to mention a recent study by the Bureau of Labor Statistics in Washington, D.C., that drew up three definitions and categorized industries according to them [see Carlson (1984)]. The smaller category included those most heavily involved in research: computers and office machines, drugs, communication equipment, electronic components, aircraft and guided missiles, and space vehicles. The next group needed a ratio of research spending to net sales that was twice the U.S. average. Twenty-eight industries are on this list: the 6 from the first group, plus chemicals, photo equipment, research and development laboratories, and 18 others. The broadest high-tech group has 48 industries included since their number of engineers, scientists, and technology-oriented workers was at least 1½ times the U.S. industrial average. This group included automobiles, tires, paints, and household appliances – hardly industries with a high-tech profile. So which industries are targeted when such recommendations are made? Drucker (1984) provides the accurate answer: When the French funded a high-powered ministry to encourage high-tech entrepreneurship, when the West Germans talked about having their own Silicon Valley, and the British and the Canadian Science Council have been proposing government aid to new high-tech enterprises, they were all concerned about the widening gap between themselves and their U.S. and Japanese competitors and realized that unless they closed this gap, their countries could not be expected to be among the leaders, among the top in international politics any more. Thus, the categorization of the Bureau of Labor Statistics misses the point: When recommending high-tech policies, the advocates do not make domestic comparisons, but *international* ones, the goal being to once again restore some nation's competitive edge. Drucker (1984), in the European context, and Daly (1979), in the Canadian one, are also on the mark when they point out that the European belief that high tech can flourish alone without being embedded in a larger, entrepreneurial economy is inaccurate, and that the problems Canada faces may be managerial rather than technological.[22]

In conclusion, neither increased government involvement in R & D nor free trade can be recommended as a universal panacea.[23] It is the movement *toward* freer trade, toward preventing any hierarchical structure from casting too firm an anchor that, sometimes, will induce entrepreneurship and innovations.[24] Decision makers in government can create and maintain such an environment – if they are statesmen rather than mere politicians.[25] Politicians will not discard outdated policies, no matter how harmful they become. Even when programs based on them have long outlived their usefulness, politicians will try to persuade the public that it is unfair to eliminate them when so many people have become dependent on them. Of course, by resisting such pressures, statesmen, although holding the society more open to creativity, hold it more open to other noncustomary acts as well. How to strike the balance? That is the art of competition – in this case among nations.

4   Conclusions

There is a central factor – the relative population growth within nations – that is a crucial variable for understanding some additional policies to be pursued in order to restore a nation's wealth. The reason for mentioning population growth just in passing in the previous chapters is that I have dealt with this relationship in detail in Brenner (1983, 1985). Repeating the detailed arguments and even part of the evidence here would take us far away from the main themes examined in this book. Nevertheless, in order to complete the picture, a brief summary concerning this relationship is given below.

For many years public attention and debate have focused on the world's "overpopulation problem." With some good reasons: Sudden increases in population or sudden contact with strangers provided one of the principal forces that set societies in motion (contacts that occurred when population started growing). At times the reaction to such contact was an entrepreneurial outburst, at times a destructive one (social instability and wars among them), within the group who perceived being threatened and falling behind. The entrepreneurial adaptation had numerous facets: The invention of agriculture in various gathering and hunting societies, and innovations in agriculture in general have occurred following sudden increases in population.[26] Changes in property rights, the substitution of custom by law, and the emergence of various institutions have been linked to population growth too. Although features of the Middle Ages have been attributed by some writers to Europe's sudden, drastically diminished population (taking into account the military technology that had already been achieved), the end of this age and the "rise of the West" have been attributed to the suddenly rising population and the resulting breakdown of customs (these events being also linked with the frequency of disturbances, of interactions among groups with different backgrounds as one can infer from the arguments presented in Chapter 5). How exactly are fluctuations in population related to innovations? The views presented in Brenner (1983, 1985) provide one answer: They show that when population suddenly increases, the kind of existence people have been accustomed to can no longer be maintained, the distribution of wealth changes, and people start betting on new, that is noncustomary, ideas, criminal or innovative.

It is the acquaintance with this evidence (rather than the idea of Malthusian starvation) that justifies worrying about population growth and leads to the conclusion that if one wants to prevent instability, one should prevent leapfrogging by keeping population stable. Although such policy eventually diminishes creativity, it diminishes destruction too. (Malthus simply forgot to take innovations in general into account, although he thought about the possibility of innovations for controlling birth rates.) As mentioned before, bringing such policy to life requires a "universalist" viewpoint among world leaders, a viewpoint that is nowhere in sight today. What is in sight is a nationalist viewpoint, the fear of falling behind and the quest for catching up. So let us make a final comment on the relationship between such a viewpoint and differential population growths within some groups and some nations.

Although some countries worry about their sudden population growth (in the Third World, where such growth started only at the beginning of this century and is very much a consequence of Western interventions done without much foresight), others worry about population decline.[27] These countries perceive bigger population as a sign of national strength (with some good reasons), while in others *once dominant* ethnic groups want to reassert their numerical superiority. Eastern European nations have started ambitious programs to increase their populations. Those in the West constantly fear the immigrant invasion from Turkey or Algeria. At the same time they are also worried about the payment of future social security benefits to an aging population. Israel, concerned about the much higher birth rate among the Arabs, promotes a national policy with a pronatalist intent. At the same time Arab nationalists are encouraging high fertility among the Arab population as a means of establishing eventual predominance over the Jewish-Israeli population (accurately arguing that democracy cannot be maintained with a significantly altered proportion). In the Soviet Union, the ethnic Russians worry about the increase in the population of non-European and Moslem peoples of the Central Asian Republics. These perceptions of linking national strength with relative population growth are not erroneous. Although "demography is *not* destiny," since outcomes in case of differential population growth depend both on political systems and "the right man being at the right place at the right time" (call this factor "chance" if you wish), abundant evidence exists to justify fears that by falling behind in numbers, a nation's life may be eventually at stake.[28] Thus, unless the alternative strategy of preventing leapfrogging is adopted, such nationalistic viewpoints imply that we may continue to run twice as fast just to stay in the same place – as Lewis Carroll's Queen in the motto to this chapter suggests.

Appendixes

Decision making and uncertainty: a dynamic approach – Appendix to Chapter 1

This appendix summarizes and extends the model presented in Brenner (1983, 1985). But elaborate discussions of some details as well as comparisons with numerous other writers' viewpoints are not repeated here.

Let us assume that people's behavior is relative, that is, their utility function (or "satisfaction") depends not only on the goods they consume but also on the percentage of people who consume similar amounts of that good. That is, let X_i be the commodity i, and $\alpha(X = X_i^0)$ the percentage of people who consume X_i^0 of it, and $\alpha(X \geq X_i^0)$ the percentage of people who consume more of it. Then, one's utility function can be written as

$$U = U(X_1^0, X_2^0, \ldots, X_n^0, \alpha(X \geq X_1^0), \alpha(X \geq X_2^0),$$
$$\ldots, \alpha(X \geq X_n^0) \mid \alpha(X = X_1^0), \alpha(X = X_2^0),$$
$$\ldots, \alpha(X = X_n^0)) \tag{2}$$

where X_i^0 represents the optimal amounts one decided to buy, taking into account his level of aspiration (represented by the conditional statements). This last condition is a translation of the "keep up with the Joneses" statement.

Note several things: This way of rewriting the utility function does not imply that all goods are consumed because somebody else is consuming them. Some $\alpha(\cdot)s$ may be equal to zero: One may think about the minimal amount of food and water necessary for survival (none of the studies in this book, however, refers to such goods). The argument that satisfaction from goods depends on perceptions of customary behavior (i.e., what do others consume) is not novel. Both Adam Smith and Marx thought this argument to be valid. Smith defined "necessaries" as "not only the commodities which are indispensably necessary for the support of life, but whatever the custom of the country renders it indecent for creditable people, even of the lowest order, to be without" (p. 399). He gives the example of the linen shirt, which the Greeks and the Romans did not use, and notes:

In the present times, through the greater part of Europe, a creditable day labourer would be as harmed to appear in public without a linen shirt, the want of which would be supposed to denote that disgraceful degree of poverty, which it is presumed nobody can well fall into without extreme bad conduct. (p. 399)

Thus, for Smith, "necessaries" are things that custom ("the established rules of decency"), as well as nature, have rendered "vital" for even the poorest. Poverty is therefore defined relative to what a society considers a "decent" standard of living. He also perceived that tastes are shaped by classes: Members of one may buy fresh coffee daily because in that social circle it is discreditable not to have it – it is a symbol of status. Still, this is not a "necessity" – unless the poorest also have this custom.

Smith's views reappear in *Capital,* where Marx suggests that there are two kinds of consumer goods: necessities and luxuries. The former are defined as ones that the "working class" uses, even if it is tobacco (thus, the criterion is not whether "physiologically" the good is "essential" to life). The fact that satisfaction is relative was emphasized by Marx too: He wrote that an owner may find a small house adequate so long as other houses in the same neighborhood are the same size. Then, if one builds a palace "the house shrinks from a little house to a hut. . . . Our desires and pleasures spring from society; we measure them, therefore, by society and not by the objects which serve for their satisfaction."[56]

The fact that a person's satisfaction depends both on the goods he consumes and how their quantity and quality can be compared to others', raises the question of who are those other persons whose consumption matters. A great number of comparisons can be made: from international ones to national ones and to local, domestic ones. The theory, of course, cannot shed light on the question with whom are comparisons made.[57] However, assumptions can be made and then predictions derived, which then can be confronted with the evidence. Suppose one assumes that international comparisons are made, and one derives the prediction that leapfrogging is more likely to lead to wars [see Brenner (1985, Chapter 1)]. One can then examine whether or not the evidence contradicts this prediction. Or one can see that migrations are legally constrained and thus decides that national comparisons should matter. Then one derives predictions on gambling or on criminal behavior, and again examines the facts, and so forth. Or one can examine periods when transportation was extremely slow, and decides that comparisons could only have been made within a village, and derives predictions on behavior in these circumstances, and so forth [see Brenner (1983, Chapters 1, 2)]. By using this methodology one eliminates from the discussion some reference groups and keeps others. In the empirical examinations one may introduce measures of fluctuations in the distribution of wealth (both local and regional) and see which ones come out significant. In Brenner (1985, Chapter 1), for example, the national and international ones seemed to play central roles – they play it again in the last two chapters of this book. Also, notice that it is the individual's perception of the different hierarchies within which he acts that matters. That is, suppose that an outsider measures that 10 percent of the relevant population owns wealth equal to $100,000, 10 percent for $200,000, and so forth up to 10 percent who own $1 million. This is *not* the distribution that matters for explaining human behavior. Rather, there are two things that matter: First, that for somebody with $600,000 within this structure, 40 percent are above him and 50 percent below; second, whether or not one expected to have $600,000. It is the *unexpected fluctuations* in these percentages that play the central roles within my views, whatever hierarchical structure one takes into account.

One can now ask this legitimate question: Why complicate the variables in the utility function since a priori not much is known either on the reference groups or on aspirations (i.e., the conditional statements), and an indirect utility function can always be rewritten as

$$V(X_1^0, X_2^0, \ldots, X_n^0) \equiv U(X_1^0, \ldots, X_n^0,$$
$$\alpha(X \geq X_1^0), \alpha(X \geq X_2^0), \ldots, \alpha(X \geq X_n^0)|$$
$$\alpha(X = X_1^0), \alpha(X = X_2^0), \ldots, \alpha(X = X_n^0)) \tag{3}$$

The answer is simple: the revised version's greater predictive power. This methodology is not novel either: Recall Becker's (1971) revised theory of choice in which purchased goods are one of the inputs into the production of "basic commodities" that directly enter preferences. That approach – just like the one pursued here – reduces the need to rely on differences in tastes (i.e., shapes of the utility function). Although Becker's approach increased the importance of differences in prices and incomes in explaining behavior, the one pursued here shows the importance of *sudden fluctuations* in one's relative standing in shaping behavior, fluctuations that are linked to the institutional structure of a society. Recall Becker's (1971) precise reformulation (it is useful not only for illustrating this methodological point but also because a revised version of his model was used in Chapter 4):

$$Z_i = f_i(X_1, X_2, \ldots, X_n, t_1, t_2, \ldots, t_p; R) \tag{4}$$

where Z_i = basic commodities
$\quad f_i$ = household production function for Z_i
$\quad X_i$ = inputs of different goods purchased into Z_i
$\quad t_i$ = inputs of different kinds of time
$\quad R$ = other variables

The utility function being then rewritten as

$$U = U(Z_1, \ldots, Z_m) \tag{5}$$

Note that outsiders do not know much about how one prepares a meal, listens to music, or studies an occupation, and this is what the Z_i represent. Neither does one know much about the value one puts on his time (what if he believes in a blissful afterworld or has cancer?). Yet the predictive power of this way of looking at individual behavior seemed to be greater than if one rewrote the utility function as

$$V(X_1, X_2, \ldots, X_n, t_1, \ldots, t_p) \equiv U(Z_1, \ldots, Z_m) \tag{6}$$

As shown in Brenner (1983), the reformulation of the utility function as done in equation (2) leads to predictions and insights that cannot be made if one looks only at the indirect utility function. While in this reformulation leap-frogging (i.e., some people falling behind others and behind their expectations, shaped by custom) explains risk-taking behavior, a traditional approach describes such behavior by imposing some constraints on the shape of the utility function.[58] But note that although the first prediction is verifiable, the second is not.

Several other features of the revised view of the utility function as in equation (2) are worth reemphasizing: (a) These revisions make sense *only* if uncertainty is taken into account in the model and the *reactions* to unexpected shocks are examined [see Brenner (1983, 1985), the first chapters and their appendixes]. (b) Since there are distinct differences between classes, it has been noted that the utility function will not be continuous. The reformulation in equation (3) reinforces this assertion: If a mansion is a symbol of status (one of the X_i's) for belonging to the "upper class," then there is a jump from one class to another and no continuity. If any class is linked with the possession of some indivisible goods (country house, Rolls Royce, Yves St-Laurent originals, prestigious neighborhoods, etc.), the assumption of discontinuity seems plausible. (c) Much attention is paid in the abstract discussions in economics to first, second, and even third derivatives of the utility function [see Arrow's (1970) measures of risk aversion]. Neither second nor third derivatives play any roles in my model (see below). As to the first, two simple assumptions are made: If X_i increases, satisfaction increases, holding other things constant (i.e., the first derivative, whenever defined, is positive); if $\alpha(\cdot)$ increases, satisfaction diminishes [i.e., the first derivative with respect to $\alpha(\cdot)$, whenever defined, is negative]. The first represents the very weak assumption that if one has more of a good, his satisfaction from it must be increased (if this statement were inaccurate, one could always increase satisfaction by either throwing part of the good away or selling it). The second implies that if one is outdone by one's fellows, in whatever hierarchy, his satisfaction is diminished. One can call this trait ambition, "keeping up with the Joneses," fear, envy, or vanity. (d) Finally, to emphasize the difference in predictive power between the model as presented here and the traditional ones, recall that the latter examine an allocational question of the following type:

$$\max U(X_1, \ldots, X_n) \quad \text{such that } \Sigma p_i X_i = I_0 \tag{7}$$

where p_i are the respective prices, I_0 is one's income, while the rest of the notations are as previously defined. What happens in this model if one's income drops unexpectedly? The individual stays poorer, the new allocation of resources is calculated – and that is it (even in models of risk aversion no further insights are gained). The contrast between this prediction and the one derived from the theory of human behavior presented here will come to the fore below.

Leapfrogging and uncertainty

Let W_0 be one's wealth and let $\tilde{W}$ be the distribution of wealth around the mean $\overline{W}_0$. This distribution defines one's perception of a certain "class" in society, a class to which this individual is expected to belong; $\alpha(\cdot)$ denotes the percentage of people who are richer than $\overline{W}_0$ in the society. Then the utility function can be defined as follows:

$$U(W_0, \alpha(W > \overline{W}_0) | W_0 \varepsilon \quad \tilde{W}_0) \tag{8}$$

where

$$\partial U / \partial W_0 > 0 \qquad \partial U / \partial \alpha < 0$$

The first derivative represents the usual assumption of the marginal utility of wealth being positive, whereas the second represents sentiments of fear (of being outdone by others), of envy, vanity, or ambition.

As shown in Brenner (1983, 1985), this reformulation of the utility function makes sense *only* when risk and uncertainty are taken into account (words that, as shown there and in chapter 1, can be precisely defined and distinguished within this model), and its usefulness stems from the predictions one can derive from it. Let us consider some of them.

Let h be the price of a lottery ticket where there is a probability p of winning a large prize H, that can jump people up on the social ladder. What factors affect people's decision to buy such tickets? The mathematical translation of this question is the following:

$$(1 - p)U(W_0 - h, \alpha(W > \overline{W}_0) | W_0 - h \varepsilon \tilde{W}_0)$$
$$+ pU(W_0 + H, \alpha(W > \overline{W}_1) | W_0 + H \varepsilon \tilde{W}_1)$$
$$> U(W_0, \alpha(W > \overline{W}_0) | W_0 \varepsilon \tilde{W}_0) \tag{9}$$

where $\tilde{W}_1$ now represents the distribution of wealth within the higher class, and $\overline{W}_1$, its mean.

Note that the way the first term is written implies that, when one individual spends the amount h on a lottery ticket, he does not take into account either that by this expenditure the mean wealth of the class he belongs to has been altered or that the distribution $\tilde{W}_0$ has been changed. These assumptions do not seem strong: If there is a large number of individuals N within his class, this individual's expenditure of lottery tickets changes the mean by h/N, a fraction that tends to zero when N is large. Also, if one of this class wins the big prize, but there was a large number of individuals with a continuous distribution of wealth over the range defining this class, $\tilde{W}_0$ is unaltered.

Let the utility function be linear in W_0 and α, and let's see under what circumstances this inequality is fulfilled:

$$U = aW_0 + b\alpha(W > \overline{W}_0) \qquad a > 0,\ b < 0 \tag{10}$$

$$\begin{aligned}
(1-p)a(W_0 - h) &+ (1-p)b\alpha(W > \overline{W}_0) \\
&+ pa(W_0 + H) + pb\alpha(W > \overline{W}_1) \\
&> aW_0 + b\alpha(W > \overline{W}_0)
\end{aligned} \tag{11}$$

If the gamble is fair, that is, $(1-p)h = pH$, condition (11) is simply reduced

$$\alpha(W > \overline{W}_1) < \alpha(W > \overline{W}_0) \tag{12}$$

which implies that the relatively poor will always participate in such games of chance (if the gamble is unfair, this condition is, of course, weakened). A similar calculation shows that the same individual who participates in such games of chance may also insure himself in order to *prevent* falling down in this pyramidal distribution of wealth – a more detailed discussion on these conditions can be found in Brenner (1983, 1985).

Let us turn to the dynamic part of the model, which illustrates under what circumstances people may bet on new ideas that previously they have avoided. Again, only some technical parts of the model will be presented; the elaborate implicit assumptions behind it, as well as philosophical implications of the model, can be found in the two previous books. The reason for presenting some features of the model here are twofold: First, I have added more precision to the model since its previous presentation; and second, it is unlikely that people who read this book have read the previous two, which dealt with subject matters far away from the field of industrial organization.

Suppose that an individual, content with his level of wealth, W_0, and the status it defines, avoids some uncertain strategies. Assume that the individual perceives that by pursuing it he may lose the amount P, which, however, may still maintain him in his "class," and gain the amount H, which may move him to a higher class, represented by the distribution $\tilde{W}_2$ and mean $\overline{W}_2$. That is,

$$U(W_0, \ \alpha(W > \overline{W}_0) \,|\, W_0 \,\varepsilon\, \tilde{W}_0) >$$
$$pU(W_0 - P, \ \alpha(W > \overline{W}_0) \,|\, W_0 - P \,\varepsilon\, \tilde{W}_0)$$
$$+ (1 - p)U(W_0 + H, \ \alpha(W > \overline{W}_2) \,|\, W_0 + H \,\varepsilon\, \tilde{W}_2) \tag{13}$$

Let's see what this condition implies for the utility function defined in equation (10):

$$aW_0 + b\alpha(W > \overline{W}_0) >$$
$$pa(W_0 - P) + pb\alpha(W > \overline{W}_0)$$
$$+ (1 - p)a(W_0 + H) + (1 - p)b\alpha(W > \overline{W}_2) \tag{14}$$

Rewritten, one obtains

$$b\alpha(W > \overline{W}_0) > (1 - p)aH - paP + pb\alpha(W > \overline{W}_0) + (1 - p)b\alpha(W > \overline{W}_2) \tag{15}$$

1. Will the individual undertake this uncertain strategy if his wealth suddenly diminishes to W_D, W_D still belonging to the distribution $\tilde{W}_0$? The translation of this question is

$$aW_D + b\alpha(W > \overline{W}_0) < pa(W_D - P) + pb\alpha(W > \overline{W}_0)$$
$$+ (1 - p)a(W_D + H) + (1 - p)b\alpha(W > \overline{W}_2) \tag{16}$$

assuming that even $W_D - P$ still belongs to the distribution $\tilde{W}_0$, and $W_D + H$ to that of $\tilde{W}_2$. The simple answer is no, since equation (16) can be rewritten as

$$b\alpha(W > \overline{W}_0) < (1 - p)aH - paP + pb\alpha(W > \overline{W}_0) + (1 - p)b\alpha(W > \overline{W}_2) \tag{17}$$

which contradicts condition (15).

2. Suppose now that $W_D - P$ may even put this individual into a lower class, whose distribution is $\tilde{W}_1$ and mean $\overline{W}_1$. Will then the individual pursue this strategy? Condition (16) is now altered to

$$aW_D + b\alpha(W > \overline{W}_0) < pa(W_D - P) + pb\alpha(W > \overline{W}_1)$$
$$+ (1 - p)a(W_D + H) + (1 - p)b\alpha(W > \overline{W}_2) \tag{16a}$$

which can be rewritten as

$$b\alpha(W > \overline{W}_0) < (1 - p)aH - paP + pb\alpha(W > \overline{W}_1) + (1 - p)b\alpha(W > \overline{W}_2) \tag{17a}$$

This and condition (15) can never be fulfilled. For if both conditions (17a) and (15) were fulfilled,

$$pb\alpha(W > \overline{W}_1) > pb\alpha(W > \overline{W}_0) \tag{18}$$

but since b is negative this would imply that

$$\alpha(W > \overline{W}_1) < \alpha(W > \overline{W}_0) \tag{19}$$

which can never be true: $\overline{W}_1 < \overline{W}_0$ implies that the percentage of people above $\overline{W}_1$ must always be greater than the percentage above $\overline{W}_0$.

3. Let's consider therefore a third possibility: Suppose that the individual's diminished wealth moved him *out* of his class. Then, instead of condition (16) one obtains

$$aW_D + b\alpha(W > \overline{W}_1) < pa(W_D - P) + pb\alpha(W > \overline{W}_1)$$

$$+ (1-p)a(W_D + H) + (1-p)b\alpha(W > \overline{W}_2) \tag{16b}$$

assuming, as before, that $W_D - P$ still belongs to the distribution $\tilde{W}_1$, and $W_D + H$ to that of $\tilde{W}_2$. Rewriting (16b) one obtains

$$b\alpha(W > \overline{W}_1) < (1-p)aH - paP + pb\alpha(W > \overline{W}_1) + (1-p)b\alpha(W > \overline{W}_2) \tag{17b}$$

let us rewrite conditions (15) and (17b) differently:

$$(1-p)b\alpha(W > \overline{W}_0) > (1-p)aH - paP + (1-p)b\alpha(W > \overline{W}_2) \tag{15a}$$

$$(1-p)b\alpha(W > \overline{W}_1) < (1-p)aH - paP + (1-p)b\alpha(W > \overline{W}_2) \tag{18}$$

Since there is a term that appears in both inequalities, the condition for both to be fulfilled is

$$(1-p)b\alpha(W > \overline{W}_0) > (1-p)b\alpha(W > \overline{W}_1) \tag{19a}$$

which, since b is negative, is always fulfilled, whatever were the original values for p, H, P. Note: These three terms are left unaltered. This assumption implies that the parameters of the utility function, a and b, still depend on expectations of belonging to the class defined by the distribution W_0. Thus, when the shock occurs, the situation that describes the individual's condition is

$$U(W_D, \ \alpha(W > \overline{W}_1) | W_D \ \epsilon \ \tilde{W}_1, W_0 \ \epsilon \ \tilde{W}_0) \tag{20}$$

since W_D belongs to a new distribution, but the parameters are the same as before, shaped by expectations of belonging to the class defined by W_0.

4. Let us now weaken somewhat the previous assumptions and assume that $W_D + H$ is just expected to *restore* one's position rather than increase it to the class represented by the distribution $\tilde{W}_2$. Then, instead of (16) one obtains

$$aW_D + b\alpha(W > \overline{W}_1) < pa(W_D - P) + pb\alpha(W > \overline{W}_1)$$

$$+ (1-p)a(W_D + H) + (1-p)b\alpha(W > \overline{W}_0) \tag{16c}$$

This condition can be rewritten as

$$b\alpha(W > \overline{W}_1) < (1-p)aH - paP + pb\alpha(W > \overline{W}_1) + (1-p)b\alpha(W > \overline{W}_0) \tag{17c}$$

For both conditions (19a) and (17c) to be fulfilled, one obtains that

$$\alpha(W > \overline{W}_0) < \tfrac{1}{2}[\alpha(W > \overline{W}_1) + \alpha(W > \overline{W}_2)] \tag{21}$$

[which is obtained by subtracting $b\alpha(W > \overline{W}_1)$ from $b\alpha(W > \overline{W}_0)$, and the left side in condition (17c) from the left side in (15), according to the simple algebraic principle that if $a > b$ and $c < d$, then $a - c > b - d$].

Other calculations, as well as numerical examples, can be found in Brenner (1983, 1985).

The contrast with the standard framework's predictions and those obtained above are evident. Since the opportunities were "there," they should have been exploited, says that framework. However, the one presented here suggests a different answer: Although the idea could have crossed some people's minds, the implementation of the new idea does not take place until some form of significant shock occurs.[59] Note that the assumption of maximization is implicitly used in this model – this motivation exactly induces individuals to alter their behavior. Thus, if because of some misfortune, they lose their wealth or suddenly perceive a threat of losing it, they bet on new ideas and some may succeed. The success will be measured as an addition to wealth (whereas the failure might not always be measured – the years of sleepless nights that finally lead nowhere, for example). Also note that the reason for avoiding dealing with changes in the variability of the distributions $\tilde{W}_0$, $\tilde{W}_1$, and so on is not just that I assumed that the utility function is linear, but a more fundamental one (which, in fact, justifies the choice of a linear utility function to start with). If one assumes that the means of the distributions W_0, W_1, and so on do not change, but the variability increases, one assumes that the dispersion of the distribution has changed. Within this model such change would require a *redefinition* of classes: This alteration, therefore, requires a different treatment than just that of a calculation of some mathematical conditions.

The noncustomary acts one undertakes may be not only of an entrepreneurial but also of a criminal nature. Both represent noncustomary acts (from the individuals' and sometimes even from the rest of the society's viewpoint), and their mathematical translation is the *same*. Therefore, this model alone cannot answer the question as to who is more likely to undertake a criminal and who an innovative act [customs and the number of people who are perceived to be in "the same boat of misfortune" provide insights into this matter – see Brenner (1983, 1985)].

How is a new equilibrium, that is, stability, achieved (or, more correctly, restored)? Note that people continue to bet on new ideas of either nature until either (a) they restore their position or (b) since society may react to the increased instability, the costs and benefits of betting on new ideas are altered, and individuals may lower their aspirations. If (a) occurs, outsiders may perceive a creation of wealth; whereas if (b) occurs, outsiders will perceive a lower level of economic activity.[60]

Now note that the same proof exactly as done above can be done with respect to *any* variable X_i that enters into one's utility function in equation (2): Just the possibility of loss P and the possibility of gain H [in expression (13)] must be translated in terms of the various variables X_i (through their relative prices and solutions of allocational problems). Although such a presentation is cumbersome, the nonaggregated form in equation (2), where each variable is represented separately, and each custom can be defined separately, has some benefits. It suggests that *any* type of shock to one's customs can be dealt with within this approach [one that occurs to the family structure in particular – see Brenner (1985, 1985) for discussion and evidence, and Chapter 2 here]. For those disturbed by attaching the word "wealth" to insurances provided by family and friends, this presentation may be more appealing. Some further comments on the model: Note that all the empirical verifications must be done in historical contexts since people's experience in the past shapes their attitudes toward risks today. Also note that the mathematical conditions examined here answered the question: What can reverse the inequality defined in condition (13)? As noted in the text, the most trivial answer is: a diminished P and an increased H. These types of alterations are discussed in the various chapters within some broader contexts (Chapter 6 in particular), and in Chapter 3 they are linked with changes in relative prices.

Let me reemphasize: This appendix is intended merely to present the essential features of my views for those unacquainted with the two previous books.[61] Further discussions on gambling, insurance, political activity, and so on, as well as some of the deeper implications of these views are not repeated here and can be found in Brenner (1983, Chapter 1 and Appendix; 1985, Chapter 1) although there only the effects of significant shocks are discussed to start with (and so the mathematical translations there fit only such cases).

Ownership and decision making – Appendix to Chapter 6

Since any studies on state-*owned* enterprises have concentrated on the second word ("ownership"), let us clarify how this notion is linked with the picture drawn in this and the previous chapters. First, let us see what the concept of ownership implies within the framework pursued here.

Ownership can be defined by the set of decisions that one can make in allocating "resources" ("resources" as defined by law and customs) without interference with other persons' or institutions' decisions (i.e., without changing the value of their resources). Note that this is a static concept that is well defined only if *no* innovations occur. (For innovations, by definition, interfere with other people's resources.) At any point of time a set of decisions is left to families, firms, and other institutions and another to governments.[25] Let us illustrate this simple relationship between ownership and decision making by an example: Suppose that the government decides to impose a regulation requiring a company to service some isolated communities. This regulation may be similar in consequence to increased government ownership of a firm's resources. The decision to regulate can also be viewed as a substitute for taxing some firms (i.e., "increased government ownership" of these firms) and subsidizing others (i.e., "diminished government ownership of these firms' resources," since the opportunity set over which they can make decisions has increased). The goal can also be achieved by the government owning the enterprise. Which of the three strategies – regulations, taxation, ownership – is chosen to achieve the goal depends on the perception of their relative effectiveness, and is another matter. In all these cases somebody in the government made up his mind that distant localities must receive a service. Thus, the *decision* of whether or not to service them and at what price was no longer left for somebody in the private sector to make. This decision thus implicitly implies an increased "ownership" of resources by the government. Briefly the issue of ownership and decision making are directly linked, and it can be rephrased in two different ways. One can either say that more decisions can be made by central authorities and less by others or that the central authority owns more resources than before about whose allocation it can decide.

The example given above, on taxes and regulations, is not novel. Posner (1971) in his "Taxation by regulation" argued, and presented evidence, that one of the functions of regulation is to perform distributive and allocative chores usually associated with the taxing or financial branches of government. This view reinforces the one also made in this chapter, that is, that perhaps the best approach to pursue is one that would study the relations of government to *all* forms of intervention. The form of the intervention is a different issue.

Notes

Chapter 1

1 As the arguments will make it clear, Say's statement that entrepreneurs are "the pivots on which everything turns" provides only part of the picture. The society and the entrepreneur are *inseparable* within this model: One's ideas, the new ones in particular, are shaped by the society within which one finds oneself.

2 The first three examples are drawn from Levitt (1960), the fourth from Solman and Friedman (1975, pp. 86–9).

3 Briefly: Implicit in the definition of markets is *somebody's* judgment about the magnitude of demand elasticities (but which, as pointed out later in the text, are not measurable). Consider this recent case as a further illustration of this statement and others made in the text. The FTC announced that it would oppose the merger of Warner Communications, Inc. and Polygram Records, Inc. But a federal judge dismissed the FTC suit to block the merger on the following grounds: Polygram would go out of business in the United States unless the merger was allowed (it was expected to lose $15 million in 1984); Warner was weak outside the United States, where Polygram is more established; Warner has no classical labels whereas Polygram does; thus the merger will be complementary. The judge, Manuel Real, also said that records face competition for the consumer dollar from other new products such as videocassettes, video games, computer software, and home taping [see Landro (1984)]. Thus the judge viewed "the market" as being that of entertainment at home rather than that of records (as the FTC seemed to perceive it). Also consider some further examples given by Levitt (1983, p. 56): The electrocardiogram substitutes a lower-paid technician for the high-paid doctor listening with a stethoscope; the consumer credit card and CRT credit and bank-balance checking machine substitute for manual credit check for each purpose; airport x-ray surveillance equipment substitutes for manual rummaging through baggage, Polaroid substitutes for film *returned* and processed ("return" implying that one's value of time plays also a role), and so forth. All these examples show how skeptical one must be of any numerical values assigned to demand elasticities and the resulting definitions of markets.

4 For a summary of the criticism see Scherer (1980) and Brenner (1985, Chapter II).

5 See Brenner (1983, 1985).

6 Festinger (1954) also argues that comparisons are made when people shape their

173

behavior, but his views are not given precision, no predictions are derived, and no rigorous attempts to try to falsify his views are presented. Zaleznik and de Vries (1975) also give to the entrepreneurs – calling them leaders – central roles. In a recent *New York Times* article (Nov. 7, 1982) Kleinfeld wrote: "What happens to the chief executive when pressure builds up? . . . He drinks, he becomes abusive, he commits crimes. He kills himself," and quotes Zaleznik saying, "I think if we want to understand the entrepreneur we should look at the juvenile delinquent. I think there are a lot of similarities." The model presented here provides a rationale for expecting such similarities. A similarity is also noted by Peters and Waterman (1982): "The champion is not a blue-sky dreamer, or an intellectual giant. The champion might even be an idea thief. But, above all, he's the pragmatic one who grabs onto someone else's theoretical construct if necessary and bull-headedly pushes it to function" (p. 207). For further discussion, see Chapter 2.

7 A similar departure point characterizes Cyert's and March's works (1955, 1956, 1963). See discussion of their arguments and evidence in Chapter 2.

8 See Brenner (1983, 1985).

9 See the modern version of this phrase in Eckstein (1978, p. 139), which is the motto of the book. But note, "luck" is needed too [see discussions on precise meaning given to this term in Brenner (1983), Chapter 1), and Brenner (1985, Appendix to Chapter 1)]. Wickenden (1980), when writing on entrepreneurship noted that "you need a great deal of luck – and not only do you need a great deal of luck, you need the type of mentality that turns *bad luck into success*. . . . Again I believe it is the sort of mind which immediately starts to examine how difficulties can be turned into opportunities that provides entrepreneurial skill" (p. 71, italics added). See discussion later in the text on how the model gives precision to these statements. Also note that one implication of the model is that the most satisfied people would be those whose anticipations have been more than fulfilled. Indeed, Freedman (1978) found in his survey that the happiest people were those with little education who earned a lot – far more than they could have anticipated. He also found that earning a lot does not guarantee happiness for the well educated. He views it as an enigma that doctors and lawyers rated themselves as relatively unhappy (although this is not an enigma in the light of the views presented here). Schoeck's (1969) observations should also be noted. He points out that whereas in English there are two words "happiness" and "luck," in German there is only one "Glück," that the word "luck" derives from Middle High German "gelücke," and that originally "happiness" meant something much like "luck" – defining a condition due to "haphazard" occurrences (p. 238). Back to the context of industrial organization and luck, Scherer (1980) concludes that on the relationship between multiplant economics of scale and the necessity of concentration, "the possibilities are complicated. A fair amount depends upon luck and the particular market segments individual firms choose to serve" (p. 117).

10 Such a broad definition is also given by Barnett (1953).

11 Comparisons with other views on entrepreneurship: the Austrians', Hoselitz's, Schultz's, Schumpeter's, Knight's, and numerous others appear in Brenner (1983), Chapter 1. Criticism on the absence of entrepreneurship in economic theory appears in Heertje (1977), Fisher (1981), and Hannah (1980, 1984) [who notes that

"bluntly, the great thing about being a successful entrepreneur is that you get rich very quickly" (1984, p. 228)]. Hannah (1980) also wrote that "there is a school of economic history which takes an ostrich-like view of these events [i.e., the lack of British entrepreneurship], claiming that entrepreneurs were faced with factor prices which prevented them from doing any better, that for reasons beyond their control the economy was predestined to decline. But their arguments have generally lacked conviction, not least because the models of profit-maximization from which their conclusions are deduced are precisely those [that reduce] the entrepreneur to the level of arithmetician" (p. 38). As an example of this approach Hannah singles out D. N. McCloskey and L. Sandberg, "From Damnation to Redemption: Judgments on the Late Victorian Entrepreneur," *Explorations in Economic History,* 9 (1971).

12 See Brenner (1983, 1985).

13 In other words, other people, revolutionaries or reactionaries, are also "entrepreneurs" who perceive the instability, but they try to exploit the opportunity for other goals. Who wins – the entrepreneurs in business or in politics – one cannot say. Discussions on these views in various historical contexts appear in Brenner (1983, 1985).

14 The comparison with Knight's (1921) views appears in Brenner (1983). Schackle (1972, pp. 409–10) made some similar points, intuitively. He argued that differences in imaginative valuations differ and such differences give rise to profit. Schumpeter (1927) directly linked entrepreneurship and profits in the following way: "Business life, like any other, consists mainly of routine work based on well-tried experience; only within boundaries of routine do people function both promptly and similarly; it is only to routine work that received theory applies; outside routine most people find it difficult – and are often unable to act; those who can are rare and therefore are not subject to competitive conditions, whence the phenomenon of profit" (p. 297). Also see Loasby (1976), Mackaay (1982, Chapter 8), in particular.

15 Also see Rapoport's (1982) discussion on game theory (pp. 69–76) as well as the notes on pp. 422–3.

16 Stevenson and Gumpert (1985), for example, note that the owners of some businesses shy from taking risks in part because they only want the business to provide a steady living. So they run their business in a way to guard what they have.

17 Discussion on the relationship between "ownership" and "decision making" appears in the appendix to Chapter 6.

18 See Cyert and March (1956, p. 47).

19 See Zaleznik and de Vries (1975) on leaders and Loasby (1976) arguing for a historical analysis. He suggests that a firm's history and financial position become elements of the analysis, in contrast to "microequilibrium theory [where] they are . . . excluded as irrelevant" (p. 214).

20 See Bennett (1981), Guiles (1985), Reich (1985), and Gates (1986). Reich's view is that Smith's biggest gamble is to challenge the corporate culture, the entrenched way of life at GM, and his opinion is that Smith's managerial innovations grew out of the long, losing battle his company fought with the Japanese. Reich also quotes Drucker and others who emphasized the role of individuals in carrying out

such changes: "Drucker once wrote: 'Whenever anything is being accomplished it is being done, I have learned, by a monomaniac with a mission.' In that sense, at least, creativity in big business is not that much different from creativity in the arts and sciences" (p. 30), and he concludes: "In their soon-to-be published book, 'Leaders,' Warren Bennis and Burt Naums of the University of Southern California suggest some of the attributes of the great chief executives. 'These intense personalities . . . do not have to coerce people to pay attention; they are so intent on what they are doing, that, like a child completely absorbed with creating a sand castle in a sandbox, they draw others in.' For Roger Smith, the auto industry is the great sandbox. And as he tosses the ideas out, he is inviting a whole company in to play with him" (p. 81). Pay attention later to some similarities with Ford's story.

21 Some economists may miss reference to the extensive theoretical literature on principal agents, asymmetric information, moral hazard, and others. The reason for avoiding discussing these topics is simple: I am not aware of a study using predictions of models incorporating these concepts that succeeded in shedding light on facts. This is not surprising: After all, what "moral hazard," for example, means that people may cheat, commit fraud, or do other illegal or noncustomary acts. If economists using the moral hazard argument wanted to do something with this term, they had to say something on the circumstances in which this hazard is more or less frequent. But they don't. As to "principal agents": First, never mind that although numerous theoretical articles have been written, the implications of not one have been verified. Fama (1980), an exponent of this literature, calls into question the need for both an entrepreneur and ownership in the theory of the firm. According to him, the two functions attributed to entrepreneurs – management and risk bearing, as well as the ownership function can be treated as naturally separate factors. According to the model presented here this statement is wrong. Also see Eliasson (1984) for criticism. Indeed, all the models using the aforementioned vocabularies remind one of Goethe's saying: When ideas fail, words come handy (today, mathematical fantasies seem to come even handier – see Chapter 5 for an explanation).

22 See extensive discussion on this and other criticism in Scherer (1980, Chapter 2).

23 See Buchanan (1979), Kirzner (1973, 1983), Loasby (1976), Mackaay (1982), Schackle (1972), and Casson (1982). Several of Schackle's (1972) observations receive clear meaning within the model presented here: For example, that "Choice is always among thoughts for it is always too late to choose among facts" (p. 280) or "Valuation is expectation and expectation is imagination" (p. 8). An example to illustrate these abstract statements: In 1945, Sewell Avery, the head of Montgomery Ward, envisioned a great postwar depression. Robert Wood, the head of Sears, Roebuck, foresaw an immense boom. Wood gambled on his faith and extended: Sears flourished. Avery hesitated and Montgomery Ward languished [see Samuelson (1985)]. Also note that part of Machlup's discussion in the text, that whatever managers choose to do can be called "profit maximization" has not much meaning within my views.

24 Also see Monsen and Downs (1965), Levitt (1983), Chapter 1 [who notes that while profit is a requisite, it is not a purpose of business (p. 6)], and summaries of

other theories in McGuire (1964). Of particular relevance is Chapter 10, where McGuire notes that most economists are acquainted with the theory of innovation and entrepreneurship set forth by Schumpeter [discussed here in Chapters 2 and 3 and in Brenner (1985), Chapters 1 and 2, respectively]. "Fewer, perhaps, know of the institutional concepts of change and progress, as described . . . by Wesley Mitchell. And even further removed from typical fare for business students are those discussions of cultural change and innovation as presented by such social scholars as H. G. Barnett and Julian H. Steward. Schumpeter . . . advocated a hero theory of innovations and progress. Mitchell and others, on the other hand, held to an environmental theory of innovation. . . . Barnett, and to some extent, Steward, would be between Mitchell and Schumpeter" (p. 233). Within the model presented here, interactions between the individual and the hierarchy within which one finds himself plays central roles, as emphasized later in the text.

25 Keynes's views are discussed in detail in Brenner (1985, Chapter 5).

26 Knight's (1921) views are discussed in detail in Brenner (1983, Chapter 1). Mueller (1976) too comments on them but attributes profits to "information." But what is "information"? See comments on this word in Brenner (1983, Appendix to Chapter 4).

27 Friedman (1975) notes that "our production functions do not include entrepreneurial capacity as a factor of production; it has, rather been regarded as determining the form of the function" (p. 101). This observation seems to be forgotten in most of the literature on industrial organization, both theoretical and empirical [when "Cobb–Douglas" functions are postulated not only for firms but for the economy as a whole (!)]. No wonder, Buchanan (1979) wrote in this context that "most modern economists have no idea of what they are doing. . . . Most modern economists are simply doing what other economists are doing" (p. 90).

28 Friedman, in true entrepreneurial fashion, advertised his ideas in numerous forms and forums, some academic others not. How can one separate his services as an "economist" (for his, let's say, own consulting firm) from that of "the entrepreneur" promoting unfashionable ideas with revolutionary fervor? Or, consider the next case: In a recent interview, Michael D. Eisner, the recently appointed head of Walt Disney Productions said that "he envisioned making Disney a 'major force' in the entertainment world. 'I think we can get entertainment (movies and television) revenues and profits to 50 percent instead of 20 percent of this company,' he added" [p. 2, Cieply (1984)]. This quote illustrates clearly not only the role of entrepreneurs and managers but also the subjective interpretation given to production functions.

29 On the meaning (or rather lack of meaning) of estimating cost functions, see Smith (1955) and, mainly, Friedman's comments on it (pp. 230–8). Also see discussion on estimating costs in the famous (more correctly infamous) Pinto case [in Solman and Friedman (1982)].

30 Evans (1959) describes how Ford and others arrived at their pricing of goods (an act that he does *not* consider essential in defining entrepreneurial activity). Edison, for example, believed that the price of a unit of electric light must be comparable to that of gas light. Later, when he turned his thoughts to the electric-traction field, he viewed success as the achievement of a cost per ton-mile that was less than that

of the steam railroad. Ford, as noted, took his guide from the salary of an "industrious American workman" (Evans (1959, p. 268), and so forth. Evans concludes that "these illustrations exhibit an almost blind faith in the ability of cost-cutting to create a profitable situation" (p. 269).

31 See Susman (1984, pp. 135–6).

32 In a sense, the approach pursued here goes in the direction Coase (1937, 1974) advocated. For, not only does it look at the *origins* of some firms, rather than the examination of behavior of existing establishments, but also looks at ideas. Clifford and Cavanagh (1985) report that 74 percent of the companies they studied got their start with an innovative product, service, or way of doing business.

33 Kleinfeld (1982) notes that there was a cartoon that appeared in the newspaper that depicted a chief executive. The tag line was: "I don't get stress. I give stress." Within the model, this is half of the truth.

34 For a different view of "teamwork," see Alchian and Demsetz (1972) and discussion on it in Brenner (1985, Appendix to Chapter 2), and Brenner and Lacroix (1986).

35 The next cases illustrate this view, as well as the previous discussion on the subjective interpretation of costs. Solman and Friedman (1982) discuss the following case: Back in 1964, IBM was trying to decide if it made sense to create a new type of computer. Bob Moore, at that time a financial executive at IBM, had the following discussion with the engineer in charge of the project: " 'What happens if we reduce your budget by two million dollars?' 'Nothing,' said the engineer. 'I mean, what will it cost the project in terms of time or quality of the product?' . . . 'Nothing' . . . 'Then why shouldn't we do it?' 'If you do, you'll simply increase the probability of failure beyond its current level' " (p. 115). Moore gave the project an additional $1 million. " 'When it came right down to it,' says Moore, 'I was betting on people' " (p. 115). Or, consider the next case: An American semiconductor enterprise in Malaysia pays factory workers a tiny fraction of American wages. It seems cost effective. But the numbers change when you compute in the cost the outbreaks of mass hysteria that have become prevalent here. "Assembly-line workers see the apparitions of evil spirits in their microscopes and fall screaming to the floor, setting off a wave of panic in the factory. . . . Before the plant can be re-opened, an exorcism ceremony must be performed by a local bomoh [a licensed healer]" (p. 125) – speaking about "objective" production functions à la Cobb–Douglas, and well-defined "cost" functions that make no reference to custom, or their breakdown. Solman and Friedman (1982) conclude: "Those among us who are vociferously pro-business may think of corporations as profoundly rational organizations, and those of us who are adamantly anti-business may think of corporations as the reincarnation of Big Brother, but in truth, the two groups believe the same myth: that big business and their executives know exactly what they are doing" (p. 118). It should be noted that in Alchian and Demsetz (1972) too, one characteristic of the firm's production process is the inseparability of the contributions of the individual factors. See comment on their work in Brenner (1985, Appendix to Chapter 2).

36 For reference and detailed discussion of this case in another context, see Jones (1983a,b).

37 For reference and discussion in a somewhat different context, see Brenner (1985, Chapter 2).

38 Schoeck (1969, pp. 23–4) discusses this and other cases in another context.

39 See Schoeck (1969, p. 19).

40 Indeed, after observing such increases some companies have made revisions, bonuses being linked either to performance relative to competitors or to a sample of manufacturing companies. See Johnson (1985). Calvo and Wellisz (1978) and Williamson (1967) also examine the relationship between hierarchy, size of firm, and the crucial role of supervision, but from a different departure point.

41 But a "too" fragile tenure of management may work in the opposite direction, since not everybody performs well under such pressures – see McCaskey (1982).

42 The views and evidence presented here and in the next chapters suggest that books on management offering quick fixes, formula, or slick techniques are useless. Managers and executives walk on the razor's edge when they try to increase productivity and profits. See Brenner and Lacroix (1986).

43 For one such model, see Bronfenbrenner (1960). He tries to reinterpret "profits" with this departure point: "a static society with constant population, tastes, natural resources, social institutions . . . and an unchanging range of technical alternatives available for use" (p. 414). Where can profits come from in such a world?

44 See Brenner (1983, Chapter 2).

45 Friedman (1955, pp. 233–4) elaborates this point, but not in the direction pursued here. He notes that in economic textbooks, the long-run conditions of equilibrium for a competitive firm are stated as "price equals marginal cost equals average cost," but he adds, correctly, that "price equals marginal cost" has a fundamentally different meaning and significance from "price equals average cost." Although the first is the goal of the firm (in the neoclassical approach), not only is the second not, but its *avoidance* is its goal.

46 See discussion in Section 1 and note 3.

47 See Sylos-Labini (1984, Chapter 1) on competition and economic growth in Adam Smith's work.

48 See Brenner (1983, chapter 6) on this point, and also recall that if one looks at the noncompensated demand curves, there is no reason for them to be downward sloping.

49 The first case draws on Levitt (1960).

50 See Main (1983). Peters and Austin (1985, p. 121) note that in the late 1940s the market for mainframe computers was estimated to be a dozen: a few to the Census Bureau, Bell Labs, Lawrence Livermore Labs. In a broader context they note that the British Secretary of War in 1910 thought that the airplane would be of no use for war purposes, that the United States lost most of its aircraft early in World War II because the perception was of threats from ground-based saboteurs, and that the French invested billions of dollars (in 1930s money) on the Maginot Line, which was flanked in a matter of hours by the flexible German tank strategy (as de Gaulle had predicted).

51 Hannah (1984) also concludes that an entrepreneur is not a "neoclassical firm" responding automatically to external signals but an actor who formulates new production functions and develops new markets. But he is skeptical of modeling en-

trepreneurship since "the logical consequence of granting entrepreneurs the creative role in shaping production and consumption is, in fact, to reduce the determinacy of their actions, and hence to increase the difficulty of modeling them in a way that captures their essence" (p. 224). However, such a model is presented here.

52 See Scherer (1980, pp. 35–7).

53 See Crain et al. (1977). Scherer (1980) also summarizes evidence that relatively unprofitable and/or undervalued corporations do run a somewhat greater risk of being taken over (p. 37), which suggests that decision makers must give the impression of doing the best for their company. Otherwise they may lose their reputation and their jobs. In another context he quotes Markham's results that "consolidations prompted by outside banks, syndicates . . . failed much more frequently than those put together by individuals with a continuing commitment to the affected industry" (p. 130), and still elsewhere he concludes the evidence on some mergers in these words: "The efficiency losses from too thinly stretched managerial resources were plainly substantial. At what cost in human displacement, disillusion, and alienation this inept game of corporate volleyball was played, we shall probably never know" (p. 138). For a case study on how the value of a firm depends on people's perceptions and managerial talents, see Solman's and Friedman's (1982) discussion of Marathon Oil (pp. 113–14).

54 Blair and Kaserman (1978) have also suggested that divergent risk perceptions provide an incentive for vertical integration. Evans's (1959) descriptions provide some concrete examples too. He notes, for example, that Charles A. Coffin, head of the Thomson-Houston Electric Company, decided in 1888 that his firm should enter the new electric-railway-equipment field, for the firm was manufacturing for the electric lighting industry whose growth possibilities he believed to be exhausted: "The company, Coffin *felt,* had to get into the new field . . . and could not afford the time to develop its own units for operating traction systems. Accordingly, Thomson-Houston bought up the Van Depoele railway equipment business and proceeded to develop for use on large scale electric railways" (p. 257).

55 Mueller (1977) argues that the persistence of above-normal profits for sustained periods is consistent with a special talents rationale for traditional entrepreneurial firms only. As the arguments presented here suggest, this statement is inaccurate – it can be linked with superior managerial talents and team performance as well. Also see Brozen (1969) who argues that the relatively high profit rates in concentrated manufacturing industries reflect their greater efficiency and their technological innovations.

Notes 56–61 refer to the Appendix for Chapter 1

56 As quoted in Springborg (1981, p. 110).

57 Reference to a very large number of authors who made the assumption that various patterns of behavior can be understood by assuming that people compare their own performance to that of others is made in Brenner (1983, 1985).

58 A note on the utility function: Although behavior is changed when people "change their minds" (a statement that within the model has a literal interpretation), note below that this does not require a change in the utility function. When considering the bet itself, the utility function stays the same. Through the betting process peo-

ple learn from experience, and *after* the bet is implemented, one can say that the parameters of the utility function have changed. This argument further justifies the historical examinations pursued here.

59 A similar point is made by Cyert and March (1955, 1956).

60 This is the process by which equilibrium (or, more correctly, stability) is restored in this model both for the individual and society.

61 Note should be taken of another view of risk taking, Kahneman's and Tversky's (1979). The difference between their and my views is clear: They, as Simon, emphasize that their goal is to provide a *descriptive* analysis rather than a theory with predictive power.

Chapter 2

1 See Brenner (1983, 1985).

2 Silver (1983) also found that the entrepreneurs had been relatively less healthy and less popular as children. They were frequently afflicted with either a small stature (the Napoleon syndrome?) or a sudden illness that prevented their participation in social and sports activities [putting them at a disadvantage compared to their peer group (p. 37)].

3 The relationship between entrepreneurial and criminal acts has been noted by numerous writers, summarized in Brenner (1983, 1985). Sharkanski (1975) for example, wrote: "It is possible that the difference between an entrepreneur and a thief is very slight. While the first aspires for promotion by showing success in initiating plans, the other wants immediate and direct material reward, exploiting influence and public resources for his own private good. It should be admitted that the discernments between thieves and entrepreneurs are thin. Maybe every thief is an entrepreneur, but not every entrepreneur is a thief" (p. 10). In a recent *New York Times* article (Nov. 7, 1982), Kleinfeld wrote: "What happens to the chief executive when pressure builds up? . . . he drinks, he becomes abusive, he commits crimes. He kills himself," and quotes Abraham Zaleznik from the Harvard Business School saying "I think if we want to understand the entrepreneur we should look at the juvenile delinquent. I think there are a lot of similarities." The model presented here provides a rationale for expecting such similarities. It is also amusing to note John D. Rockefeller's memory of his education. He had a father who was an itinerant vendor of quack medicine, a sometime fugitive from the law, and a poor provider at best. He is said to have boasted, "I cheat my boys every chance I get. I want to make 'em sharp" [see Solman and Friedman (1982, p. 176)].

4 Elsewhere Hannah (1980) notes: "The facts are reasonably well accepted. Although [a] constellation of industries was growing between 1900 and 1930, it was not growing as fast in Britain as in America and Germany. And when you study the attempts to set up companies in these leading sector industries, you usually find that there were relatively few British people involved in trying to set them up in Britain. The role of the immigrant or of the foreign company is large and the hypothesis which inevitably suggests itself is that native British entrepreneurs did

not see this opportunity" (p. 38). In other words, when facing the same factor prices, immigrants ventured into new businesses that local entrepreneurs were reluctant to. The model presented in Chapter 1 presented a rationale for expecting such behavior. The evidence on immigrants leads Hannah (1984) to this remark: "I sometimes wonder whether the clearest historical lesson one could derive for the present government might not lead to a policy recommendation that a new Statue of Liberty should be erected in London's derelict dockland. On it would be written: "Give me your Tamils, your Hong Kong Chinese, your East African Asians" (p. 230). In a recent article McGrath (1983) notes that "Asian Americans are only about 1.5% of the U.S. population, but what they lack in numbers they make up for in achievement. Out of 40 Westinghouse finalists, nine were born in Asia and three others were of Asian descent. Some 10% of Harvard's freshman class is Asian American. While no more than 15% of California high school graduates are eligible for admission to the University of California system, about 40% of Asian Americans qualify." At the same time he notes that "for many Asians, stress is the price of survival. Nearly half the 160 Vietnamese students at Brigthon High School in Boston left their families in Vietnam or in refugee camps." Also see Hume (1985) for emerging evidence on them. But see Brenner (1983, 1985) for the disadvantages associated with population growth, due to migration in particular, when considering some broader perspectives.

5 Dahmèn (1970) also attributes the rising number of new firms founded by workers in the wood-joinery industries in the 1930s to the decline in employment opportunities for carpenters and joiners due to the rise in the popularity of prefabricated interior fittings (p. 267).

6 Mensch (1979), concerned about the accuracy of his data, compares it with those presented by other writers and finds that they too have noted that innovations tend to cluster.

7 See Arieti (1976) and Brenner (1983, Chapter 7). In this broader context also the following observations should be noted. Hannah (1984) points out that: "The reward system of British company directors is significantly less performance-related than that in the United States. This explains why U.S. profitability is higher, many conclude (*Economist*, 1982). Yet Japanese managers' rewards are even less closely related to performance than British ones, and so we need to introduce other factors into our explanation of performance" (p. 225). An answer is suggested by Christopher (1983) in *The Japanese Mind*, who argues that every Japanese achievement is rooted in the dictates of a primitive tribe and shaped by a sense of impending catastrophe and the overwhelming need to survive. According to him these urges, as well as a shortage of land and natural resources, explain the sometimes violent Japanese reaction to the outside world and their intense competition. Gilder (1981) first notes that "economics can predict events only to the extent that it can explain the incentives and psychology of business" (p. 50) and then concludes that "few businesses begin with bank loans, and small businesses almost never do" (p. 51), and "in every case, *setbacks* led to innovation and renewed achievement" (p. 53, italics added). Berthold Leibinger, a German entrepreneur, whose company had $85 million in revenues in 1983 notes that he faces a problem of succession. His three children are unlikely to take command, and Anders (1984) notes that this

puts him in a "common German predicament" [although considering the evidence here and in Brenner (1985), this seems to be an international one]. "If he brings in professional managers, they will be younger, contented Germans who won't be motivated by the same survival worries that have made him push so hard since 1945" (p. 18). The links with the views presented in Chapter 1 are obvious.

8 But collusion may not have in these circumstances the "evil" purpose and negative connotation that most economists assign to it. See Dewey (1979). The ambivalent reaction to this and other forms of leapfrogging is again apparent in the following sequence of events. Silicon Valley legend holds that the way to get rich is to become entrepreneurial, and evidence abounds. Yet the valley has also a darker side, see Lindsey (1983). Some losers in the valley tried to find wealth in spying. While William B. Hugle's and James D. Harper, Jr.'s contemporaries (such as Robert N. Noyce, Gordon Moore, Charles Sporck, Jerry Sanders, etc.) founded companies that made not only for them, but sometimes even for their janitors and clerical workers (who took stock options) millions of dollars, neither of them made it "big." Both owned companies that went bankrupt in 1975, which is the year that, according to the FBI, they first met in Warsaw with Polish agents. Others seemed to take less drastic steps when some leapfrogging occurred, and their attempts seemed to be related with "mere" stealing of trade secrets. According to Peter Stone, the state judge in Santa Clara, the number of trade-secret suits has grown exponentially during the last several years. Although it is not always easy to know who is the victim in these suits, the rationale behind them seems to be related to a perception of leapfrogging: Often the employers left behind sue, although there is no evidence that the employees who left committed a criminal act (but the suits and their threat slow down the competition – see Chapters 3 and 4 for further discussion on this point). Sometimes the previous employees seemed to commit criminal acts. Gregory Wald, a Palo Alto attorney, argues that ideas belong to the employer who paid employees to think, and "just because you thought of [an invention] it doesn't make it your idea" (Larson 1984, p. 14). Note that according to the views presented in Chapter 1, this opinion is accurate: Some entrepreneurs and managers may succeed in providing incentives for their subordinates to bet on new ideas. Recall too (as explained in Chapter 1) that these incentives are imposed by making progress within a corporation less predictable and positions less insured – policies now pursued by Roger Smith at GM, Richard Snyder at Simon and Schuster, or in the past by Deupree at Procter & Gamble. These managers seemed to succeed whereas others, as the evidence presented here suggests, did not; although even the successful ones worried about internal disruptions. Both Deupree (at P & G) and Sloan and Smith (at GM) perceived that the major obstacle for the implementation of their new strategy was the traditional way of thinking that developed as a result of some unexpected, early success ("too much Ivory thinking" as some executives at P & G put it).

9 See Berkowitz (1983).

10 Speaking of demand curves in Chapter 1: Reynolds's view suggests that people's perceptions matter. If they think that a certain good of a good quality can be produced for, let's say, $2,000, they will not trust someone who will sell that good for $500. So they may be ready to buy it for $2,000 but not for $500. The suc-

cessful entrepreneur in this market will be one that, for a while, sells for the higher rather than the lower price. The source for Reynolds's story is Solman and Friedman (1982).

11 One can also call the actor "an idea thief."

12 See Solman and Friedman (1982, pp. 177–81).

13 See Schisgall (1981).

14 One should not jump to any deterministic conclusions. "Luck" plays a role in this model; see discussion on its meaning within the model presented in Chapter 1 in Brenner (1985, Appendix to Chapter 1), and Brenner (1983, Chapter 1, p. 25). Wickenden's (1980) remark captures part of the argument (although not its deeper meaning), where he states: "You need a great deal of luck – and not only do you need a great deal of luck, you need the type of mentality that turns bad luck into success. It is not always appreciated how often what appears on the face of it to be a disaster can be turned to one's advantage. Again I believe it is the sort of mind which immediately starts to examine how difficulties can be turned into opportunities that provides entrepreneurial skill" (p. 71). Also see Hughes's (1973) detailed description of the lives of a few American entrepreneurs. Also note that adversity can take numerous forms. Shapero (1975) notes that a common kind of displacement occurs when a person is fired. He interviewed 109 individuals who formed companies in Austin, Texas. In 65 percent of the cases, the role or primary reason for the venture was negative, that is, the types of comments heard were: "I was fired," "I worked for the company for 10 years, day and night, and they brought in their idiot son as my boss," and so forth. According to Michael Tushman from the Columbia Business School [quoted by Alter (1983)], this is not an unusual reaction, but part of what he calls the "who the hell is the guy but the owner's son" syndrome.

15 But consider the following facts: Hannah (1980) notes that "if you compare the portfolio of shares in small and medium-sized companies over the seventies with a portfolio of large companies, you will see that it is better to have been investing in small companies. For the skeptical I quote as evidence a chart published in *The Economist* [chart accompanying article entitled "Why Wall Street Looks Oversold," October 20, 1979] showing the 1974–79 differential between AMEX (American Stock Exchange) shares and the New York Stock Exchange shares, broadly an indication of the difference between small and large companies in the U.S." (p. 57). Bleakley (1984) provides the following information: "When a prospective investor in the Mutual Shares Corporation checks out the fund's roster of holdings, a first glance can be troubling. One finds bonds of at least half a dozen companies that are in bankruptcy proceedings, shares in more than a dozen corporations that are being liquidated and dozens of stocks that are selling well below their book value. But what may seem at first to be a junkyard of mistakes is actually a treasure trove of hidden values, says Max Heine, the 73 year old president and co-founder of the fund. . . . By sticking doggedly to that belief, the . . . fund has racked up one of the best records in the mutual fund fraternity. It currently is ranked sixth out of more than 600 funds for its most recent 12-month improvement in price per share, and it is first out of 92 funds in the growth and income category, according to Lipper Analytical Securities. Over the past 10 years, it

ranks eighth.'' Can traditional economic theory explain these facts? It should be noted that (maybe not accidentally) Mr. Heine came to the United States from Germany in 1934.

16 Quinn (1979) made a similar observation: ''Because the inventor/entrepreneur works out of his own home, his overhead cost is minimal. He invents to avoid costs. He uses sweat capital instead of dollars for materials or equipment. As a result, failure cost is low and not publicly visible'' (p. 21). There are numerous recent examples: In 1976, William Millard borrowed $250,000 from a venture capital firm called Marriner & Co. This helped him build his Computerland Corp. valued at $2 billion in 1985 (see ''Unwanted Angel at Computer Land,'' *Newsweek*, March 25, 1985, p. 72). A. E. Paulson, founder of Gulfstream Aerospace worked for TWA as a mechanic and moonlighted at an auto-repair garage. In 1951, he set up his own business, converting passenger planes into cargo aircraft, and in 1978, starting to build airplanes on his own. In April 1984, when his company, Gulfstream, went public, he collected $85 million in cash and stock worth $551 million [see Taylor (1984) for this and numerous other similar success stories]. Barmash (1985) describes the rise of two entrepreneurs, Milton Petrie and Leslie Wexner, in the women's apparel business from scratch to over $1 billion in sales in 1984. Sylvan N. Goldman was the inventor of the shopping cart. As the owner of two struggling grocery-store chains in the depths of the Depression, Goldman noticed that shoppers stopped buying when their baskets got too heavy to carry. So he mounted the baskets on wheels and started a retailing revolution [and the idea was transformed into an empire worth $200 million in 1984, when he died (see *Newsweek*, December 10, 1984, p. 97)]. Cox (1985) notes Alfred Taubman's history: The son of German immigrants, growing up during the Depression, an indifferent student saddled with dyslexia and a slight stutter, started a contracting business with a $5,000 loan at the age of 25. Today he is the largest shareholder of Manufacturers National Bank of Detroit, owner of Sotheby, and so on.

17 Schumpeter makes two additional observations: First, he too frequently refers to the ''social pyramid,'' a pyramid that plays a crucial role in the formal model presented in Brenner (1983, 1985), and suggests that one always needs a symbol to recognize a social class and to distinguish it from other social classes [according to him, marriage can serve as such a symbol (p. 141)]. Second, he writes that one way to jump classes is ''to do something altogether different from what is . . . ordained to the individual,'' in particular ''to become an entrepreneur – which does not, of itself, constitute class position, but *leads* to class position'' (pp. 173–74). One should also note that the incentive to gamble depends on the customs and laws of the society [see Brenner (1983, 1985)]. For Schumpeter's view on this point and comparison with others see Brenner (1983, Chapter 1) and chapter 2 in Brenner (1985) on progressive taxation. Also, the point that an increased number of potential competitors may induce one to innovate sooner has been made by Barzel (1968) and Fethke and Birch (1982).

18 See more on this point in Brenner (1985, Appendix to Chapter 1).

19 Schiff and Lewin (1968) discuss this issue in detail. According to them the introduction of the smoothing technique was motivated by the management desire to project an image of company growth (p. 51). The budget incorporates varying

degrees of slack because managers bargain about the performance criteria by which they will be judged throughout the year – see Chapter 1 on this point. They say that "organizational slack, in the Cyert and March view, arises unintentionally in the bargaining process and its primary role is to stabilize performance despite fluctuations in the firm's environment," but "we believe as does Williamson – contrary to Cyert and March – that managers consciously and intentionally . . . bargain for organizational slack" (p. 51) and conclude that "to maximize personal goals while achieving the goals of the firm requires a slack environment" (p. 51). Within the model presented here, every individual pursues only one, personal goal, and no normative statements are made.

20 Schiff and Lewin (1968) also conclude that their results "amply support behavioral implications of the occurrence of slack as an unintended result of the budget and control system, especially where the system is based on the traditional accounting model of the firm" (p. 62). "Contending that the traditional system, contrary to expectations, does not result in maximal use of resources, we have shown on the basis of our pilot study how management can and does create slack to achieve attainable budgets and to secure resources for gathering their personal goals and desires" (p. 62). Their conclusion is different: Although in my model "stability" plays the central role, in the one Schiff and Lewin rely upon, "maximal use of resources" is used as the criterion for judgment.

21 Without providing a formal model, Sir J. Stamp in his 1926 study on inheritance stated that in the United States "inequality of wealth . . . stirs men to effort, to emulation, to ambition" (p. 363). On the subject of inheritance, see Gabrielle Brenner (1985). Also see note 7 and Alter (1983) whose discussion suggests that Leibinger's case (mentioned in note 7) is not unusual. In the United States 7 out of 10 family firms either are sold, go public, or fold before being passed on to the second generation. They also note that although these are exceptions, most family companies seem either to collapse or pass into other hands with the retirement of the entrepreneur who initiated them, perhaps because the children lack their parents' toughness.

22 See Hoselitz (1963) for discussing the evidence in another context.

23 The change is expressed clearly by a young Tabanan nobleman, whom Geertz cites as saying: "They have taken the government away from us – all right, we will capture the economy" [as quoted in Hoselitz (1963), p. 40; Geertz's study is quoted in Hoselitz (1963)].

24 Hoselitz (1963) also notes "that most restrictive regulations imposed upon the aristocracy and of sanctions preventing it to participate in business practices stem from the time after 1600. For example, we may refer to Duke Johann Adolph of Holstein-Gottorf, who stated in 1615 that business activities were not proper for noblemen. And the consequence of this attitude was that the Holstein nobility, which before 1600 had participated to some extent in trade and money–lending activities – came to be influenced by this new principle of aristocratic behavior" (pp. 43–4).

25 Such a broad definition is also given by Barnett (1953), who investigates innovations in all domains too. In the popular literature, Gilder (1981) is emphasizing entrepreneurship in a preaching manner.

26 Miller (1949) presents evidence that only a minority of business and political elite came from the relatively lower classes. Note his evidence does not contradict the hypothesis: First, the business and political elite may be conservative rather than entrepreneurial. Second, as shown, it is *not* the origins that matter but sudden *adversity*. Also see articles in Backman (1983) or by Toulouse (1983), and note that although the definitions are different, the topics examined – "originality," "innovativeness" – seem to be similar to ours.

Chapter 3

1 See Guyon (1983).
2 Roland Martin, a Sony vice-president, illustrates these arguments when he describes his company's strategy: "In order to stay *ahead,* the next time you are able to change models, you have to introduce a more innovative product, or find a way to produce the same thing at a lower price," and Dick Komiyama, another Sony vice-president, adds: "If we don't obsolete ourselves, someone else will" [see Landro (1981)]. Not all the companies have this attitude at all times. Solman and Friedman (1982) remark that "keypunch video technology was an easy technical step for IBM to take. But if it were taken, untold thousands of customers would terminate their leases on the card punchers and switch to video. . . . So IBM stood pat, and Inforex became one of the hottest high-technology companies of the early 1970s" (p. 36).
3 Solow [quoted in Skeoch (1972)] makes a similar point: "The multifaceted dynamics of technological advance and industrial transformation – the underpinnings of increased productivity – are almost wholly excluded from the preview of Establishment economics. The notion that a competitive price-directed market is the underlying economic reality lingers on a fixation even of those who proclaim the organizational revolution" (p. 1). Schumpeter (1939) wrote that "no other than ordinary routine work has to be done in this stationary society, either by workmen or managers. Beyond this there is, in fact, no managerial function – nothing that calls for the special type of activity which we associate with the entrepreneur. Nothing is foreseen but repetition of orders and operations, and this foresight is ideally borne out by events" (p. 17). Hayek (1972) made the same points in an article written in 1946. He argued that economists assumed away the competitive process by assuming that all the demands are known and all innovations made. Hayek, as Kirzner and as the Austrian school, justly viewed competition as a discovery process, and not a final, static equilibrium. According to them, and according to the approach pursued here, equilibrium theory, which eliminates the entrepreneur, can provide no help in illuminating the competitive process. Also see Armentano (1982) and Fisher et al. (1983) on this point.
4 As quoted by Loasby (1976, p. 203).
5 See Nisbet (1982, pp. 284–8) making some similar observations.
6 This view is not exactly novel: Coase's (1937) argument, when explaining the nature of firms, is founded on the premise that in an exchange prices and partners have to be discovered [remarking on the assumption of equilibrium theory that prices are given, that "this is clearly not true of the real world" (p. 390)].

7 The point that prices and partners must be discovered is also made in Loasby (1976). A detailed discussion on Texas Instruments' strategies can be found in Solman and Friedman (1982). Note that the strategy of cutting prices was introduced when Texas Instruments was still a relatively small company. If this same strategy had been undertaken by a big corporation it would have been labeled "predatory." For the price charged was less than the *observed* marginal and average costs. The costs Texas Instruments' managers took into account existed only in their minds.

8 See Davis (1984).

9 Hart (1962), in his examination of the problems of the size of firms and their growth, concludes that there is a large stochastic component in the forces that determine them, and so one cannot adopt a deterministic explanation. According to him, one should expect that the growth and decline of firms should depend on the quality of their management, government policies, internal and external political situation, and so forth.

10 The fact that full, rather than quoted, prices are pertinent also suggests that the relative prices that matter for understanding human behavior have a subjective interpretation. This conclusion implies that questions of interest that can be refuted will concern indicators other than prices – more about that is said later in this chapter when the meaning of full prices is further clarified. Meanwhile recall the example given in Chapter 1 on the competition between the producers of diapers. The innovation of fitted diapers was greatly appreciated because of the time it saved. No competition in price could have added so much to the value of this product. Thus, the fact that *observed* prices may be relatively stable when there are a relatively small number of firms does not imply collusion and lack of competition. It is just the case that in such circumstances the managers have greater incentives to compete with other strategies (since price cuts are the easiest to imitate). Also Schumpeter's (1942) observation is worth quoting: "As soon as quality competition and sales effort are admitted into the sacred precincts of theory, the price variable is ousted from its dominant position" (p. 84). As an illustration of this argument, consider the following case: in Dunbar, Pa., Pechin's Shopping Village has a bad location, a slipshod look, a pockmarked parking lot, no piped-in-music, and a $30 million yearly business. Its low prices, like coffee for a nickel, and free meals for senior citizens (as of June 1984) keep a loyal core of customers coming from as far away as Ohio, West Virginia, and Maryland. The founder, Sullivan D'Amico, opened the store in 1967 and says: "It costs me a little bit of money to give free meals. But I'd have to give it to the government any way, so I might as well give it to the people. And it does me more good than putting an $800 ad in the paper." Thus the zero price for the meal, the nickel for coffee and for doughnuts, and the monetary "loss" they impose reflect investments in advertising, in attracting a group of customers. This is a competitive response to the strategies of other businesses that may be better located, more visible. Of course, no negative connotation can be given to these practices, although some economists may call them "tie-in" arrangements and "predatory pricing" (i.e., selling below "marginal costs") and give such connotations. D'Amico's story appears in "Forget the frills: 5 cent cup of coffee will draw the crowd," *The Gazette,* Montreal,

June 28, 1984. Carlton (1984) also emphasizes how erroneous it is to focus attention on price as the exclusive mechanism to allocate resources: "Nonprice rationing is not a fiction, it is a reality of business and may be the efficient response to economic uncertainty" (p. 4). Also see Johnson (1976).

11 Briefly: Price equilibrium is only one of the visible signs that a balance of forces has been achieved in the society and stability is maintained. That this is not a very interesting case to examine (Arrow–Debreu efforts notwithstanding) is also Williamson's (1967) opinion. In his survey he agrees with Kaldor that static equilibrium provides no role for management and quotes Robinson (1934) to support his views: "In Mr. Kaldor's long period we shall not only be dead but in Nirvana, and the economics of Nirvana . . . is surely the most fruitless of sciences" (p. 250). See extensive discussion of these points in Loasby (1976, pp. 64–8) and Ayres (1944, Chapter 1). Ayres emphasizes that the intent of the principle of just price during the Middle Ages, for example, "was to freeze the orders of society in the proportions they assumed in the Middle Ages. What was interdicted was neither commerce, nor wealth but the increase of commerce at the expense of feudal powers" (p. 28).

12 See Stocking and Watkins (1948).

13 See the extensive evidence on food riots in England and France in Rudé (1981), Lefebvre (1973), and Bridenbaugh (1968), to just randomly mention a few writers who touched on this subject.

14 See Stocking and Watkins (1948).

15 See discussion on the two approaches in Goldschmid et al. (1974, pp. 162–245).

16 See Posner (1976, Chapter 2).

17 This approach is also pursued by Fisher (1979).

18 Maybe it is useful to recall with this example the subjective interpretation of "full prices" and that measuring areas under "demand curves" make not much sense.

19 Of course, these conclusions have been reached at times, without, however, providing uniform background that allows one to reach them and without providing an alternative approach that could suggest what is the nature of questions that should be asked. Dean (1954), for example, remarked that "generally speaking, competition to the businessman, is whatever he has to do to get business away from his rivals and whatever they do to take sales away from him" (p. 108) and on price differentiation he notes, "charging different prices to different people makes the economist suspect price discrimination, roughly defined as price differences that are not 'justified' by cost differences. . . . Price discrimination may also be employed to acquire, perpetuate, or abuse market power. . . . The businessman sees his structure of price discounts as an instrument of competitive strategy in fighting for position in different sectors of the market" (p. 109). Evans (1959), who describes what he would view as entrepreneurial acts, also points out that "the pricing of goods has been omitted from his major decisions" (p. 253).

20 There is an extensive literature on "predatory pricing" that gives a criterion to identify it [Areeda and Turner (1975), for example] and that criticizes the criterion [Posner (1976), on the basis that the criterion is useful in *static* circumstances only]. More recently Ordover and Willig (1981) give an alternative definition of predation, one, that in contrast to Areeda's and Turner's, which referred to diver-

gence between prices and marginal costs, is the following: "Predatory objectives are present if a practice would be unprofitable without the exit it causes, but profitable with the exit" (p. 9). But considering the evidence presented later in this chapter on inventions and the relationship between changes in prices and a firm's changed plans, this definition is as impractical as Areeda's and Turner's is irrelevant. Moreover, Ordover's and Willig's later reasoning seems peculiar: They remark that "the introduction of a new product exhibits a predatory objective if the firm can only recoup its investment by the exercise of such additional monopoly power." This is certainly perverse reasoning: Isn't it inventions and innovations that our society today seems to encourage? What else can restore or increase wealth? So how can one perceive their introduction as "predatory" and attribute negative connotations to it?

21 Also see extensive discussion on profits being an unreliable signal of monopoly power in Demsetz (1973) and Schwartzman (1973).

22 See Fisher et al. (1983).

23 According to Utterback (1969, p. 30), in the scientific instrument industry, 17 percent of its 1960 sales were of products not in existence in 1956, ranking the industry second on this measure only to the aircraft industry. At the less aggregated level, according to Pearson (1982, p. 22), 3M Corporation has a record of introducing new products at such a rate that between 20 and 25 percent of any year's sales are from products introduced within the immediate past five years. At Hewlett-Packard in 1981, 75 percent of the sales were generated by products introduced during the preceding five-year period [Hammond 1982, p. 124)].

24 Even without easy entry by new firms, competition will be equally effective if existing firms can readily expand. Thus, even if entry is difficult, the question whether or not a particular firm has monopoly power does not directly depend on its current share of the market but on what would happen to its share if it attempted to charge high prices. This, in turn, depends on the ability of existing competitors to expand, which has the same effect as entry. Similar points are made in Fisher et al. (1983). As illustration, consider the fashion and entertainment industries: There are numerous small textile manufacturers and numerous singers that are virtually unknown. Yet dominant firms in both industries exist: Yves Saint-Laurent, Pierre Cardin, Calvin Klein, Ralph Lauren in fashion (generating sales close or over the billion-dollar mark), Spielberg and Lucas in the movies, previously the Beatles, now Michael Jackson in singing. So why should economists be surprised to find similar distributions (due to talent and chance) in other domains? The distributions posed a puzzle because entrepreneurial talent played no clear role in their models and the comparison with the aforementioned domains was avoided since the managerial talents and innovative strategies of businessmen are less recognizable and identifiable than those of some artists, singers, or fashion designers.

25 A critical survey of these theories can be found in Stigler (1968a,b) and Posner (1976).

26 The source for this case is Solman and Friedman (1982, pp. 127–30); Wesley Cohen's work was part of his Ph.D. dissertation at Yale.

27 The source of information is Evans (1959) in his section titled "To be left behind is too risky" (pp. 257–8).

28 See Freeman (1983), discussion starting p. 85.

29 Scherer (1980, pp. 148–9) remarks that concentration rises rapidly in differentiated durable–goods industries because of "chance."

30 This section draws, in part, on a research report prepared by Plouffe (1985), and the sources for the cases are ABA (1974–80, 1977, 1984).

31 The concept is also consistent with the recommendation Scherer (1980, p. 244) makes: "Some assumptions have to be made by a potential entrant calculating the profitability of entry. The economist too must build a theory upon assumptions conforming, one hopes, as closely as possible to the thought processes of real-world entrepreneurs." This is exactly the approach pursued in this book.

32 A final point on the traditional notion of competition and on a recent development. Scherer (1980) notes that one of the benefits of competition was perceived to be that it solves "the economic problem *impersonally,* and not through the personal control of entrepreneurs or bureaucrats" (p. 13). Frequently economists failed to note that such anonymity has also costs and not only benefits, of more fraud occurring, and that this type of anonymous exchange may be an adaptation to a rising and more mobile population. These points are elaborated in Brenner (1983, Chapter 2) and Brenner (1985, Chapter 3). During the last week of March 1986, the Supreme Court made a decision in the *Zenith* case ruling that "lawyers claiming predatory pricing will be shown the door" (editorial, *Wall Street Journal,* April 1, 1986). Back in 1974, Zenith argued that the Japanese firms had conspired for the past 20 years (!) to sell televisions in the United States below cost. The court said they wouldn't, couldn't, and didn't. The court found that Zenith and RCA still have 40 percent of the U.S. TV market, about the same as in the 1970s. Judge Frank Easterbrook, of the Seventh Circuit, thought the Japanese "were just engaged in hard competition," and Justice Powell wrote in his Zenith decision that "cutting price in order to increase business is the very essence of competition."

Chapter 4

1 See Telser (1964) and Schudson (1984).

2 Although many models and empirical researches have spoken of depreciation of advertising, they have never pointed out clearly that the question they are examining is, in simple language, how quickly people forget things, what types of ads they recall at all, and so on [see summary of such studies in Comanor and Wilson (1979)]. These questions are related to the way people memorize and retain information, and they are raised in this chapter, which is an extension of Brenner and Brenner (1982).

3 See Nelson (1974) and Stigler (1968).

4 See Goldschmid et al. (1974) and Comanor and Wilson (1974, 1979). Note that advertising is examined here from a completely different viewpoint than in Comanor and Wilson (1974), in particular since competition is defined differently in the previous chapter than in neoclassical economics.

5 See Schelling (1960, p. 56) and Scherer (1980, pp. 190–1).

6 By this we do not say that people have a rigid biological constraint on their memory capacity: Although this is constrained by biology, diverse means such as associations, books, and computers are used as an extension of memory. But com-

pared with the actual memory, which by analogy with computer science we would call direct-access memory, all the mechanical and electric extensions are costly in either money terms (computers) or time (search in books). Moreover, the storage of information in artificial memories is itself a memory-consuming operation: In order to retrieve a piece of information, one must remember in which book or tape it was stored.

7 A survey on memory and the distinction between conscious and unconscious memory is presented in Jaynes (1976), although the main thrust of the book is flawed [see Brenner (1983)].

8 One can argue that, once one has the catalog at home, one does not have to rely on memory. But consider the following scenario: A consumer receives the catalog and glances at it. Some time later, he sees one of the items in the catalog in a store at $15. However, he recalls that in the Sears catalog it was "fourteen something." Of course, a consumer will remember numbers he frequently uses more than numbers he does not frequently use. And some numbers he will not round; phone numbers, of course, are of no use if rounded.

9 This can be casually observed in the 1970 Neiman-Marcus Christmas catalog: A fur coat is $100,000; jewels $5,000. On the other hand, a nightgown (item with more substitutes) is priced at $19.95.

10 One can also argue that the prices discussed here may help in advertising: One can claim that all one's prices are below $10, which may mean nothing more than that all one's prices are $9.99. But basically, this explanation is similar to our own: Implicitly, it is based on the assumption that people will *remember* the below $10 statement.

11 See Brenner (1983, Chapter 2) for references and for shedding light on features of primitive societies by taking into account our limited capacity to memorize.

12 See Dolan (1982) and Abrams (1980) for reference on the case studies quoted in this paragraph.

13 See Abrams (1982).

14 See discussion in Brenner (1983, Chapter 7) and Brenner (1985a, Chapter 7). As Alsop (1985) notes, companies need more emotional hooks in their ads, such as music, to make their products stand out in people's minds – once again a relationship to memory.

15 See Hackett (1983).

16 This and the other cases in this paragraph appear in Kneale (1983).

17 Of course, just like with the $2.99 type advertising feature, if many enterprises and institutions start using "famous faces," viewers may turn out. Alsop (1985) summarizes recent surveys that this seems to be happening. Meyers (1982) quotes other surveys that suggest that in advertising "it pays to be creative. . . . Memorable commercials get the public attention more easily. . . . You don't have to see them as often to make your point."

18 See Schudson (1984).

19 For a review of the controversy, see Comanor and Wilson (1979).

20 See Telser (1964), Schudson (1984), Brozen (1974), and literature referenced in the concluding section.

21 This, as well as other sources are referenced in Schudson (1984, Chapter 3).

22 See *Newsweek*, May 6, 1985, p. 56.

23 See Schudson (1984, p. 98–9).

24 Part of this section draws on Brenner and Courville (1983).

25 See answers to this question discussed in Brenner (1983, Chapters 2–4).

26 See Clinard and Yeager (1980, p. 77) and Saddler (1983).

27 See Scammon and Semenik (1982), Furth (1978), and Armstrong et al. (1979). Note, however, that if the company's use of words *was* noncustomary, the charge of "deception" could have been made. This reservation should also be kept in mind when subjective claims in advertising are called "fraudulent." Whether or not they are depends on customary interpretations. Also, the data presented in this chapter do not suggest that people take ads literally: They distinguish between "information" given by noninterested parties and the ones disseminated by those who are.

28 The source is Solman and Friedman (1982).

29 The sources are Abrams (1983) and Alsop (1985). On the trend of substituting traditional ads by national news stories, see Lipman (1986).

30 The source for this case is Clinard and Yeager (1980).

31 Clinard and Yeager (1980, p. 82) also note that the Heinz Company is said to have given information to the FTC about Campbell's "marbles in the can" soup advertisement (in which marbles were inserted to show that there is meat in it. It is unclear why this ad is misleading: Since meat does not float, how do you remind people, when they glimpse at a picture, that the soup has meat in it?); later Campbell reported to the government that Heinz had too much mold in its ketchup. In 1979, Heinz sued Campbell for monopolizing the canned soup business. Clinard and Yeager (1980) remark that "present and former employees, including executives, and particularly those who are *disgruntled*, are often sources of information" (p. 82). Note that according to the views presented in Chapters 1 and 2 these employees' accusations cannot always be trusted. Recently, Baumol and Ordover (1985) make some similar points.

32 See Pace (1982).

33 See Saddler (1983).

34 See Schudson (1984, pp. 95–9).

35 Others too have found that in determining their advertising budgets firms resort to rules of thumb [see survey in Schudson (1984, Chapter 1)]. San Augustine and Foley (1975) found that large American advertisers rely on "essentially illogical" approaches when setting their budgets, a finding Gilligan replicates. This leads Schudson (1984, p. 17) to the conclusion that in contrast to the prediction based on models of "marginal analysis," in practice, decisions are made differently – as indeed one would expect from the views presented in this book. Indeed, as Schudson (1984, p. 85) remarks, the most quoted line about advertising among businessmen is one attributed to various people, ranging from F. W. Woolworth to Lord Leverhulme: "I know that at least half of my advertising money is being wasted. My problem is – I do not know which half."

36 This evidence suggests that advertising does not hurt the poor, as some claim. See this point elaborated from a different angle, in Schudson (1984, pp. 119–22). Also note that one of Schudson's (1984) conclusions is consistent with the broader ap-

proach pursued in this book. He wrote that "the department stores did less to provide equality in consumption than to encourage a democracy of aspirations and desire. They contributed to the democratization of envy" (p. 151).

37 Schudson (1984) concludes that "while advertising may be today a 'barrier to entry' . . . it was not a barrier in the late nineteenth century. What was a barrier was the extensive marketing organization and the long-term ties between executives and managers and jobbers and retailers that constituted the human side of the organization: that was not easy for newcomers to duplicate" (p. 167). Schudson does not explain why the situation today is different. He explains the growing importance of advertising in the American economy by the increased mobility of the population and the resulting diminished face-to-face economic relation (p. 167). This feature of diminished face-to-face interactions is used in Brenner (1983, 1985) to explain numerous additional phenomena. Also see Brozen (1974) on raising the question of how the "barrier-to-entry" view of advertising emerged and persisted.

Chapter 5

1 This approach is by no means unusual: This is Barnett's (1953) departure point. Usher (1955) too notes that "there is no difference in the general character of the behaviour of entrepreneurs and technologists. Entrepreneurs and executive directors invent new concepts of social ends and new procedures in social action. . . . But these acts of insight are dispersed through a highly diversified array of acts of skill which are often incorrectly classified because there are generalized to a greater degree than acts of skill in the fields commonly regarded as skilled and professional" (p. 49).

2 See Scherer (1980), p. 432 in particular.

3 Also see discussion in Johnson (1975). Ogburn (1947) repeats the same point when he concludes "in the discussions in the preceding paragraphs about the future effects of the wartime inventions there is a margin of error depending upon the factor of human will. In so far as the discussions have concerned social effects of the past, this factor need not concern us" (p. 88). It is interesting to note that Merton (1973) makes some similar points, when he argues that multiple discoveries are the rule rather than the exception in science. But he later admits that without the few, like Freud and others, the discovery may be lost: "Such focalizing may turn out to be a distinctive function of eminent men and women of science" (p. 452). This argument implies that one needs the eminent men in science as much as one needs entrepreneurs. Without them nobody would read the article written by the noneminent scientist or appreciate its importance. The information would be lost, forgotten, and thus provide no contribution to science. Thus Merton's argument that "the individual man of scientific genius is the functional equivalent of a considerable array of other scientists of varying degrees of talent" (p. 381) is wrong. Without the *courage* of the few eminent ones to pursue their ideas against many odds, these ideas might never be developed. It is also unclear what Merton means by the fact that "in an enlarged unsociological conception, men of scientific genius are . . those whose discoveries . . . would eventually be rediscovered" (p. 381). Some within 10 years? Others within 100 years, when

discoveries made before have already been forgotten? So can the focus be regained?

4 See the evidence discussed in detail in Freeman (1983), Johnson (1975), Scherer (1980), and Kamien and Schwartz (1982).

5 Mansfield (1968) remarks that survey work suggests that firms often use a rule of thumb in allocation of R & D funds. The typical target allocation is a percentage of sales that is determined with reference to the industry *average*. Note the similarity with decisions on expenditures on advertising, as noted in the previous chapter.

6 See Scherer (1980, p. 412).

7 See *Time* (April 9, 1984), Peters and Austin (1985, Chapter 9). Ohmae (1982) also notes that in Japan smaller companies have been able to capture significant market shares from formidable rivals such as Mitsubishi, Toshiba, Hitachi, and Canon, through innovations. He also notes that some of the ''grand'' old Japanese businessmen made it to the top with little formal education and little connection to the business establishment.

8 See detailed discussion of this and other cases in Peters and Austin (1985, Chapter 9).

9 The evidence presented in this section contradicts Arrow's (1962) and Usher's (1971) viewpoints. According to them, a firm realizing monopoly profits on its current product calculates the profit from innovation as the difference between its current profits and the profits it could realize from the new product, whereas the newcomer regards the profit from the new product as gain. Thus, according to them the newcomer always has a greater incentive to innovate (Arrow used this argument for process innovation, whereas Usher used it for product innovation). But why would one seller behave like that? Only if he does not take into account the threat of entry could such arguments somehow be justified. However, firms do not appear to neglect such threats. Also see discussion on diversification later in the chapter.

10 On what defines a ''new product,'' see extensive discussion in Buzzel and Nourse (1967, Chapter 2).

11 Recall, however, that considerations of ''minor'' and ''major'' are subjective and after-the-fact constructs: For some people the innovation in Coca-Cola's taste seemed so significant that they were willing to carry out a minirevolution in order to restore order. But I doubt that social scientists will ever count this change in their measures of innovation. Also see detailed discussion later in the text on the definition of ''important new products.''

12 Asinof (1985) notes that small companies, if they are innovative, can get help from numerous quarters. Omnicad Corp., a tiny computer-aided design company and AT&T became partners, AT&T making a $5 million equity investment, agreeing to provide research and development funds, and giving Omnicad equipment discounts in return for additional shares. ''If you're AT&T, how do you catch IBM?'' asks Edwin A. Goodman, a partner in Hambro International Venture Fund. ''You don't do it with 20 years of research and development. You do it by buying and investing in innovative small companies. Roughly 50 corporations have formal programs to make direct venture investments, double the number in [1982]. . . .

Since 1980, the number investing through venture-capital funds has increased six fold to about 150'' (p. 33).

13 Consider the case Cooper and Schendel (1982, p. 328) examine: In 1934 when GM introduced the first mainline diesel electric locomotive, the producers of steam locomotives could look back upon two earlier threats they had survived: the electric locomotive, and, in the 1920s, passenger cars with individual gasoline-powered engines. Both of these captured only small segments of the American locomotive market. There was no indication that the next threat, the diesel electric, would destroy the traditional industry within 15 years. So how could calculations be made, but based on gut feeling (i.e., subjective probabilities, costs, benefits)? As noted, some economists, recognizing the inability to deal with the issue of creativity, admitted that economic models have more to say on the diffusion of innovations than on innovations themselves. But are the causes of diffusion really different than those of the innovations themselves? After all, individuals and the institutions within which they work must depart from their customary behavior; thus it is the motivation that leads them to behave so that must be examined. Indeed, Hufbauer's (1966) evidence does not give support to the idea that the distinctions can lead to useful insights. He prepared a list of 56 plastics, synthetic rubbers, and fibres and identified the first producer in a large number of countries. One result of his study was that it enabled comparisons between countries and firms not only in terms of numbers of innovations (defined by him as the world's first producer) but also in terms of ''imitation'' (defined as first producer in a particular country after the innovation). This evidence shows that countries with the highest ''innovation'' rate also had the shortest imitation lag. Also see discussion of Hufbauer's evidence in Freeman (1983, p. 60).

14 This long, complex decision-making process that brings an innovation to life is incompatible with theories of the firm that postulate a high degree of accuracy in investment calculations, accuracy in the estimation of costs and benefits, or probabilities of success and failure [also see Freeman (1983, p. 25) on this point]. Thus, unsurprisingly, the mathematically more complex models summarized in Kamien and Schwartz (1982), which introduce probability distributions and game theory, are not more illuminating since they too do not deal either with creativity, differences of opinions, or changes in risk-taking behavior. Also notice that the managers of existing firms cannot be blamed for being unable to make calculations when a new product is introduced. Based on what? Indeed, Freeman (1983) notes that the ''more advanced'' portfolio selection methods, which have been developed by statisticians and management consultants, are seldom used. ''In the U.S., Baker and Pound . . . found that a few of the techniques had been used occasionally and then discarded in favor of simpler 'rule of thumb' methods or discounted cash flow . . . calculations. These methods are strongly biased towards short-term pay-back and the system in which they are used is frequently project-based rather than portfolio based. Their widespread use probably discourages the more radical type of innovation, which would find more favour either in fairly sophisticated selection systems or without any very formal system. A survey in Sweden in 1971 confirmed that only simple quantitative methods were used in Swedish industry . . . and [another] concluded that in the European chemical industry project selec-

tion remains a pragmatic and intuitive art" (p. 157). Freeman also notes that few top managers support technological forecasting, and none initiated it, and that in most companies he studied "the planning and control of R & D expenditures appears haphazard at best" (p. 166). So why is it done? It insures some managers: If their venture fails, they can say that they have done their best and even asked the "experts."

15 Scherer (1984) also notes that "it is at least conceivable that certain inventions with very high 'best guess' benefit-cost ratios require unusually bold, farsighted, time-consuming departures from orthodox technology, with extraordinary attendant uncertainties and risks. . . . Such cases are probably rare . . . and thus cannot safely be squeezed into the mold of an orthodox profit-maximizing model" (p. 140). The last part of the statement is accurate, but not the first: Whose perception is it that such cases are "rare"? How can an outsider state whether an investment of $100,000 is "routine" or "extraordinary"? For some, losing $100,000 may be small change, for others it means bankruptcy and loss of reputation too.

16 See Gould (1984), Gleick (1985), and Ben Yehuda (1985, p. 111).

17 Also recall that Copernicus was an excellent physician, who also translated poetry from ancient Greek into Latin; Leonardo da Vinci was a man of all trades; Hutton had his training in medicine, later turned to geology, and also wrote a theory of rain, gravitation, heat, light, and electricity.

18 See Trattner (1938, p. 143).

19 See Roe (1953, 1972). Also recall the negative shocks these scientists had early in their lives [leading Murray (1925) to ask: "Is early disappointment an element of later success?" (p. 24)] and the similarity with the evidence presented in Chapter 2: Jenner's father died when he was 5, Simpson's mother when he was 9, Copernicus was 10, Darwin 8, when they lost a parent, and so on [see Murray (1925), Trattner (1938), and McCaskey (1982)]. Galileo was unemployed and thought about moving to the Byzantine empire (Goran 1974, p. 63); Dalton was the son of a poor hand-loom weaver; Rumford of a poor farmer; and Kepler's life was filled with financial difficulties and mishaps [see Trattner (1938)]. Freud and Einstein were Jewish, encountering antisemitic reactions from an early age [see Trattner (1938, p. 375), who also notes that Einstein's family fortunes were always thin, but in Italy they were at low ebb (p. 377)]. Note that Lord Charles Cavendish was a man of enormous wealth. Although he made discoveries, he *never* published them or gave the slightest sign that there were of value. He watched men advocating theories that he had demonstrated to be wholly erroneous, without interfering in the debate [see Murray (1925, pp. 341–2)]. His example not only does not contradict the prediction of the model but seems consistent with it, since the model makes predictions about bringing ideas *to life*. Also recall that such early disappointments may lead to revenge as well. Marat, who once wrote a chemical treatise, turned down as devoid of interest by Lavoisier, was deeply envious of Lavoisier's success, with devastating results. Lavoisier died on the guillotine on May 8, 1794, in part because of Marat's relentless attacks on him. Barnett (1953, pp. 77–84, 136–46, 402) and Schoeck (1969) also examine the role of deprivation, resentment, and envy in all fields of human activity.

20 See Schoeck (1969, p. 91).

21 See Murray (1925), Trattner (1938), Gould (1984), and Gleick (1985).

22 In addition to the books mentioned in the text see Frankel (1976), Wallis (1979), Ben-David (1977), and also recall Einstein's answer to Walter Kaufman. Kaufman was a professor of physics who had been measuring the relation between charge and mass in electrons when Einstein, an *outsider* – a 26-year-old employee of the Swiss patent office – published the special theory of relativity. Kaufman declared the theory to be incompatible with his experimental findings. "So much worse for your findings and the limited theoretical vision that informs them" [see Joravsky (1983)]. See the Wernerian episode in Trattner (1938, pp. 54–6); recall that Dalton was ridiculed for his pictorial presentation of chemical compounds – his atoms were regarded as "false," "unnecessary" (pp. 85–90). Loasby (1976) notes that, in general, when evidence conflicts with the model, it is the evidence that is found wanting (p. 210, also recall Sims's experience with the military establishment). McCaskey (1982) also reaches this conclusion and adds that, in general, psychologists have researched the various ways people will not engage in a problem, how they will deny, distort, and create myths and illusions to defend against hearing bad news (p. 72). It is a regular pattern: See the most recent extensive discussion in Ben Yehuda (1985).

23 See Goran (1974, p. 91); note the reference to being an "outsider."

24 As quoted in Murray (1925, pp. 313–4).

25 See Murray (1925) and Trattner (1938).

26 See extensive summary of evidence in Ben Yehuda (1985) and a detailed description in Johanson and Edey (1982). Barnett (1953) notes that "new ideas are frequently scouted by scientists not because of their intrinsic merits but because they do not conform to existing doctrine" (p. 68), examines features of "science" by pointing out that the primary urge of some may be for recognition, wealth, and status (pp. 101–3), and concludes: "The impartial observer, however, will find that this ideal (of open-mindedness toward new ideas) is less frequently realized in practice than is generally claimed and supposed. Most scientists are not the dispassionate seekers after truth that these self-concept and popular stereotype demands. . . . For the present we are concerned with the dependence upon authority as an extrinsic consideration in the evaluation of new ideas. . . . Every area of knowledge . . . has its big names whose opinions in science and out of it carry weight and prevail over the views of lesser lights just because they are recognized authorities" (pp. 68–70). Lewontin (1984) also suggests that "scientists are curious about nature, but the search for truth among them is generally the pathway by which they search for status" (p. 22). Recall how dismayed both Newton and Darwin were on learning that somebody else had come up with "their" theories. Barnett also emphasizes the similarities in reactions that competition provokes in various fields of activity: "Modern businessmen incline to the view that competition is an essential spur to progress. . . . Its implication is that human beings are inherently lazy and, unless they are forced to exert themselves by the economic threat of rivals, they will relax in a rut. In so far that the theory singles out competition to the exclusion of other incentives . . . it is certainly in error. There are many other inducements to increase activity and to raise the level of aspiration of the individual. There is no denying, however, that within the frame of reference implied by the proposition, competition is a stimulus of great importance" (p. 72).

The evidence presented in this and in Brenner (1983, 1985) seems consistent with this view. Although in this book competition has been emphasized, it has been noted that numerous other incentives can shock people out of their customary behavior. Barnett also takes note of the fact that competition may induce not only innovative acts (in a positive sense) but also "spreading of damaging rumors, canards, and fictions about opponents – mudslinging it is popularly called" (p. 74).

27 Although, apparently it needs reminders; see Ben Yehuda (1985), Merton (1973) and Joravsky (1985). Note, however, that this argument does *not* imply that all scientific knowledge is no more than privately agreed upon opinion expressed by a group of "experts." It is more: At its origin this knowledge may have been linked with some observations, which later generations, however, either misinterpreted or proved to be inaccurate. Also see Johanson and Edey (1982).

28 The reason for this reaction is not always the one Kuhn (1962) mentions, namely the uncertainty about whether or not the idea will turn out to be accurate. If this was the case, scientists should at least look at the evidence. But they frequently simply do not, thus contradicting Kuhn's explanation. Some points similar to those made in the text are made in Crozier (1970, p. 51). Perhaps one should add that the arts are no exception to the rule: Recall Van Gogh, Modigliani, Herman Melville (the critics called what we view today as masterpieces "sheer moonstruck lunacy"), Mark Twain (early critics called his work "the veriest trash . . . rough, coarse, and inelegant"), Edgar Allan Poe, and so on. The behavior of leading philanthropists may not be an exception to the regularity noted in the text either. In the 1984 annual conference J. Irwin Miller and Alan Pifer, two respected spokesmen for philanthropy (Pifer being president emeritus of the Carnegie Corporation) complained that many foundations shied away from new, untried, or controversial undertakings, preferring to follow fashions in grant making. Mr. Miller is quoted as saying that "as the world around us becomes more confusing and in many ways more terrifying, foundations appear to be impelled to play it safer and safer. . . . Increasingly we fund conferences and studies whose proceedings immediately begin their long accumulation of dust on some library shelf, but also cause no criticism and are good for some nice lunches" (Teltsch 1984).

29 As quoted in Schoeck (1969, p. 171). Merton (1973) wrote that "the practice of seeking to trivialize what can be shown to be significant is a well-known manifestation of resistance" (p. 384).

30 Schoeck (1969) notes that sometimes "even primitive people realize that because some of their fellows are courageous enough to defy the envious eye, they prosper. The Tiv are a pagan people numbering some 800,000. . . . Ten years ago an anthropologist gave an account of their economic system: 'Tiv are very scornful of a man who is merely rich in subsistence goods (or today, in money), they say . . . that jealous kinsmen of a rich man will bewitch him and his people by means of certain fetishes in order to make him expend his wealth in sacrifices. . . . A man who persists in a policy of converting his wealth into higher categories instead of letting it be dispersed by his dependents and kinsmen is said to have a 'strong heart.' . . . He is both feared and respected." The word *tsav* indicates the magic substance of the heart which fends off envy. Not everyone has it. Is a person in any way outstanding, if only as a singer, dancer, hunter? He has some *tsav*, though

perhaps only a little. Is a man healthy, possessed of a large family and prosperous farms? He is a man of *tsav,* or he could not have warded off the envy of others either in its physical or mystical expression'' (pp. 56–7). Today we would call ''tsav,'' ''courage.'' Browning (1985) shows that today a stroke of luck is bad news in Japan, if one isn't insured: A golfer's hole in one means spending between $2,000 to $5,000. Why? Since there is the widespread notion that good luck should be shared: '' 'If you keep the luck all for yourself, you will be thrown under a curse,' the chairman of Nippon Steel Corp., Japan's largest steel company, told a Japanese gold magazine recently.''

31 A similar point is made by Barnett (1953), although in a different context, when he writes: ''The Samoan instance affords an excellent illustration. The innovations that loom so large to the Samoan are trivial if not imperceptible. . . . Moreover, one who takes the trouble to analyze them finds that they all fall within the framework of a limited pattern. Toleration is within an extremely narrow range, and variations are correspondingly minute. . . . Bunzel's analysis of Pueblo Indian pottery making reveals the same psychology. Potters prided themselves upon their artistic freedom and fancied that their products were unique to themselves. . . . The student of southwestern Indian pottery, however, finds that the departures are in reality only a reworking of traditional elements on a very limited scale. The same conclusions are to be drawn from O'Neale's study of Yurok and Karok Indian basketry'' (pp. 57–8). Barnett also summarizes discussion of fashion in this context (p. 57), and notes that ''among things, emphasis is placed upon novelty in intimate possessions, such as clothes, body ornamentation (among women), houses, automobiles, and foods. Among ideas, praises are reserved for originality in the arts and crafts, the professional skills, and in economic enterprises but are withheld from novelty in religious, social and political thinking'' (p. 101). The reason cannot be that many new ideas may turn out to be inaccurate. For we know that the old, established ones have turned out to be such too.

32 Indeed, when Lyell was eventually proven wrong, and admitted it, all scientists viewed this recognition as an example of heroism, Darwin writing that ''considering his age, his former views, and position in society, I think his conduct has been heroic on this subject'' [as quoted in Murray (1925, p. 58)]. But one calls an act ''heroic'' only if it is rare and unexpected. So there are exceptions: The contemporary Russian physicist P. L. Kapitsa confessed: ''As you grow older, only younger students can save you from a premature hardening of the brain.'' Kapitsa quoted his own teacher, Ernest Rutherford, as saying: ''You know that only thanks to my students do I keep on feeling young'' (as quoted in Goran (1974), p. 64). Of course, such an attitude requires some humility. Also see Ben Yehuda (1985) on the points raised in this paragraph in the text.

33 Or, as Newton put it ''no great discovery is ever made without a bold guess'' [quoted in Goran (1974, p. 91)]. One should not be surprised therefore at Trattner's (1938) following observation: ''Often what has passed for a theory has been nothing more than a baseless hypothesis. Much that has been paraded with a pretence at wisdom has proven to be singularly sterile, a masquerade of confused terminology and incomprehensible absurdities. It is a strange irony that men in their efforts to be logical and reasonable have so frequently spoken nonsense and

written idiocies. Only an unusual mind can resist the temptation of pseudoclarity. True intellectual enterprise does not consist simply in listing mere data; the theorist does more than elucidate the obvious" (p. 7) . . . "a theory cannot be a tissue of self-contained hypothesis. Just to sit down and suppose something and then work out the consequences may be an exercise in imagination, but that is not science. A theory as such refers beyond itself and is relative to something which is real and not hypothetical. Facts must suggest the theory" (p. 8). Note both Newton's and Trattner's references to "boldness," a point also made by Broad (1984): "It seems, then, that there is usually a way to discover new scientific landscapes, even if it means detours along the way. But it takes one final ingredient, according to Carruthers (a well-known physicist), that is perhaps the least 'scientific' of all. You have to have confidence. You must be bold. Confronting confusion for a long time or roaming incessantly from field to field takes verve. Of all the ingredients, he says, this is the hardest to systematize and convey." McCaskey (1982) summarizes similar points: "As we have seen, groups need a common map to function effectively. A creative person, in contrast, needs the strength to withstand a group's desire to maintain using a map already in place. . . Being creative requires the courage to resist social pressures and to risk being alone" (p. 114). So, in science, as in every field, if one wants to keep its practitioners happy (a passive state of mind) rather then exulted, teach them (as Isak Dinesen reminded herself) to be bold, to be bold, but not to be too bold. Such teaching helps keep things stable. Also see note 30 on "courage," in a different situation, but related context.

34 Kuhn (1962) also writes that "only when scientists encounter [a] . . . type of phenomena, the recognized anomalies whose characteristic feature is their stubborn refusal to be assimilated to existing paradigms" (p. 97) will new theories emerge. "Paradigms provide all phenomena except anomalies with a theory-determined place in the scientist's field of vision" (p. 97); he concludes that as in manufacture so in science, retooling is an extravagance to be reserved for the occasion that "demands it" (p. 76). Sounds convincing? Not quite, since recall that the anomaly may be in the eye of the beholder, just like *perceptions* of demand, as the evidence in the world of business presented in the previous chapters suggested, and the evidence on the long list of "forgotten scientists" [the title of one of the chapters in Murray's (1925) book and the subject of Ben-David's (1977) study] suggests too. Also recall that although Merton (1973) may be right in stating that the institutional goal of science is the extention of certified knowledge, since that is what a hierarchy is interested in for maintaining stability, it would be inaccurate to conclude that such a goal promotes innovations or discoveries. Just the contrary.

35 See Cohen (1985, p. 46) and also Ben-David (1977). Einstein [as quoted in Trattner (1938, pp. 400–1)] points out additional reasons why this might be the case: "Many kinds of men devote themselves to science, and not all for the sake of science herself. There are some who come into her temple because it offers them the opportunity to display their particular talents. To this class of men science is a kind of sport in the practice of which they exult. . . . There is another class of men who come into the temple to make an offering of their brain pulp in the hope of securing a profitable return. These men are scientists only by the chance of some

circumstance which offered itself when making a choice of career. If the attending circumstance had been different they might have become politicians or captains of business. Should an angel of God descend and drive from the temple of science all those who belong to the categories I have mentioned, I fear the temple would be nearly emptied.'' See Barnett (1953) who elaborates on the various incentives that motivate scientists. Kuran (1986) examines scientists by looking at their integrity and their incentives for preference falsification (that is, like Kepler, writing his uncritical treatise on astrology, when he no longer believed in the idea, in order ''to avoid starvation'').

36 See note 32, on Lyell, and notes 31 and 33 on boldness in general, in science, in particular.

37 McCaskey (1982) makes a similar point: ''Another block to creative thinking is the tendency of groups to treat reality as defined by hard facts only. We have seen that each person's ''reality'' is in part a social construct. If a group is rigidly limited by common sense perceptions, members remain locked into familiar ways of patterning and understanding events'' (p. 113). Also see Einstein's reply to Kaufman, note 22.

38 See Barnett (1953) for making similar observations.

39 Of course, if later, suddenly, circumstances change, people may discover the once discarded idea and then state, as Murray (1925) does, that ''oftentimes a great mind comes too soon. The age in which he lives is not prepared for him. The philosopher Kant is reported to have said to Stägemann in 1797: 'I have come too soon; after a hundred years people will begin to understand me rightly, and will then study my books anew and appreciate them.' Robert Mayer felt exactly that way about his work and so did Gregor Mendel. Young realized that the prestige of Newton was too firmly rooted for men to give his ideas a fair hearing. 'He was one of the most clear-sighted men who ever lived,' once declared Helmholtz in a tribute to Young, but he had the misfortune to be greatly superior in sagacity to his contemporaries. They gazed on him with astonishment, but could not always follow the bold flight of his intellect, and thus a multitude of his most important ideas lay buried and forgotten in the great tome of the Royal Society of London, till a later generation in tardy advance remade his discoveries and convinced itself of the accuracy and force of his inferences.'' (p. 153).

40 Anaxagoras, a century before Pythagoras, had been cast into an Athenian jail for maintaining that the sun was not a heavenly chariot daily driven by the gods through the skies. Copernicus, who was aware of this story, permitted the publication of his manuscript only on his deathbed, although he did communicate his results to a wide circle of friends. It reached even Pope Leo X who was not worried about the heliocentric idea. But Luther and Melanchthon were and realized the full menace to the Catholic Church's dogma [see Trattner (1938, pp. 18–28)]. Karl Friedrich Gauss shrank from publishing his results because he feared the hostility his ideas might excite (also see note 39 on Young's fears). Others published, without any impact: Green (1793–1841) published his striking essay on the application of mathematical analysis to the theories of magnetism and electricity in 1828, without any effect until 1845, when Lord Kelvin noticed it. That's 17 years; it took 20 years for both Newton's *Principia* and Gauss's *Disquisitiones Aritmeticae* to gain

recognition [see Murray (1925, pp. 317–49) for detailed discussion on this and numerous other examples]. Remember the 19 years it takes, on average, for an innovation in business to find its market?

41 See Boorstin (1983).

Chapter 6

1 See Brenner (1983, 1984a, 1985), Brenner and Courville (1986).

2 See, for example, Delion (1978) who justifies state-owned enterprises in terms of rationalizing the "national scale of economic functions," Finbow (1983) who justifies them in terms of "infrastructure," "basic industries," and others, criticized by Tupper and Doern (1981) who "explain" it by "pragmatism," which they say, quoting Reginald Whitaker, " 'is usually an excuse for an explanation which remains to be given.' The term is a vague, theoretical catch-all that provides little insight into the confluence of ideological, material, technological, and jurisdictional imperatives that underpin the state's expansion" (p. 11).

3 See Borcherding (1983). Note that the intervention occurred in times of crisis – see discussion later in this chapter.

4 Almost all the studies referenced in this chapter repeat these points: See Leibenstein (1978, Chapter 8), Prichard (1983), Tivey (1966), Vernon and Aharoni (1981) and so forth.

5 This argument is based on Coase's (1937) well-known observation, which is descriptive rather than predictive, that the market mechanism is not always used because it is costly to use it. Thus some transactions are internal to the firm.

6 This rationale for government intervention is by no means unique. Jones and Mason (1982), for example, remark that in Malaysia, the government has a conscious policy of improving the lot of the ethnic Malay population, in part by integrating them into the entrepreneurial class. One vehicle has been the establishment of public enterprises. They note that ethnic Chinese and Indian entrepreneurs could readily have undertaken such activities without public enterprise intervention and conclude that "efficiency" has thus been subordinated to what is perceived as a higher social goal (p. 42). In the United States such encouragement seems to be done by regulations (affirmative action, etc.).

7 This point is important: As Walsh notes: "Like U.S. public enterprises, those of West Germany are not products of socialist movements or of explicit ideologies of public ownership. Since the feudal lords ran profitable enterprises and medieval cities provided services essential for local trade and commerce, certain economic and administrative activities – particularly warehousing, ports and markets – have been considered governmental responsibilities" (p. 313). Why? We do not always know. We cannot question the origins of *all* our customs, of all the things that we grow up being used to and being taught to practice. In particular, government budgets and policies, toward state-owned enterprises in particular, can never be reexamined all together, as compared to all possible alternatives. See Klein (1976) on an elaboration of this point and Coombes (1971), who also notes the lack of questioning for state-ownership in Sweden (p. 182).

8 Trebat (1983) remarks that in Brazil public ownership of the railroads dates from

the beginning of the twentieth century and is rooted in particular circumstances: "The policy of government guaranteed rates of return on foreign investment in the railroads had resulted in a heavy strain on the government budget. After a point, it became apparent that it would be cheaper to nationalize the foreign lines rather than to continue the profit remittance policy. Large parts of the foreign-owned rail network were purchased" (p. 40). Again, no evidence of economies of scale as a rationale for government. Rather, it is a response to crises due to errors made in the past. Also see Lukasiewicz (1976).

9 See Robson (1960). At this point one can already ask: Why is today the argument on "Natural monopoly" so frequent, in spite of the lack of evidence? The answer may be that for economists trapped in the lines of thought of the neoclassical tradition, whose language nonsocialists have adopted, that was the main justification – within their view of the world – for state intervention. This is one of the conclusions that Primeaux (1985) reaches when examining the Alaska Public Utilities case, stating that "perhaps an argument could be made that regulators may be hostile toward direct electric competition because where it exists it reflects serious flaws in the theory of natural monopoly. Much of the justification of the whole regulatory process rests upon that theory. Consequently, anything that tends to indicate weakness in the theory automatically raises serious questions about the value and purpose of regulation" (p. 18). Also see Loasby (1976, p. 69).

10 In Marxist analysis, welfare expenditures are perceived as an investment in social control made necessary by the disruptive impact of capitalism. See Klein (1976) and O'Connor (1973). Although there may be a superficial resemblance between this and my arguments, see discussion on significant differences in Brenner (1985, Chapter 5) and mainly Brenner (1985, Chapter 7).

11 Similar conclusions have also been reached by Rodrick (1982), who remarks that "the principal factor responsible for S.O.E. creation in the bauxite-aluminium industry . . . is the well-known, if poorly understood, phenomenon of economic nationalism in the third world" (p. 200). Trebat (1983) too concludes that "the argument can be made that the creation of public enterprise in Brazil has been almost accidental, that is, the result of historical circumstances, such as balance of payment crisis, rather than conscious government policy. Suzigan, for example, observes: "The rise of the State as entrepreneur did not result from any planned action and its ideological motivation does not extend beyond the economic nationalism that was in vogue at the time that some of these sectors were created" (p. 30). . . . "Particular historical events leading to the creation of public enterprises may also outweigh economic factors. For example, natural disasters such as earthquakes or depressions [but why are 'depressions' 'natural'?] may mandate state intervention to avoid collapse of vital services. A massive earthquake aided the Chilean Popular Front to honor an electoral pledge to strengthen the public sector during the 1930's. The Italian experience in public enterprise can be traced to widespread government intervention in faltering enterprises during the Depression" (p. 35).

12 See Brenner (1983, 1985).

13 As Davis et al. (1965) note: "The United States needed an extensive transport and communications network before its internal market was large enough to support a

modern industrial economy. Again, in the modern world some economically feasible power source is required before development can begin; however, because of technological indivisibilities, minimum plant size is frequently so large that the underdeveloped economy cannot profitably utilize its output in the foreseeable future'' (p. 163). Note that both arguments are implicitly linked with expectations for population growth, which, where immigration is concerned depends on political decisions.

14 See Brenner (1983, 1985).

15 For a summary see Brenner (1983, 1985).

16 And the individual, in turn, perceives the turn in the emotional tidal wave. See concluding section on this point.

17 Recall also some similar observations made by Rostow (1950): ''War and German occupation left behind a heritage of shattered institutions. Almost by default, governments had to seize the initiative in starting Europe on the road to recovery. On the continent especially, neither the private institutions nor the private investment resources existed to reconstruct railways and other basic facilities. And even where resources and institutions were reassembled, the environment lacked the stability – the confidence – . . . to invest money on a large scale for long periods. By default rather than from ideological persuasion, governments and their civil servants took over a substantial part of the function of risk taking and investment. In this process the nationalization of industry has figured, but it figured only as an incident to a much wider sequence of events'' (pp. 109–10).

18 This argument does not exclude the possibility that the decision to change the goals was erroneous. Making mistakes is an inherent part of the model. But since mistakes are costly and diminish wealth, the model suggests mechanisms for correction.

19 Hughes concludes that: ''Too little social control led to the great turnabout of 1911–1914, when the federal nonmarket control establishment was launched in the name of reform. Nearly a century later we need to change the mixture again and let in more freedom'' (p. 242). The same suggestion emerges in Davis et al. (1965) when they examine the history of railways, attributing the current problems, in part, to regulations that have not been changed in spite of the altered circumstances. Also see L'Hériteau (1972) on the changing goals, and the studies in Vernon and Aharoni (1981), Grassini's in particular. Implicitly, Olson's (1982) argument too can explain the change in goals in broad contexts.

20 See Mackay and Reid (1979), and Reid (1977) on specific discussion on the political markets and criticism on existing models, and Brenner (1983, 1985) for detailed discussion on the implications of this argument. It may seem, at first sight, paradoxical that many economists have adopted this view of the political market, when, with minuscule variations they themselves followed the ideas of Smith, Keynes, and some other brand names. But, maybe, after all, this situation is not so paradoxical. For those who follow this approach did not really form their own opinion, but received it, almost unquestioned, from older generations. So they may extrapolate their own behavior to their view of politics too.

21 But his argument, relying on Becker's, that ''rational expectations'' characterize the market for political influence, is questionable when viewed through the light

of the model, where the word "rational" is not a useful concept. (The word that can be used is "expectations that people got *accustomed* to," which of course has very different implications.) Why Borcherding believes in this idea, considering the Hitlers, Maos, Stalins, and so forth of modern history seems a puzzle (since he seems to take a historical perspective when looking at the subject).

22 How skeptical one must be of numbers whenever one looks either at state owner-ship or the state as part of a transaction also comes to the fore when one looks at the following interpretation of some facts: "Presumably for theological reasons, the U.S. government tends to shield workers against the risk of unemployment by granting contracts to private enterprise or by the creation of pseudo-private enter-prises, such as CONRAIL, rather than resorting to state ownership. Public services are also supplied through government by contract. . . . The major advantage of contracts is that they offer a detour around a conservative belief system. . . . They permit elected officials to claim balanced budgets and conservative economic pol-icies while distributing projects and contracts funded by public debt. . . . Incen-tives for efficiency, productivity, and management improvement are weak in that portion of the private sector for which the government is the major customer and in which the cost-plus contract and variations of it are commonplace. . . . These efforts put free enterprise rhetoric to work in extracting private profit from govern-ment expenditure" [p. 167, Aharoni (1983), quoting, in part, Walsh (1978)]. It should also be noted that the method suggested in the text requires the so-called counter-factual analysis, which demands a lot of imagination, is rarely done, even more rarely done well, and even then it is unclear why it is useful.

23 The broad approach pursued here is not unusual. Muzaffer (1981) too remarks that the analysis of public enterprises requires taking into account the "*total* social system consisting of economic, political, and societal subsystems" (p. 51).

24 See Ricklefs (1985).

Note 25 refers to the Appendix for Chapter 6.

25 Once Rostow (1950) made the observation that "the phrase 'government and pri-vate enterprise' is derived mainly from American experience, one might almost say from American political controversy" (p. 105).

Chapter 7

1 See Baumol (1984). Note that the standard, static international trade relationship does not apply here: although exchange is still profitable, the innovations in one country lower the other country's "budget constraint."

2 Various definitions given to "industrial strategies" are examined in Brenner and Courville (1986) in detail.

3 See Stern (1937).

4 Ozaki (1984) notes that "what is the industrial policy of a strong nation . . . is an unresolved issue" (p. 68). According to the views presented here, it is not so much that this issue is unresolved, but in a static situation, when somebody is and ex-pects to stay on top, the issue is simply not raised. When one is on top, although improvements might be possible, why bother? Who would be able to tell that indeed there was improvement? Moreover, those under may even notice that they

are falling behind. However, what will happen when a nation suddenly gets to a position higher than expected can be described. According to Safran (1984) the Saudis are looking to reduce risks, to avoid confrontations, to postpone tough decisions since they became, almost overnight, financial giants. Thurow (1985) summarizes events that occurred in West Germany following their "economic miracle": Wealth was redistributed, labor costs rose, profits shrank, the entrepreneurial spirit waned. Although nearly $500 million was spent on microchip research and in Japan half that amount, the Japanese captured 40 percent of the world sales, while the Europeans together only 10 percent, in part because innovations were not brought to life. In Holland, according to Reeves (1985), the new riches of giant natural gas fields have subsidized schemes that add up to guaranteed support for everyone, whether they work or not. Dutch egalitarianism is such that at Royal Dutch/Shell and Philips, average earnings of top management are only five times the pay of the lowest laborer. The combined welfare, unemployment, and disability payments can add up to more than working people earn. The biggest problem seems to be with the "disablement list," which provides that Dutch workers who become ill or are injured, whether on or off the job, are entitled, at public expense, to up to 80 percent of their previous pay for a year and then 70 percent until they are 65. In 1985 this list reached 800,000 people. Also recall the discussion in Chapter 2 [on Nauru, Wiener's (1982) evidence, etc.].

5 In a recent book, Amos Perlmutter (1985) writes that the Israelis are "not a nation, not yet. It is an exiled people still in the desert longing for the flesh of Egypt. It cannot be considered a nation until the Negev and Galilee are settled; until millions of Jews immigrate to Israel; and until moral standards necessary to the ethical practice of politics and the high values of Zionism are sustained. This is neither a mob nor a nation. It is a people still chained to their exilic past." But how does one build a nation? In Israel, among others ways, by subsidizing settlements in the Negev and Galilee. In Canada, in 1879, the country's first Prime Minister, Sir John A. Macdonald, proclaimed the "National Policy." It called for a railroad to link the Canadian east and west, reversing the cheaper north-south trade. Also high tariffs were enacted to foster the development of local industry. In 1911, the Liberal Prime Minister, Sir Wilfrid Laurier, lost an election when he urged abandoning the National Policy and striking a free-trade deal with the United States. Prime Minister Mackenzie King negotiated such a deal in 1948, then pulled back at the last minute. Schlossstein (1984) also argues that industrial policy is just another name for economic nationalism.

6 See Ozaki (1984, p. 68).

7 See Wolf (1984) and Schlossstein (1984) and also note that almost daily the Japanese are accused of dumping, cheating, lying, and of waging economic war without any rules, although the charges are frequently superficial, to put it mildly. Wolf, for example, objects not to trade barriers but to Japan's social structure and its customs. He suggests that Japanese should eat American food, importing grain products, beef, citrus, thus not only eliminating half of their U.S. trade surplus but providing the Japanese with a more nourishing diet. One better not comment on such reasoning.

8 In a recent poll, 53 percent of Americans answered "yes" to the question: Is the military threat from the Soviet Union constantly growing and a real, immediate

danger to the United States? See Clymer (1985). How such perceptions of leap-frogging are linked with wars, see Brenner (1985).

9 See Pine (1985) and Murray (1985).

10 See Roberts (1984).

11 Needless to point out that none of the economic models in the field of international trade, those that imply "free trade" in particular, deal with defense, nationalism, or other such "marginal" issues. . . . See Robinson's (1962) criticism of some of these models. Also, models that discussed these issues within the normative frame-work of "welfare economics" are useless (as is, in fact, all of the so-called welfare economics), based like the rest of mainstream economics on static models. See Brenner (1983) and Brenner and Courville (1986) for criticism.

12 See "Get Rich Quick," editorial, *The Wall Street Journal*, August 21, 1984. Although this perception may be inaccurate, Lionel Olmer, former U.S. Under-secretary of Commerce warns that this perception may not only constrain trade but the West's own development. For he perceives a danger in losing the benefits of rapid sharing of technology in the West as far greater than the risk of the Russians being able to exploit Western inventions, especially as changes are coming so fast. See Lewis (1986), who seems puzzled by the fact that growth is linked to defense spending. But, as the arguments and evidence presented here and in Brenner (1983, 1985) suggest, she should not be.

13 See "Israel-Argentina Jet Deal Blocked by U.S.: Report," *The Gazette*, August 28, 1985.

14 See Sayle (1985) and Robinson (1962).

15 See Freeman (1983, Chapter 9).

16 See Murray (1985) and Fauriol and Kopperl (1985) and note that the issue of protection is also linked with the problem of debt. Samuelson (1985) discusses this aspect and suggests some policies.

17 As quoted in "A Little Principle," editorial, *The Wall Street Journal*, December 19, 1985.

18 See Sease (1985).

19 Among others they want to achieve this goal by setting up computer systems that will measure, color code, and inspect fabric as it comes off their looms. The information will be transmitted to small computers at the apparel factories before the bolts of cloth arrive. That way there will be no need for the apparel factory to redo the job.

20 This is Samuelson's (1984) conclusion too in the context of the auto industry.

21 Also recall the evidence interpreted in the previous chapters.

22 The policies criticized here have been recommended in Canada by Britton and Gilmour (1978), on whose views the Science Council's *Forging the Links* (1979) seems to have been based. Their goal is "technological sovereignty" defined as "the ability to *develop* and *control* the technological capability necessary to ensure . . . economic and hence . . . political self-determination" (p. 14) – note the nationalistic goal. They suggest that the policies should be oriented toward these goals: "1. Increasing the demand for indigenous Canadian technology. 2. Expand-ing the country's potential to produce technology. 3. Strengthening the capacity of Canadian firms to absorb technology. 4. Increasing the ability of Canadian firms

to import technology under conditions favorable to Canadian industrial development" (p. 48). These four goals can be reduced to just one that can be expressed in a simple sentence: "Make Canadians smarter." For the first objective is to increase the demand for "indigenous Canadian technology." But what is this technology if not some Canadians' bright, new ideas? The second objective is to expand the country's potential to produce technology. What does "producing technology" mean? First, people must have the motivation to acquire some skills and, second, entrepreneurs and good managers must be willing to take risks and bet on new ventures, using these skills. The third and fourth objectives can also be reduced to similar statements. So, the Science Council's view is that the problem of the Canadian economy is the lack of innovative drive – a good diagnosis. But what is the treatment the Council suggests? It suggests: "1. Conduct, in cooperation with industry, an internal review of suppliers to pinpoint firms with a high innovative capacity so that policies can be targeted to specific firms or industries [p. 49]. 2. Actively solicit from such firms industrial proposals with a high degree of innovative content and be ready to provide special support for such innovations [p. 49]. 3. Develop specific programs that help the innovative Canadian supplier *expand* the department's or government's own base requirements to the larger similar needs of wider markets [p. 49, italics added]. 4. Train government officials to recognize innovative capacity and provide them with incentives to develop flexible procedures to facilitate positive interaction with the private sector" (p. 49). The reader will recognize the vagueness of the proposals as well as the familiar "pick the winners" strategy. The recommendation assumes that there is a theory or set of rules by which one can recognize "innovative capacity" (note: According to the Council not only must innovations be identified but also the capacity for making them!). It also presumes government officials can undertake the task. But who can teach the government officials to pick winners? These points are made in Brenner and Courville (1986). Britton and Gilmour (1978) also attribute the lack of innovations to foreign ownership and the phenomenon of "truncation," never raising the question as to how that can prevent Canadians from being entrepreneurial and innovative. Also, they may not have been aware of the fact that at least in England the relationship between foreign ownership and performance was positive. Wiener (1981), summarizing the evidence, notes that even before World War I, much of the output of the rapidly growing new industries was produced by American firms operating in Britain. Two of the four largest electrical machinery producers, British Westinghouse and British Thomson-Houston were American owned, while a third, Siemens, was German owned (the remaining one, GEC, was controlled and managed by a German immigrant). By the end of the 1950s, "the most efficient firms in Britain were predominantly enterprises that have been started by immigrants as early as 1940, were controlled by minorities (Quakers or Jews, chiefly), or were branches of international corporations" (p. 203). In the fifties and sixties American firms operating in Britain consistently earned higher rates of return on capital than their British competitors, their success being "roughly proportioned to the degree of U.S. control. . . . By the close of the seventies, a similar comparison could be made with German and Japanese subsidiaries" (pp. 203–4). As one can infer, such performances are linked with entrepreneurship and features of society rather than ownership. According to Bergier (1973) this was also the case during the Industrial Revolution. Also see Thurow (1985).

23 One should not be surprised to find that whatever were the advocated principles, free trade never had a chance. Although the United States took the initiative organizing the General Agreement on Tariffs and Trade (GATT) and has been, since 1947, the focus of conferences aiming to reduce trade barriers, GATT is so riddled with exceptions and is so vague that it permits almost anything. According to Jackson (1969), from the beginning, the language in which the agreement was written was so obscure that nobody really understood it. Senator Eugene D. Millikin, at hearings of the Senate Committee on Finance in 1951 said that "anyone who reads the GATT is likely to have his sanity impaired," while Herbert Feis, an adviser to the State Department on the charter for the International Trade Organization said in an article in *International Organization* (Madison, February 1948) that "only the learned can communicate with it and then only in code." But Winthrop Brown, one of the draftsmen of GATT, when testifying at hearings of the Senate Committee on Finance in 1951 said: "I think your difficulty . . . is the inherent complexity of the subject. . . . I must admit I am thoroughly confused." No wonder: Since nobody knows, for example, what is an "export subsidy." When Japan won the bid to build an additional bridge over the Bosphorus, it called its subsidy "foreign aid" [see Ingrassia (1985)]. The U.S. Commerce Department helps run trade fairs abroad [see Clarck (1984)]. The United States also invented another loophole in GATT: Persuading trade partners to use "voluntary quotas" (and using such persuasions for the steel and auto industries). Nobody should be too pontifical about free trade.

24 This conclusion implies not only a movement toward freer trade but also abolishing subsidies, some regulations or, in general, protective measures of any kind, of any sector or bureaucracy. In Chapter 6, privatization was recommended in these circumstances. In recent years New Zealand has done just that. Why? A number of people in New Zealand's planning council noted that although in the mid 1950s New Zealand had the third highest per capita gross domestic product, following the United States and Canada, by 1978 its position had slipped to twenty-second – and it is the labor government who is dismantling the subsidies and regulations rather than the conservatives. See Shaw and Stroup (1985).

25 As already emphasized in previous chapters, how one motivates subordinates in an enterprise is, in part, culturally determined. How culture and motivations are linked in Japan see Buruma (1984), Kanata (1983), studies edited by Thurow (1985), Takashi's in particular, Chira (1985), Bennett (1986).

26 Also see Nelson (1984) and North (1981).

27 See Teitelbaum (1985).

28 See Brenner (1985), McNeill (1982), and Johnson (1983) on linking differential population growth with the rise of destructive outbursts (in Algeria, for example) and Brenner and Deutsch (1986) for examining similar relationships elsewhere.

References

Chapter 1

Alchian, Armen A., and Harold Demsetz, "Production, Information Costs and Economic Organization," *American Economic Review,* 62/5 (December, 1972): 177–95.

Arrow, Kenneth J., *Essays in the Theory of Risk-Bearing,* Amsterdam: North-Holland, 1970.

Barnett, H. G., *Innovation: the Basis of Cultural Change,* New York: McGraw-Hill, 1953.

Baumol, William J., "Entrepreneurship in Economic Theory," *American Economic Review,* Papers and Proceedings, 59 (1968): 64–71.

Becker, Gary S., *The Economics of Discrimination,* Chicago: University of Chicago Press, 1959.

Becker, Gary S., *Economic Theory,* New York: Knopf, 1971.

Bennett, Amanda, "GM's Smith Wants Leaner Firm, More Rivalry Among Its Divisions," *Wall Street Journal,* May 21, 1981, pp. 29–30.

Blair, Roger, and David L. Kaserman, "Uncertainty and the Incentive for Vertical Integration," *Southern Economic Journal,* (July 1978): 266–72.

Boyer, Kenneth D., "Industry Boundaries" in Calvani, T., and J. Siegfried (eds.), *Economic Analysis and Antitrust Law,* Boston: Little, Brown, 1979, pp. 88–106.

Brenner, Reuven, *History – The Human Gamble,* Chicago: University of Chicago Press, 1983.

  Betting on Ideas: Wars, Invention, Inflation, Chicago: University of Chicago Press, 1985.

Brenner, Reuven, and Robert Lacroix, "The Workplace: Compensations, Efforts and Hierarchies," working papers no. 2586, Centre de Recherche et Développement en Economique (C.R.D.E.), 1986.

Bronfenbrenner, Martin, "A Reformulation of Naïve Profit Theory," *Southern Economic Journal,* in W. Breito, and H. M. Hochman (eds.), *Readings in Microeconomics,* Hinsdale: Dryden Press, 1971, pp. 411–22.

Brozen, Yale, "The Significance of Profit Data for Antitrust Policy," in Y. F. Weston and S. Peltzman (eds.), *Public Policy toward Mergers,* Pacific Palisades: Goodyear, 1969, pp. 110–27.

Buchanan, James, *What Should Economists Do?* Indianapolis: Liberty Press, 1979.

Calvo, Guillernmo A., and Stanislaw Wellisz, "Supervision Loss of Control, and the Optimum Size of the Firm," *Journal of Political Economy,* 86/5 (1978): 943–52.

Casson, Mark, *The Entrepreneur,* Totowa, N.J.: Barnes & Noble, 1982.

Chamberlin, Edward H., *The Theory of Monopolistic Competition,* Cambridge: Harvard University Press, 1933.

Cieply, Michael, "Disney Yields to Pressure from Holders, Names Gisner, Wells to Head Company," *Wall Street Journal,* Sept. 24, 1984, p. 2.

Clifford, Donald K., Jr., and Richard E. Cavanagh, *The Winning Performance: How America's High-Growth Midsize Companies Succeed,* New York: Bantam Books, 1985.

Coase, Ronald H., "The Nature of the Firm," *Economica,* 4 (1937): 386–405.

"The Market for Goods and the Market for Ideas," *American Economic Review,* 64 (1974): 384–91.

Crain, W. M., Thomas Deaton, and Robert Tollison, "On the Survival of Corporate Executives," *Southern Economic Journal,* 43 (January 1977): 1372–75.

Cyert, R. M., and J. G. March, "Organizational Structure and Pricing Behavior in an Oligopolistic Market," *American Economic Review,* 45 (1955): 129–39.

"Organizational Factors in the Theory of Oligopoly," *Quarterly Journal of Economics,* 70 (1956): 44–64.

A Behavioral Theory of the Firm, Englewood Cliffs, N.J.: Prentice-Hall, 1963.

Demsetz, Harold, "Industry Structure, Market Rivalry, and Public Policy," *Journal of Law and Economics,* 16 (April, 1973): 1–10.

Drucker, Peter F., "Reform Executive Pay or Congress Will," *Wall Street Journal,* April 24, 1984.

Eckstein, Otto, *The Great Recession,* New York: North-Holland, 1978.

Eliasson, Gunnar, "Micro Heterogeneity of Firms and the Stability of Industrial Growth," *Journal of Economic Behaviour and Organization,* 5/3–4 (1984): 249–74.

Evans, Heberton G., "Business Entrepreneurs, Their Major Functions and Related Tenets," *Journal of Economic History,* 19 (June, 1959): 250–70.

Fama, Eugene F., "Agency Problems in the Theory of the Firm," *Journal of Political Economy,* 88/2 (April, 1980): 288–308.

Festinger, Léon, "Theory of Social Comparisons Processes," *Human Relations,* 7 (1954): 117–40.

Fisher, Malcolm R., "The Entrepreneur, the Economist and Public Policy," Working Paper No. 81-013, The University of New South Wales, Australian Graduate School of Management, December, 1981.

Ford, Henry, *My Life and Work,* New York: Doubleday, Page, 1923.

Freedman, Jonathan, *Happy People: What Happiness Is, Who Has It and Why,* New York: Harcourt Brace Jovanovich, 1978.

Friedman, Milton, "Comment" in *Business Concentration and Price Policy,* NBER, Princeton: Princeton University Press, 1955, pp. 230–38.

Price Theory, 1962, Chicago: Aldine, 1975.

Friedman, Murray M., *The Research and Development Factor in Mergers and Acquisitions,* Study no. 16, U.S. Congress, Senate Committee on the Judiciary, Subcommittee on Patents, Trademarks and Copyrights, 85th Cong., 2nd sess., 1958.

Gates, Bruce, "Clay Model Set Ford on Road to Profits," *Financial Post,* February 15, 1986.

Guiles, Melinda G., "GM's Smith Presses for Sweeping Changes But Questions Arise," *Wall Street Journal,* March 14, 1985.

Hannah, Leslie, "Entrepreneurs and the Social Sciences," *Economica,* 51 (1984): 219–34.

"The Entrepreneur in History," in *The Prime Mover of Progress,* London: Institute of Economic Affairs, 1980, pp. 31–41.

Heertje, Arnold, *Economics and Technical Change,* London: Weidenfeld and Nicholson, 1977.

Hughes, Jonathan, *The Vital Few,* 1965, Oxford: Oxford University Press, 1973.

Jewkes, John, David Sawers, and Richard Stillerman, *The Sources of Inventions,* New York: Macmillan, 1958.

Johnson, Robert, "Big Executive Bonuses Now Come with a Catch: Lots of Criticism," *Wall Street Journal,* May 15, 1985.

Jones, Stephen, R. G., "An Economic Model of Conformist Behavior," Discussion Paper No. 83-15, Department of Economics, University of British Columbia, May, 1983a.

"Tradition: An Economic Analysis," Discussion Paper No. 83-16, Department of Economics, University of British Columbia, May, 1983b.

Kahneman, David, and Amos Tversky, "Prospect Theory: An Analysis of Decision Under Risk," *Econometrica,* 47/2 (March, 1979): 263–91.

Keynes, John M., *Treatise on Probability,* London: Macmillan, 1921.

The General Theory of Employment Interest and Money, 1936, London: Macmillan, 1970.

Kirzner, Israel M., *Competition and Entrepreneurship,* Chicago: University of Chicago Press, 1973.

Perception, Opportunity and Profit, Chicago: University of Chicago Press, 1983.

Kissinger, Henry, *Years of Upheaval,* Boston: Little, Brown, 1982.

Kleinfeld, N. R., "The Chief Executive Under Stress," *New York Times,* November 7, 1982.

Knight, Frank H., *Risk, Uncertainty and Profits,* 1921, Chicago: University of Chicago Press, 1971.

Landro, Laura, "Merger of Warner Unit, Polygram Angers Troubled Record Industry," *Wall Street Journal,* April 12, 1984.

Leibenstein, Harvey, *General X-Efficiency and Economic Development,* Oxford: Oxford University Press, 1978.

Levitt, Theodore, "Marketing Myopia," *Harvard Business Review,* (July–August, 1960): 45–56.

The Marketing Imagination, New York: The Free Press, 1983.

Loasby, Brian J., *Choice, Complexity and Ignorance,* Cambridge: Cambridge University Press, 1976.

Lynch, Harry H., *Financial Performance of Conglomerates,* Boston: Harvard Business School, 1971.

Machlup, Fritz, "Marginal Analysis and Empirical Research," *American Economic Review,* 36 (September, 1946): 519–54.

Mackaay, Ejan, *Economics of Information and Law*, Boston: Kluger–Nijhoff, 1982.

Main, Jeremy, "Help and Hype in the New-Products Game," *Fortune*, February 7, 1983.

Mandeville, Bernard, *The Fable of the Bees*, New York: Capricorn Books, 1962.

Marris, Robin, *The Economic Theory of 'Managerial' Capitalism*, New York: Free Press, 1964.

Marshall, Alfred, *Principles of Economics*, London: Macmillan, 1920.

McCaskey, Michael B., *The Executive Challenge*, Marshfield: Pitman Publishing, 1982.

McGuire, Joseph W., *Theories of Business Behavior*, Englewood Cliffs, N.J.: Prentice-Hall, 1964.

Monsen, R. J. and Anthony Downs, "A Theory of Large Managerial Firms," *Journal of Political Economy*, 73/3 (1965): 221–36.

Mueller, Dennis C., "Information, Mobility and Profit," *Kyklos*, 29/3 (1976): 419–48.

"The Persistence of Profits Above the Norm," *Economica*, 44/176 (November, 1977): 369–80.

Needham, Douglass, "Substitutability Criteria for Market Definition" in Calvani, T., and J. Siegfried (eds.) *Economic Analysis and Antitrust Law*, Boston: Little, Brown, 1979, pp. 78–83.

Nelson, Richard R., and Sidney G. Winter, *An Evolutionary Theory of Economic Change*, Cambridge, Mass.: Harvard University Press, 1982.

Pagels, Heinz, *Perfect Symmetry*, New York: Simon and Schuster, 1985.

Peltzman, Sam, "The Gains and Losses from Industrial Concentration," *Journal of Law and Economics*, 20 (October, 1977): 229–63.

Peters, Thomas J., and Nancy Austin, *A Passion for Excellence*, New York: Random House, 1985.

Peters, Thomas J., and Robert H. Waterman, Jr., *In Search of Excellence*, New York: Harper & Row, 1982.

Posner, Richard A., *Antitrust Law*, Chicago: University of Chicago Press, 1976.

Rapoport, Anatol, "Introduction" in Carl von Clausewitz, *On War*, Edited by A. Rapoport, London: Penguin, 1982, pp. 11–83.

Reich, Gary, "The Innovator," *New York Times Magazine*, April 21, 1985.

Robinson, Joan, *The Economics of Imperfect Competition*, London: Macmillan, 1933.

Samuelson, Robert J., "The Great Postwar Prosperity," *Newsweek*, May 20, 1985.

Schackle, G. L. S., *Epistemics and Economics*, Cambridge: Cambridge University Press, 1972.

Scherer, F. M., *Industrial Market Structure and Economic Performance*, Chicago: Rand McNally, 1980.

Schoeck, Helmut, *Envy*, New York: Harcourt, Brace & World, 1969.

Schumpeter, Joseph A., *Imperialism and Social Classes*, 1919, 1927, Paul Sweezy (ed.), New York: Augustus M. Kelly, 1951.

"The Theory of the Business Cycle," *Economica*, 7 (December, 1927): 286–311.

Silver, Morris, *Enterprise and the Scope of the Firm*, Oxford: Martin Robertson, 1984.

Simon, Herbert A., *Administrative Behaviour*, New York: Macmilllan, 1957.

"Theories of Decision-Making in Economics and Behavioral Science," 1959, in E. Mansfield (ed.), *Microeconomics Selected Readings*, New York: Norton, 1971: pp. 85–98.

Smith, Adam, *The Wealth of Nations*, New York: Modern Library, 1937.

Smith, Caleb A., "Survey of the Empirical Evidence on Economies of Scale," in *Business Concentration and Price Policy*, NBER, Princeton: Princeton University Press, 1955, pp. 215–30.

Solman, Paul, and Thomas Friedman, *Life and Death on the Corporate Battlefield*, New York: Simon and Schuster, 1982.

Spengler, Joseph J., "Hierarchy vs. Equality: Persisting Conflict," *Kyklos,* 21·(1968): 217–38.

Springborg, Patricia, *The Problem of Human Needs and the Critique of Civilisation*, London: George Allen and Unwin, 1981.

Stevenson, H. H., and D. E. Gumpert, "The Heart of Entrepreneurship," *Harvard Business Review* 63 (March–April, 1985): 85–95.

Stigler, George J., "Monopolistic Competition in Retrospect," in *The Organization of Industry*, Homewood, Ill.: Richard D. Irwin, 1968: 309–21.

Stocking, George W., and Myron W. Watkins, *Cartels or Competition*, New York: The Twentieth Century Fund, 1948.

Susman, Waren I., *Culture as History: The Transformation of American Society in the Twentieth Century*, New York: Pantheon Books, 1984.

Sylos-Labini, Paolo, *The Forces of Economic Growth*, Cambridge, Mass.: MIT Press, 1984.

Wickenden, Keith, "Idea into Action – An Unsolved Problem," in *The Prime Mover of Progress*, London: Institute of Economic Affairs, 1980, pp. 68–73.

Williamson, Oliver E., *The Economics of Discretionary Behavior: Managerial Objectives in a Theory of the Firm*, Englewood Cliffs, N.J.: Prentice-Hall, 1964.

"Hierarchical Control and Optimum Firm Size," *Journal of Political Economy*, 75/2 (April 1967): 123–38.

Zaleznik, Abraham, and Manfred F. R. Kets de Vries, *Power and the Corporate Mind*, Boston: Houghton Mifflin, 1975.

Chapter 2

Alter, Jonathan, "Calvin and the Family Firm," *Newsweek,* December 12, 1983.

Anders, George, "German Bosses Stress Consensus Decisions, Technical Know-How," *Wall Street Journal,* September 25, 1984.

Arieti, Silvano, *Creativity: The Magic Synthesis*, New York: Basic Books, 1976.

Aristotle, *The Politics.* New York: Penguin Books, 1980.

Asch, Peter, and J. J. Seneca, "Is Collusion Profitable?" *Review of Economics and Statistics,* 58/1 (February, 1976): 1–12.

Backman, Jules (ed.), *Entrepreneurship and the Outlook for America.* New York: The Free Press, 1983.

Barmash, Isadore, "The Acquisition Kings of Women's Apparel," *New York Times,* March 31, 1985.

Barnett, H. G., *Innovation: The Basis of Cultural Change*, New York, McGraw-Hill, 1953.

Barzel, Yoram, "Optimal Timing of Innovations," *Review of Economics and Statistics*, 50 (August, 1968): 348–55.

Berkowitz, Peggy, "Stalking Bell-Northern Telecom Set to Battle AT&T Unit in Phone-Gear Market," *Wall Street Journal*, December 29, 1983.

Berna, James J., *Industrial Entrepreneurship in Madras State*, New York: Asia Publishing House, 1960.

Bleakley, Fred R., "Picking Losers Who Come Out on Top," *New York Times*, May 6, 1984.

Braithwaite, John, *Inequality, Crime and Public Policy*, London: Routledge and Kegan Paul, 1979.

Brenner, Gabrielle A., "Why Did Inheritance Laws Change?" *International Journal of Law and Economics*, 5 (June, 1985): 91–106.

Brenner, Reuven, *History – The Human Gamble*, Chicago: University of Chicago Press, 1983.

  Betting on Ideas: Wars, Invention, Inflation, Chicago: University of Chicago Press, 1985.

Brown, William H., "Innovation in the Machine Tool Industry," *Quarterly Journal of Economics*, 71 (August, 1957): 406–25.

Carr-Hill, R.A., and N.H. Stern, *Crime, the Police and Criminal Statistics*, New York: Academic Press, 1979.

Carr-Saunders, A.M., H. Mannheim, and E.G. Rhodes, *Young Offenders*, London: Cambridge University Press, 1942.

Chapman, S.J., and F.J. Marquis, "The Recruiting of the Employing Classes from the Ranks of the Wage-Earners in the Cotton Industry," *Journal of the Royal Statistical Society*, 75 (February, 1912): 293–313.

Chiswick, Barry R., "The Effects of Americanization on the Earnings of Foreign Born Men," *Journal of Political Economy*, (1978) Vol. 8: 897–923.

Christopher, Robert C., *The Japanese Mind: The Goliath Explained*, New York: Linden Press/Simon and Schuster, 1983.

Collins, Orvis F., David G. Moore, and Darab B. Unwalla, *The Enterprising Man*, East Lansing: Michigan State University, Bureau of Business and Economic Research, 1964.

Cox, Meg, "To Sotheby's Boss, Selling Art is Much Like Selling Root Beer," *Wall Street Journal*, September 18, 1985.

Cyert, R.M., and J.G. March, "Organizational Structure and Pricing Behavior in an Oligopolistic Market," *American Economic Review*, 45 (1955): 129–39.

  "Organizational Factors in the Theory of Oligopoly," *Quarterly Journal of Economics*, 70 (1956): 44–64.

Dahmèn, Erik, *Entrepreneurial Activity and the Development of Swedish Industry 1919–1939*. Homewood: Irwin, 1970.

Dalton, Hugh, *Some Aspects of the Inequality of Income in Modern Communities*, 2nd ed., London: Routledge and Kegan Paul, 1925.

Dewey, Donald, "Information, Entry and Welfare: The Case for Collusion," *American Economic Review*, 69/4 (September, 1979): 587–94.

Evans, Heberton G., "Business Entrepreneurs, Their Major Functions and Related Tenets," *Journal of Economic History,* 19 (June, 1959): 250–70.

Fethke, Gary C., and John J. Birch, "Rivalry and the Timing of Innovations," *Bell Journal of Economics* 13 (Spring, 1982): 272–9.

Gigot, Paul A., "The Smallest Nation Has a Rare Problem: Too Much Wealth," *Wall Street Journal,* September 29, 1983.

Gilder, George, *Wealth and Poverty,* New York: Basic Books, 1981.

Glueck, E. T., and S. Glueck, *Unravelling Juvenile Delinquency,* New York: Harper & Row, 1950.

Gottschalk, Earl C., "Promotions Grow Few as 'Baby Boom' Group Eyes Managers' Jobs," *Wall Street Journal,* October 22, 1981.

"More Women Start Up Their Own Business with Major Success," *Wall Street Journal,* May 17, 1983.

Grabowski, Henry G., and Dennis C. Mueller, "Life-Cycle Effects on Corporate Returns on Retentions," *Review of Economics and Statistics,* 57 (November, 1975): 400–16.

Graham, Ellen, "The Entrepreneurial Mystique," *Wall Street Journal.* A Special Report, May 20, 1985.

Hannah, Leslie, "The Entrepreneur in History," in *The Prime Mover of Progress,* London: Institute of Economic Affairs, 1980, pp. 31–41.

"Entrepreneurs and the Social Sciences," *Economica,* 51 (1984): 219–34.

Hoselitz, Bert, "Entrepreneurship and Traditional Elites," *Explorations in Entrepreneurial History,* 2nd series Vol. 1 (1963): 36–49.

Hughes, Jonathan, *The Vital Few,* 1965, London: Oxford University Press, 1973.

Hume, Ellen, "Indochinese Refugees Adapt Quickly in U.S. Using Survival Skills," *Wall Street Journal,* March 21, 1985.

Kamin, Jacob Y., and Joshua Ronen, "The Effects of Corporate Control on Apparent Profit Performance," *Southern Economic Journal,* 45/1 (July, 1978): 181–91.

Klein, Burton H., *Dynamic Economics.* Cambridge: Harvard University Press, 1977.

Kleinfield, N.R., "The Chief Executive Under Stress," *New York Times,* November 7, 1982.

Landes, David S. "French Entrepreneurship and Industrial Growth in the Nineteenth Century," *Journal of Economic History,* 9 (1949): 45–61.

"Statistical Study of French Crises," *Journal of Economic History,* 10/1 (May, 1950): 195–212.

Lardner, James, "A Producer-Director-Actor-Memoirist," *New York Times Book Review,* September 11, 1983, p. 11.

Larson, Erik, "In High-Tech Industry, New Firms Often Get Fast Trip to Courtroom," *Wall Street Journal,* August 14, 1984.

Levinson, Harry, *Executive Stress.* New York: Harper & Row, 1970.

Levitt, Jr., Arthur, and Jack Albertine, "The Successful Entrepreneur: A Personality Profile," *Wall Street Journal,* August 29, 1983.

Lindsey, Robert, "Some Losers in Silicon Valley Said to Find Wealth in Spying," *New York Times,* October 23, 1983.

MacFarlane, Alan, *The Origins of English Individualism,* Oxford: Basil Blackwell, 1978.

Mack, Ruth P., *The Flow of Business Funds and Consumer Purchasing Power*. New York: Columbia University Press, 1941.

Malcolm, Andrew H., *The Canadians*, New York: New York Times Books, 1985.

Marshall, Alfred, *Industry and Trade*, London: Macmillan, 1932.

McGrath, E., "Confucian Work Ethic," *Time*, March 28, 1983, p. 64.

Mensch, Gerhard, *Stalemate in Technology*, Cambridge: Ballinger, 1979.

Miller, William, "American Historians and the Business Elite," *Journal of Economic History*, 9 (May, 1949): 184–208.

Mills, C. Wright, "The American Business Elite: A Collective Portrait," *Journal of Economic History*, 5 (1945): Supplement: 20–44.

Palmer, John, "Some Economic Conditions Conducive to Collusion," *Journal of Economic Issues*, 6 (June, 1972): 29–38.

Quinn, James B., "Technological Innovation, Entrepreneurship, and Strategy," *Sloan Management Review*, 20 (Spring 1979): 19–30.

Reader, W.J. *ICI: A History*, 2 vols., Oxford: Oxford University Press, 1970, 1975.

Roberts, Edward B., "Entrepreneurship and Technology: A Basic Study of Innovators; How to Keep and Capitalize on Their Talents," *Research Management*, 11/4 (July, 1968): 244–66.

Ronen, Joshua (ed.), *Entrepreneurship*, Lexington: Lexington Books, 1983.

Rubinstein, W.D., *Men of Property*, New Brunswick: Rutgers University Press, 1981.

"Sir John Ellerman" in D.J. Jeremy (ed.), *Dictionary of Business Biography*, Vol. 2, London: Butterworths, 1984.

Sarachek, Bernard, "American Entrepreneurs and the Horatio Alger Myth," *Journal of Economic History*, 38 (1978): 439–56.

Schiff, M., and A.Y. Lewin, "Where Traditional Budgeting Fails," *Financial Executive*, 36 (May, 1968): 57–62.

Schisgall, Oscar, *Eyes on Tomorrow: The Evolution of Procter & Gamble*, Chicago: J.G. Ferguson/Doubleday, 1981.

Schumpeter, Joseph A., *Imperialism and Social Classes*, 1919, 1927. Edited by Paul M. Sweezy, New York: Augustus M. Kelley, 1951.

Shapero, Albert, "The Displaced Uncomfortable Entrepreneur," *Psychology Today*, 11 (November, 1975): 83–8, 133.

Sharkanski, I., "Government Corporations as a Tool for Economic Development – Possibilities and Problems," *Organization and Management* (in Hebrew) (June 1975).

Silver, A. David, *The Entrepreneurial Life*, New York: Wiley, 1983.

Smith, Adam, "The History of Astronomy," in *Essays on Philosophical Subjects*, Indianapolis: Liberty Classics, 1980, pp. 33–106.

Smith, Randall, "Real-Estate Superstar Wields Many Weapons and Is Fast on His Feet," *Wall Street Journal*, August 29, 1983.

Solman, Paul, and Thomas Friedman, *Life and Death on the Corporate Battlefield*, New York: Simon and Schuster, 1982.

Stamp, Sir Josiah, "Inheritance as an Economic Factor," *Economic Journal*, 36 (September, 1926): 339–74, 1926a.

"Note on 'Inheritance as an Economic Factor'," *Economic Journal*, 36 (December, 1926): 687, 1926b.

Stocking, George W., and Myron W. Watkins, *Cartels or Competition?* New York: Twentieth Century Fund, 1948.

Taussig, F.W., and C.S. Joslyn, *American Business Leaders,* New York: Macmillan, 1932.

Taylor, Alexander L., "Making a Mint Overnight," *Time,* January 23, 1984.

Tocqueville, Alexis de, *L'Ancien Régime,* M.W. Patterson (trans.), Oxford: Oxford University Press, 1956.

Toulouse, Jean-Marie, and Noël Bélanger, "L'entrepreneur: une ressource particulière," mimeographed, Ecole des Hautes Etudes Commerciales, November 1983.

Walker, N.D., *Crime and Punishment in Britain,* Edinburgh: Edinburgh University Press, 1965.

Wickenden, Keith, "Idea into Action – An Unsolved Problem," in *The Prime Mover of Progress,* London: Institute of Economic Affairs, 1980, pp. 68–73.

Wiener, Martin J., *English Culture and the Decline of the Industrial Spirit 1850– 1980,* Cambridge: Cambridge University Press, 1981.

Wohl, R. Richard, "The 'Rags to Riches Story': An Episode of Secular Idealism," in Reinhard Bendix and Seymour Martin Lipset (eds.), *Class, Status and Power,* New York: Free Press, 1953, pp. 388–95.

Chapter 3

ABA, *Antitrust Section, Monograph no 1, Mergers and the Private Antitrust Suit: The Private Enforcement of Section VII of the Clayton Act and Law,* Chicago: American Bar Association, 1977.

Antitrust Law Development, Third Supplement, Chicago: American Bar Association, 1974–80.

Antitrust Section, Antitrust Law Developments, 2nd ed. Chicago: American Bar Association, 1984.

Areeda, Phillip, and Donald F. Turner, "Predatory Pricing and Related Practices Under Section 2 of the Sherman Act," *Harvard Law Review,* 88 (1975): 697–733.

Armentano, Dominick T., *Antitrust and Monopoly. Anatomy of a Policy Failure,* New York: Wiley, 1982.

Ayres. C.E., *The Theory of Economic Progress,* Chapel Hill: University of North Carolina Press, 1944.

Bartkus, Robert E., "Innovation Competition: Beyond Telex vs. IBM," *Stanford Law Review,* 28 (January, 1976): 285–331.

Baumol, William J., and Janusz A. Ordover, "Use of Antitrust to Subvert Competition," *Journal of Law and Economics,* 28/2 (May, 1985): 247–65.

Becker, Gary S., *The Economic Approach to Human Behavior,* Chicago: University of Chicago Press, 1976.

Bork, Robert H., *The Antitrust Paradox: A Policy at War with Itself,* New York: Basic Books, 1978.

Brenner, Gabrielle A., and Reuven Brenner, "Innovations and the Competition Act," in W. Block (ed.), *Reaction: the New Combines Investigation Act,* Vancouver: Fraser Institute, 1986, pp. 117–40.

Brenner, Reuven, *History – The Human Gamble,* Chicago: University of Chicago Press, 1983.

Betting on Ideas: Wars, Invention, Inflation, Chicago: University of Chicago Press, 1985.

Brenner, Reuven, and Léon Courville, *Gasoline Marketing,* Toronto: Shell Canada Ltd., 1982.

Bridenbaugh, Carl, *Vexed and Troubled Englishmen 1590–1642,* New York: Oxford University Press, 1968.

Calvani, Terry, "The Mushrooming Brunswick Defense: Injury to Competition, Not to Plaintiff," *Antitrust Law Journal,* 50/2 (1981): 319–45.

Carlton, Dennis, "Market Behavior with Demand Uncertainty and Price Inflexibility," *American Economic Review,* 68 (September, 1978): 571–87.

"The Rigidity of Prices," Working Paper, Graduate School of Business, University of Chicago, November 1984.

Choffray, Jean-Marie, and Gary L. Lilien, *Market Planning for New Industrial Product,* New York: Wiley, 1980.

Clearwaters, Keith I., quoted in "Innovations, Competition and Antitrust Laws," *Research Management,* 21/3 (May, 1978): 4.

Coase, Ronald H., "The Nature of the Firm," *Economica,* new series, 4 (1937): 386–405.

Davis, Bob, "Divining Defense Plans Is Art for Military Electronics Firms," *Wall Street Journal,* September 20, 1984, p. 33.

Dean, Joel, "Competition as Seen by the Businessman and by the Economist," in Harvey W. Huegy (ed.), *The Role and Nature of Competition in Our Marketing Economy,* Bureau of Economic and Business Research, University of Illinois, 1954, pp. 8–15.

Demsetz, Harold, "Industry Structure, Market Rivalry and Public Policy," *Journal of Law and Economics,* 16 (April, 1973): 1–9.

Erickson, Myron L., *Antitrust and Trade Regulations: Cases and Materials,* Columbus: Grid, 1977.

Evans, Heberton G., "Business Entrepreneurs, Their Major Functions and Related Tenets," *Journal of Economic History,* 19 (June, 1959): 250–70.

Fisher, Franklin M., "Diagnosing Monopoly," *Quarterly Review of Economics and Business,* 19/2 (Summer, 1979): 7–33.

Fisher, Franklin M., John J. McGowan, and Joen E. Greenwood, *Folded, Spindled, and Mutilated: Economic Analysis and U.S. vs. IBM,* Cambridge: MIT Press, 1983.

Freeman, Christopher, *The Economics of Industrial Innovation,* Cambridge, Mass.: MIT Press, 1983.

Gee, Edwin A., and C. Tyler, *Managing Innovation,* New York: Wiley, 1976.

Goldschmid, Harvey J., H. Michael Mann, and J. Fred Weston, *Industrial Concentration: The New Learning,* Boston: Little, Brown, 1974.

Guyon, Janet, "The Public Doesn't Get a Better Potato Chip Without a Bit of Pain," *Wall Street Journal,* March 25, 1983, p. 1.

Hammond, D.L., "R&D in the Electronics Industry," in W.N. Smith et al. (eds.), *Industrial R&D Management,* New York: Marcel-Dekker, 1982.

Hart, P.E., "The Size and Growth of Firms," *Economica,* new series, 24 (1962): 29–39.

Hayek, F.A., "The Meaning of Competition," in *Individualism and Economic Order,* Chicago: Henry Regnery, 1972, pp. 92–106.

Hibner, Don T., Jr., "Litigation as an Overt Act – Development and Prognosis," *Antitrust Law Journal,* 46/3 (1977): 718–29.

Ijiri, Yuji, and Herbert A. Simon, "Business Firm Growth and Size," *American Economic Review,* 54 (March, 1964): 77–89.

Jentes, William R., "Assessing Recent Efforts to Challenge Aggressive Competition as an 'Attempt to Monopolize'," *Antitrust Law Journal,* 49/3 (1980): 937–52.

Johnson, James C., "How Competitive Is Delivered Pricing?" *Journal of Purchasing and Materials Management,* 12 (Summer, 1976): 26–30.

Landro, Laura, "Technology, Competition Cut Price of Electronics Gear as Quality Rises," *Wall Street Journal,* December 1, 1981, p. 37.

Lefebvre, Georges, *The Great Fear of 1789,* Princeton: Princeton University Press, 1973.

Loasby, Brian J., *Choice, Complexity and Ignorance,* Cambridge: Cambridge University Press, 1976.

Markham, Jesse W., "The Nature and Significance of Price Leadership," *American Economic Review,* 41 (December, 1951): 891–905.

McEntee, Joseph L., and Robert C. Kahrl, "Damages Caused by the Acquisition and Use of Monopoly Power," *Antitrust Law Journal,* 49/1 (1980): 165–200.

McMurray, Scott, "Salomon's Innovative, Risky Style Creates Profits and Some Problems," *Wall Street Journal,* September 17, 1984, p. 31.

Merger Case Digest, Section of Antitrust Law, American Bar Association, Chicago, Ill., 1982.

Nisbet, Robert, *Prejudices,* Cambridge, Mass.: Harvard University Press, 1982.

Ordover, Janusz A., and Robert D. Willig, "An Economic Definition of Predation: Pricing and Product Innovation," *Yale Law Journal,* 91/8 (1981): 8–53.

Pearson, John W., "Organizing the R&D/Manufacturing/Marketing Interface in a Large Diverse Product Line Company," in W.N. Smith et al. (eds.), *Industrial R&D Management,* New York: Marcel-Dekker, 1982.

Ploufe, Alain, "Le recours aux lois antimonopoles afin d'éliminer la compétition," Rapport de recherche présentée à la Faculté des Etudes supérieures, Université de Montréal, décembre, 1985.

Posner, Richard A., *Antitrust Law,* Chicago: University of Chicago Press, 1976.

Robinson, E.A.G., "The Problems of Management and the Size of Firms," *Economic Journal,* 44 (1934): 240–54.

Rudé, George, *The Crowd in History 1730–1848,* 1964, London: Lawrane and Wishart, 1981.

Scherer, F.N., *Industrial Market Structure and Economic Performance,* Chicago: Rand McNally, 1980.

Schumpeter, Joseph A., *Business Cycle,* 1939, New York: McGraw-Hill, 1964.
   Capitalism, Socialism and Democracy, 1942, New York: Harper Torch Books, 1962.

Schwartzman, David, "Competition and Efficiency, Comment," *Journal of Political Economy,* 81/3 (June, 1973): 756–65.

Simon, Herbert A., and Charles P. Bonini, "The Size Distribution of Business Firms," *American Economic Review,* 48 (September 1958): 607–17.

Skeoch, C.A. (ed.), *Canadian Competition Policy,* Kingston: Industrial Relations Center of Queen's University, 1972.

Solman, Paul, and Thomas Friedman, *Life and Death on the Corporate Battlefield,* New York: Simon and Schuster, 1982.

Stigler, George J., "Industrial Organization and Economic Progress," in Leonard R. White (ed.), *The State of the Social Sciences,* Chicago: University of Chicago Press, 1956, pp. 269–82.

"Perfect Competition, Historically Contemplated," *Journal of Political Economy,* 55/1 (February, 1957): 1–17.

"A Theory of Oligopoly," in *The Organization of Industry,* Homewood, Ill.: Richard D. Irwin, 1968a, pp. 39–63.

"The Kinky Oligopoly Demand Curve and Rigid Prices," in *The Organization of Industry,* Homewood, Ill.: Richard D. Irwin, 1968b, pp. 208–34.

Stocking, George W., and Myron W. Watkins, *Cartels or Competition?* New York: Twentieth Century Fund, 1948.

Utterback, James M., "The Process of Technical Innovation in Instrument Firms," Ph.D. dissertation, MIT, January 1969.

Vawter, Robert R., and Sharyn B. Zuch, "A Critical Analysis of Recent Federal Appellate Decisions on Predatory Pricing," *Antitrust Law Journal,* 51/3 (1982): 401–21.

Williamson, O.E., "Hierarchical Control and Optimum Firm Size," *Journal of Political Economy,* 75 (1967): 123–38.

Chapter 4

Abrams, Bill, "Practice of Naming New Products Upset by Ruling on Trademarks," *Wall Street Journal,* October 16, 1980.

"Wisconsin Entrepreneur Grandly Dreams about an Empire Built on Phone Numbers," *Wall Street Journal,* November 29, 1982.

"Some New Ads May Rekindle Burger Battle," *Wall Street Journal,* March 4, 1983.

Alsop, Ronald, "Jaded TV Viewers Tune out Glut of Celebrity Commercials," *Wall Street Journal,* February 7, 1985.

"When Is a TV Ad not an Ad? When It's Hyped as Event," *Wall Street Journal,* March 21, 1985.

"Liquor Ads Look less Macho as Female Drinking Increases," *Wall Street Journal,* June 6, 1985.

Armstrong, Gary, N. Gurol, and F.A. Russ, "Detecting and Correcting Deceptive Advertising," *Journal of Consumer Research,* 6 (December, 1979): 237–96.

Baumol, William J., and James A. Ordover, "Use of Antitrust to Subvert Competition," *Journal of Law and Economics,* 28/2 (May, 1985): 247–67.

Becker, Gary S., *Economic Theory,* New York: Knopf, 1971.

Benham, Lee, "The Effect of Advertising on the Price of Eyeglasses," *Journal of Law and Economics*, 15 (October, 1972): 337–52.

Brenner, Gabrielle A., and Reuven Brenner, "Memory and Markets, or Why are You Paying $2.99 for a Widget?" *Journal of Business*, 55/1 (1982): 151–8.

Brenner, Harvey M., *Mental Illness and the Economy*, Cambridge: Mass.: Harvard University Press, 1973.

Brenner, Reuven, *History – The Human Gamble*, Chicago: University of Chicago Press, 1983.

　Betting on Ideas: Wars, Invention, Inflation, Chicago: University of Chicago Press, 1985.

Brenner, Reuven, and Léon Courville, "Fraud among Buyers and Sellers: Legal and Market Remedies," Study prepared for Consumer and Corporate Affairs, Canada, 1983.

Brozen, Yale, "Entry Barriers: Advertising and Product Differentiation," in Goldschmid, Harvey J. et al. (eds.) *Industrial Concentration: The New Learning*, Boston: Little, Brown, 1974.

Clark, Kenneth, *Civilisation*, London: BBC and John Murray, 1969.

Clinard, Marshall B., and Peter C. Yeager, *Corporate Crime*, New York: The Free Press, 1980.

Comanor, William S., and Thomas A. Wilson, *Advertising and Market Power*, Cambridge: Harvard University Press, 1974.

　"Advertising and Competition: A Survey," *Journal of Economic Literature*, 17 (June, 1979): 453–76.

Dolan, Carrie, "Concocting Zingy New Names Starts Turning into a Business," *Wall Street Journal*, August 5, 1982.

Furth, Joseph, "Is F.T.C. Action in Listerine Case Legal?" *Advertising Age*, June 5, 1978.

Galbraith, John K., *The New Industrial State*, 2d ed., New York: Deutsch, 1972.

Gilligan, Colin, "How British Advertisers Set Budgets," *Journal of Advertising Research*, 17 (February, 1977): 47–9.

Glassman, M., and W.J. Pieper, "Processing Advertising Information: Deception, Salience, and Inferential Belief Formation," *Journal of Advertising*, 9, no. 1, 1980: 3–10.

Goldschmid, Harvey J., H. Michael Mann, and J. Fred Weston (eds.), *Concentration: The New Learning*, Boston: Little, Brown, 1974.

Hackett, Regina, "Too Kool," *Seattle Post-Intelligencer*, July 29, 1983.

Handler, Milton, "False and Misleading Advertising," *Yale Law Journal*, 39 (1929): 22–51.

Jaynes, Julian, *The Origins of Consciousness in the Breakdown of the Bicameral Mind*, Boston: Houghton Mifflin, 1976.

Katz, Elihu, and Paul F. Lazarsfeld, *Personal Influence*, New York: The Free Press, 1955.

Kneale, Dennis, "Advertisers Use Music Groups to Reach Young Consumers," *The Wall Street Journal*, July 28, 1983.

Lipman, Joanne, "As Network TV Fades, Many Advertisers Try Age-Old Promotions," *Wall Street Journal*, August 26, 1986.

Meyers, William, "Where Pizazz Pays Off," *New York Times*, December 5, 1982.

Nelson, Philip, "Advertising as Information," *Journal of Political Economy*, 82/4 (July/August, 1974): 729–54.

Newsweek, "Procter & Gamble's Old Devil Moon," May 6, 1985.

Pace, Eric, "There's a Song in Their Art," *New York Times*, May 2, 1982.

Posner, Richard A. "Regulation of Advertising by the F.T.C.," Washington: American Enterprise Institute, November (1973).

Prescott, Eileen, "Word-of-Mouth: Playing on the Prestige Factor," *Wall Street Journal*, February 7, 1984.

Saddler, Jeanne, "F.T.C. Easing Rules Requiring Firms Support Ad Claims," *Wall Street Journal*, July 21, 1983.

San Augustine, A.J., and W.F. Foley, "How Large Advertisers Set Budgets," *Journal of Advertising Research*, 15 (October, 1975): 11–16.

Scammon, Debra L., and Richard J. Semenik, "Corrective Advertising: Evolution of the Legal Theory and Application of the Remedy," *Journal of Advertising*, 11/2 (1982): 10–20.

Schelling, Thomas C., *The Strategy of Conflict*, Cambridge, Mass.: Harvard University Press, 1960.

Scherer, F.M., *Industrial Market Structure and Economic Performance*, 2nd ed., Chicago: Rand McNally, 1980.

Schmalensee, Richard, *The Economics of Advertising*, Amsterdam: North-Holland, 1972.

Schudson, Michael, *Advertising, the Uneasy Persuasion*, New York: Basic Books, 1984.

Sears Roebuck Catalog, Chicago: Sears, 1980.

Sears Roebuck Consumer Guide, 1900, Reprinted. Northfield, Ill.: BDI Books, 1970.

Simon, Julian, *Issues in the Economics of Advertising*, Urbana: University of Illinois Press, 1970.

Singer, M., and F. Ferreira, "Empirical Research on Misleading Advertising: A Review," Working Paper, University of Manitoba, 1982.

Solman, Paul, and Thomas Friedman, *Life and Death on the Corporate Battlefield*, New York: Simon and Schuster, 1982.

Steiner, Robert L., "Does Advertising Lower Consumer Prices?" *Journal of Marketing*, 37 (1973): 19–26.

Stigler, George, "The Economics of Information," in *The Organization of Industry*, Homewood, Ill.: Richard D. Irwin, 1968, pp. 171–90.

Taylor, Gordon R., *The Natural History of the Mind*, 1979, New York: Penguin, 1981.

Telser, Lester G., "Advertising and Competition," *Journal of Political Economy*, 72/6 (December, 1964): 537–62.

Totman, Richard, *Social Causes of Illness*, New York: Pantheon Books, 1979.

Chapter 5

Arrow, Kenneth J., "Economic Welfare and the Allocation of Resources for Inventions," in R.R. Nelson (ed.), *The Rate and Direction of Inventive Activity*, Princeton, N.J.: Princeton University Press, 1962: 609–26.

Asinof, Lynn, "Small Firms Turn to Big Business for Capital, Markets, Technical Aid," *The Wall Street Journal,* November 5, 1985, p. 33.

Barnett, H.G., *Innovation: The Basis of Cultural Change,* New York: McGraw-Hill, 1953.

Belshaw, Cyril S., "In Search of Wealth. A Study of the Emergence of Commercial Operations in the Melanesian Society of Southeastern Papua," *American Anthropologist Memoir,* 80 (February, 1955):

Ben-David, Joseph, "Organization, Social Control, and Cognitive Change in Science," in Y. Ben-David and T. Clark (eds.), *Culture and Its Creators: Essays in Honor of Edward Shils,* Chicago: University of Chicago Press, 1977, pp. 244–65.

Ben-Yehuda, Nachman, *Deviance and Moral Boundaries,* Chicago: University of Chicago Press, 1985.

Boorstin, Daniel J., *The Discoverers,* New York: Random House, 1983.

Brenner, Reuven, *History – The Human Gamble,* Chicago: University of Chicago Press, 1983.

    Betting on Ideas: Wars, Invention, Inflation, Chicago: University of Chicago Press, 1985.

Broad, William J., "Tracing the Skeins of Matter," *New York Times Magazine,* May 6, 1984.

Browning, E.S., "A Stroke of Luck Is Bad News in Japan If One Isn't Insured," *Wall Street Journal,* August 12, 1985.

Buzzel, Robert D., and Robert E.M. Nourse, *Product Innovation in Food Processing,* Boston: Harvard University, Division of Research, Graduate School of Business, 1967.

Carr, E.H., *What is History?* 1961, Middlesex: Penguin Books, 1982.

Choffray, Jean-Marie, and Guy L. Lilien, *Market Planning for New Industrial Products,* New York: Wiley, 1980.

Clark, Colin, *The Conditions of Economic Progress,* London: n.p., 1940.

Cohen, Bernard I., *Revolution in Science,* Cambridge, Mass.: Harvard University Press, 1985.

Comanor, W.S., "Research and Technical Change in the Pharmaceutical Industry," *Review of Economics and Statistics,* 47 (May, 1965): 182–91.

Cooper, A.C., and D. Schendel, "Strategic Responses to Technological Threats," in M.L. Tushman and W.L. Moore (eds.), *Readings in the Management of Innovations,* Boston: Pitman, 1982: 325–34.

Cooper, Robert G., "Most New Products *Do* Succeed," *Research Management,* 26/6 (November–December, 1983): 20–5.

Crozier, Michel, *La Société bloquée,* Paris: Seuil, 1970.

Dean, Robert C., Jr., "The Temporal Mismatch-Innovation's Pace vs. Management's Time Horizon," *Research Management,* 17/3 (May, 1976): 12–5.

Dobb, Maurice, *Political Economy and Capitalism,* London: n.p., 1937.

Fisher, Franklin M., John J. McGowan, and Joen E. Greenwood, *Folded, Spindled, and Mutilated: Economic Analysis and U.S. vs IBM,* Cambridge: MIT Press, 1983.

Frankel, E., "Corpuscular Optics and the Wave Theory of Light: the Science and

226   **References**

Politics of a Revolution in Physics,'' *Social Studies of Science,* 6 (1976): 141–84.

Franklin, Roger, *The Defender: the Story of General Dynamics,* New York: Harper & Row, 1986.

Freeman, Christopher, *The Economics of Industrial Innovation,* Cambridge, Mass.: MIT Press, 1983.

Gee, Edwin A., and Chaplin Tyler, *Managing Innovation,* New York: Wiley, 1976.

Gilfillan, S.C., *The Sociology of Invention,* Chicago: Follets, 1935.

Gleick, James, ''The Man Who Reshaped Geometry,'' *New York Times Magazine,* December 8, 1985.

Gluckman, Max, *Politics, Law and Ritual in Tribal Society,* New York: Mentor Books, 1965.

Goran, Morris, *Science and Anti-Science,* Ann Arbor: Ann Arbor Science Publishers, 1974.

Gould, Stephen J., ''Triumph of a Naturalist: Review of E.F. Keller's *A Feeling for the Organism,*'' *New York Review of Books,* March 29, 1984.

Hadley, Arthur, *The Straw Giant: Triumph and Failure, America's Armed Forces,* New York: Random House, 1986.

Hamberg, D., *R & D: Essay on the Economics of Research and Development,* New York: Random House, 1966.

Henderson, J.M., and Richard E. Quandt, *Microeconomic Theory,* New York: McGraw-Hill, 1971.

Hilton, Peter, *New Product Introduction for Small Business Owners,* Washington, D.C.: Small Business Administration, 1961.

Hopkins, David S., ''New Product Winners and Losers,'' Report no. 773, The Conference Board, 1980.

Hsien-Chin, Hu, ''The Chinese Concept of 'Face','' *American Anthropologist,* 46 (1944): 45–64.

Hufbauer, G.C., *Synthetic Materials and the Theory of International Trade,* London: Duckworth, 1966.

Jewkes, J., D. Sawers, and R. Stillerman, *The Sources of Invention,* 1958, 2nd ed., New York: Norton, 1969.

Johanson, Donald, and Maitland Edey, *Lucy: the Beginnings of Humankind,* New York: Warner Books, 1982.

Johnson, P.S., *The Economics of Invention and Innovation,* London: Martin Robertson, 1975.

Joravsky, David, ''Unholy Science,'' *New York Review of Books,* October 13, 1985.

Kamien, Morton I., and Nancy L. Schwartz, *Market Structure and Innovation,* Cambridge: Cambridge University Press, 1982.

Keynes, John M., *The General Theory of Employment, Interest and Money,* 1936, London: Macmillan, 1970.

Kuhn, Thomas S., *The Structure of Scientific Revolutions,* 1962, Chicago: University of Chicago Press, 1970.

''Reflections on My Critics,'' in I. Lakatos and A. Musgrave (eds.), *Criticism and the Growth of Knowledge,* Cambridge: Cambridge University Press, 1970, pp. 231–78.

Kuran, Timur, "Preference, Falsification, Social Conservatism, and Ideological Conformism," Working Paper, Department of Economics, University of Southern California, January 1986.

Landes, David S., *Revolution in Time,* Cambridge, Mass: Harvard University Press, 1983.

Lewontin, R.C., "A Simple Problem Science Can't Solve," *New York Review of Books,* April 12, 1984.

Loasby, Brian J., *Choice, Complexity and Ignorance,* Cambridge: Cambridge University Press, 1976.

MacKay, Charles L.D., *Extraordinary Popular Delusions and the Madness of Crowds,* 1841, New York: Harmony Books, 1980.

Malinvaud, Edmond, *Leçons de Théorie Microéconomique,* 1968, Paris: Dunod, 1982.

Mansfield, Edwin, *The Economics of Technological Change,* New York: Norton, 1968. *Technical Change,* New York: Norton, 1971.

Mansfield, Edwin, "Firm Size and Technological Change in the Petroleum and Bituminous Coal Industries," in Thomas D. Duchesneau, *Competition in the U.S. Energy Industry,* Cambridge: Ballinger, 1975, pp. 317–47.

McCaskey, Michael B., *The Executive Challenge,* Cambridge, Mass.: Harvard University Press, 1982.

Merton, Robert K., *The Sociology of Science,* Chicago: University of Chicago Press, 1973.

Miller, R., and D. Sawers, *The Technical Development of Modern Aviation,* London: Routledge, 1968.

Murray, Robert H., *Science and Scientists in the Nineteenth Century,* London: Sheldon Press, 1925.

Nelson, Richard R., "Incentives for Entrepreneurship and Supporting Institutions," *Weltwirtschaftliches Archiv,* 120 (1984): 646–72.

Nelson, Richard R., and Disney G. Winter, *An Evolutionary Theory of Economic Change,* Cambridge, Mass.: Harvard University Press, 1982.

Ogburn, William F., "How Technology Changes Society," *The Annals,* 249 (January, 1947): 81–8.

Ohmae, Kenichi, "Japan's Entrepreneurs Battle the Goliaths," *Wall Street Journal,* December 20, 1982.

Pegram, Roger M., and Earl L. Bailey, *The Marketing Executive Looks Ahead,* The Conference Board of Canada, 1967.

Pessemier, Edgar A., *Product Management,* New York: Wiley, 1977.

Peters, Tom, and Nancy Austin, *A Passion for Excellence,* New York: Random House, 1985.

Polanyi, Michael, *Scientific Thought and Social Reality,* New York: International Universities Press, 1979.

Raiga, Eugène, *L'Envie,* Paris: Librairie Félix Alcan, 1932.

Roe, Anne, *The Making of a Scientist,* New York: Dodd & Company, Mead, 1953. "Patterns in Productivity of Scientists," *Science,* 176, (May, 1972): 940–1.

Roman, Daniel D., *Research and Development Management,* New York: Appleton, 1968.

Rossman, Joseph, "War and Invention," *American Journal of Sociology*, 36 (1931): 325–33.

Samuelson, Paul A., *Foundations of Economic Analysis*, 1947, New York: Atheneum, 1971.

Schackle, G.L.S., *The Years of High Theory*, Cambridge: Cambridge University Press, 1967.

Scherer, F.M., *Industrial Market Structure and Economic Performance*, Chicago: Rand McNally, 1980.

   Innovation and Growth: Schumpeterian Perspectives, Cambridge, Mass.: MIT Press, 1984.

Schmookler, Jacob, "Inventors Past and Present," *Review of Economics and Statistics* (August, 1957): 321–33.

Schoeck, Helmut, *Envy*, New York: Harcourt, Brace and World, 1969.

Schumpeter, Joseph A., *Capitalism, Socialism and Democracy*, 1942, New York: Harper, 1962.

Solman, Paul, and Thomas Friedman, *Life and Death on the Corporate Battlefield*, New York: Simon and Schuster, 1982.

Stekler, H.O., "Technological Progress in the Aerospace Industry," *Journal of Industrial Economics*, 15 (1967): 312–30.

Stern, Bernhard, "Resistances to the Adoption of Technological Innovations," in U.S. Government Report of the Subcommittee on Technology: *Technological Trends and National Policy*, Washington, 1937, pp. 39–66.

Sturmey, S.G., *The Economic Development of Radio*, London: Duckworth, 1958.

Sylos-Labini, Paolo, *The Forces of Economic Growth*, Cambridge, Mass.: MIT Press, 1984.

Teltsch, Kathleen, "Foundations Warned Against Complacency," *New York Times*, April 29, 1984.

Time, "Picture Perfect," April 9, 1984.

Trattner, Ernest R., *Architects of Ideas*, 1938, Westport, Connecticut: Greenwood Press, 1966.

Usher, A.P., "Technical Change and Capital Formation," *Capital Formation and Economic Growth*, National Bureau of Economic Research, 1955, pp. 523–50. Reprinted in N. Rosenberg (ed.), *The Economics of Technological Change*, Middlesex: Penguin, 1971, pp. 43–72.

Van Deusen, Edmund, "The Inventor in Eclipse," *Fortune*, December, 1954.

Varian, Hal R., *Microeconomic Analysis*, 1978, New York: Norton, 1984.

Wallis, Roy (ed.), *On the Margins of Science: The Social Construction of Rejected Knowledge*, University of Keele Press, 1979.

Chapter 6

Aharoni, Yair, "Charting the Iceberg: Visible and Invisible Aspects of Government," in S.E. Spiro and E. Yuchtman-Yaar (eds.), *Evaluating the Welfare State*, New York: Academic Press, 1983, pp. 161–74.

Aitken, H.G.J., "Defensive Expansionism: The State and Economic Growth in Canada,'' in W.T. Easterbrook and M.H. Watkins (eds.), *Approaches to Canadian Economic History,* Toronto: McClelland and Steward, 1961, pp. 183–222.

Anastassopoulus, Jean-Pierre C., ''The French Experience: Conflicts with Government,'' in R. Vernon and Y. Aharoni (eds.), *State-Owned Enterprise,* London: Crown Helm, 1981, pp. 99–117.

Ashley, C.A., and R.G.H. Snails, *Canadian Crown Corporations,* Toronto: Macmillan, 1965.

Brenner, Reuven, *History – The Human Gamble,* Chicago: University of Chicago Press, 1983.

''Crowding-out and the Fable of the Bees,'' study prepared for the Economic Council of Canada, 1984a.

''State-owned Enterprises – Practices and Viewpoints,'' in *Government Enterprise: Roles and Rationale,* Ottawa: Economic Council of Canada, 1984b, pp. 12–69.

Betting on Ideas: Wars, Invention, Inflation, Chicago: University of Chicago Press, 1985.

Brenner, Reuven and Léon Courville, ''Industrial Strategy: Inferring What It Really Is,'' in D.G. McFetridge (ed.), *Economics of Industrial Policy and Strategy,* Toronto: University of Toronto Press, 1986: 47–83.

Borcherding, Thomas E., ''Toward a Positive Theory of Public Sector Supply Managements,'' in J.R.S. Prichard (ed.), *Crown Corporations,* Toronto: Butterworth, 1983, pp. 99–184.

Borins, Sandford F., ''World War II Crown Corporations: Their Functions and Their Fate,'' in Prichard, J.R.S. (ed.), *Crown Corporations,* Toronto: Butterworth, 1983, pp. 447–75.

Buchanan, J., and Tideman, N., ''Gasoline Rationing and Market Pricing: Public Choice in Political Democracy,'' Research Paper No. 808231-1-12, Center for Study of Public Choice, Virginia Polytechnic Institute, January, 1974.

Chandler, Marsha A., ''The Politics of Public Enterprise,'' in Prichard, J.R.S. (ed.), *Crown Corporations,* Toronto: Butterworth, 1983, pp. 185–218.

Coase, Ronald H., ''The Nature of the Firm,'' *Economica,* 4, new series (1937): 386–405.

Cochran, Thomas C., ''Land Grants and Railroad Entrepreneurship,'' *Journal of Economic History,* Supplement X, (1950): 53–67.

Coombes, David, *State Enterprise – Business or Politics?* London: Allen & Unwin, 1971.

Davis, Lance E., Jonathan R.T. Hughes, and Duncan M. McDougall, *American Economic History,* Homewood, Ill.: Irwin, 1965.

Delion, André, ''Les enterprises publiques en France,'' in André Gélinas (ed.), *L'enterprise publique et l'intérêt public,* Toronto: L'Institut d'Administration Publique du Canada, 1978: 119–47.

Demsetz, H. ''Why Regulate Utilities?'' *Journal of Law and Economics,* 11 (1968): 55–65.

Finbow, Robert, ''The State Agenda in Quebec and Ontario, 1960–1980,'' *Journal of Canadian Studies,* 18/1 (Spring, 1983): 117–35.

Foster, George M., ''The Anatomy of Envy: A Study in Symbolic Behavior,'' *Current Anthropology,* XIII/2 (April, 1972): 165–202.

Fournier, Pierre, "The National Asbestos Corporation of Quebec," in A. Tupper and G.B. Doern (eds.), *Public Corporations,* Montreal: Institue for Research on Public Policy, 1981, pp. 353–65.

Grassini, Franco A., "The Italian Enterprises: The Political Constraints," in R. Vernon and Y. Aharoni (eds.), *State-Owned Enterprise,* London: Crown Helm, 1981, pp. 70–85.

L'Hériteau, Marie-France, *Pourquoi des Entreprises Publiques?* Paris: Presses Universitaires de France, 1972.

Hillhouse, A.M., *Municipal Bonds: A Century of Experience,* New York: Prentice-Hall, 1936.

Hughes, Jonathan, *The Governmental Habit: Economic Controls from Colonial Times to the Present,* New York: Basic Books, 1977.

Jones, Leroy P., and Edward S. Mason, "Why Public Enterprise," in L.P. Jones (ed.), *Public Enterprise in Less-developed Countries,* Cambridge: Cambridge University Press, 1982, pp. 17–48.

Klein, Rudolf, "The Politics of Public Expenditure: American Theory and British Practice," *British Journal of Political Science,* 6 (1976): 401–32.

Lakoff, Sanford A., *Equality in Political Philosophy,* Cambridge: Cambridge University Press, 1964.

Langford, John W., "Air Canada," in A. Tupper and G.B. Doern (eds.), *Public Corporations,* Montreal: Institute for Research on Public Policy, 1981, pp. 251–85.

Laux, Jeanne K., and Maureen A. Molot, "The Potash Corporation of Saskatchewan," in A. Tupper and G.B. Doern (eds.), *Public Corporations,* Montreal: Institute for Research on Public Policy, 1981, pp. 189–221.

Leibenstein, Harvey, *General X-Efficiency Theory & Economic Development,* Oxford: Oxford University Press, 1978.

Loasby, Brian J., *Choice, Complexity and Ignorance,* Cambridge: Cambridge University Press, 1976.

Lukasiewicz, J., *The Railway Game,* Toronto: McClelland and Steward, 1976.

Mackay, Robert J., and Joseph D. Reid, "On Understanding the Birth and Evolution of the Securities and Exchange Commission: Where Are We on the Theory of Regulation?" in *Regulatory Change in an Atmosphere of Crisis,* New York: Academic Press, 1979, pp. 101–21.

Marina,William, "Egalitarianism and Empire," in Templeton, K.S., Jr. (ed.), *The Politization of Society,* Indianapolis: Liberty Press, 1979, pp. 127–67.

Martinelli, Alberto, "The Italian Experience: A Historical Perspective," in R. Vernon and Y. Aharoni (eds.), *State-Owned Enterprise,* London: Croom Helm, 1981, pp. 85–99.

McNeill, William H., *The Pursuit of Power,* Chicago: University of Chicago Press, 1982.

Middletown, P. Harvey, *Railways of Thirty Nations,* New York: Prentice-Hall, 1937.

Muzaffer, Ahmad, "Political Economy of Public Enterprise," in L.P. Jones (ed.), *Public Enterprise in Less-developed Countries,* Cambridge: Cambridge University Press, 1981, pp. 49–65.

Nelson, James R., "Public Enterprise: Pricing and Investment Criteria," in W.G.

Shepherd (ed.), *Public Enterprise,* Lexington: Lexington Books, 1976, pp. 49–76.

Noreng, Oystein, "State-Owned Oil Companies: Western Europe," in R. Vernon and Y. Aharoni (eds.), *State-Owned Enterprise,* London: Crown Helm, 1981, pp. 133–45.

North, Douglass C., *Structure and Change in Economic History,* New York: Norton, 1981.

O'Connor, J., *The Fiscal Crisis of the State,* New York: St. Martin's Press, 1973.

Olson, Mancur, *The Rise and Decline of Nations,* New Haven: Yale University Press, 1982.

Posner, Richard A., "Taxation by Regulation," *Bell Journal,* 2/1 (Spring, 1971): 22–49.

Prichard, J. Robert S. (ed.), *Crown Corporations in Canada,* Toronto: Butterworth, 1983.

Primeaux, Walter J., "Dismantling Competition in a Natural Monopoly," *Quarterly Review of Economics and Business,* 25/3 (Autumn, 1985): 6–21.

Pryor, Frederic L, "Public Ownership: Some Quantitative Dimensions," in W.G. Shepherd (ed.), *Public Enterprise,* Lexington, Mass.: Lexington Books, 1976, pp. 3–23.

Reid, J., Jr., "Understanding Political Events in the New Economic History," *Journal of Economic History,* 37 (June, 1977): 302–28.

Ricklefs, Roger, "Concerns Nationalized by France Put Profits Ahead of Social Goals," *Wall Street Journal,* April 18, 1985.

Robson, William A., *Nationalized Industry and Public Ownership,* Toronto: University of Toronto Press, 1960.

Rodrick, Dani, "Changing Patterns of Ownership and Integration in the International Bauxite-Aluminium Industry," in L.P. Jones (ed.), *Public Enterprise in Less-developed Countries,* Cambridge: Cambridge University Press, 1982, pp. 189–215.

Rostow, W.W., "Government and Private Enterprise in European Recovery," *Journal of Economic History,* Supplement X (1950): 105–113.

Rotstein, Abraham, "The Origins of the Canadian Wheat Board," in *Government Enterprise: Roles and Rationale,* Economic Council of Canada, 1984, pp. 69–103.

Schoeck, Helmut, *Envy,* New York: Harcourt, Brace & World, 1969.

Schumpeter, Joseph, *Capitalism, Socialism and Democracy,* 1942, New York: Harper & Row, 1950.

Sheahan, John B., "Experience with Public Enterprise in France and Italy," in W.G. Shepherd (ed.), *Public Enterprise,* Lexington, Mass.: Lexington Books, 1976: 123–83.

Shepherd, William G. (ed.), *Public Enterprise,* Lexington, Mass.: Lexington Books, 1976.

Stevenson, Garth, "Canadian National Railways," in A. Tupper and G.B. Doern (eds.), *Public Corporations,* Montreal: Institute for Research on Public Policy, 1981, pp. 319–53.

Tivey, L.J., *Nationalization in British Industry,* London: Jonathan Cape, 1966.

Trebat, Thomas Y., *Brazil's State-Owned Enterprises,* Cambridge: Cambridge University Press, 1983.

Trebilcock, M.J., and J.R.S. Prichard, "Crown Corporations: The Calculus of Instrument Choice," in J.R.S. Prichard (ed.), *Crown Corporations,* Toronto: Butterworth, 1983, pp. 1–99.

Tupper, Allan, "Pacific Western Airlines," in A. Tupper and G.B. Doern (eds.), *Public Corporations,* Montreal: The Institute for Research on Public Policy, 1981, pp. 285–319.

Tupper, Allan, and G. Bruce Doern (eds.), *Public Corporations and Public Policy in Canada,* Montreal: Institute for Research on Public Policy, 1981.

Vernon, Raymond, and Yair Aharoni (eds.), *State-Owned Enterprise in the Western Economies,* London: Crown Helm, 1981.

Vining, A.R., "Provincial Hydro Utilities," in A. Tupper and G. B. Doern (eds.), *Public Corporations,* Montreal: The Institute for Research on Public Policy, 1981, pp. 149–89.

Walsh, Ann-Marie H., *The Public's Business,* Cambridge, Mass.: MIT Press, 1978.

Chapter 7

Baumol, William, "On Productivity Growth in the Long Run," *Atlantic Economic Journal,* 12/3 (December, 1984): 5–10.

Bennett, Amanda, "American Culture Is Often a Puzzle for Foreign Managers in the U.S.," *Wall Street Journal,* February 12, 1986.

Bergier, Y.F., "The Industrial Bourgeoisie and the Rise of the Working Class 1700–1914," in C.M. Cipolla (ed.), *The Industrial Revolution,* Glasgow: Fontana, 1973.

Brenner, Gabrielle A., and Reuven Brenner, "Innovation and the Competition Act," in W. Block (ed.), *Reaction: the New Combines Investigation Act,* Vancouver: Fraser Institute, 1986, pp. 117–40.

Brenner, Reuven, *History – The Human Gamble,* Chicago: University of Chicago Press, 1983.
  Betting on Ideas: Wars, Invention, Inflation, Chicago: University of Chicago Press, 1985.

Brenner, Reuven, and Léon Courville, "Industrial Strategy: Inferring What It Really Is," in D.G. McFetridge (ed.), *Economics of Industrial Policy and Strategy,* Toronto: University of Toronto Press, 1986, pp. 47–83.

Brenner, Reuven, and Antal Deutsch, "Terrorism – From a Somewhat Different Angle," working paper, University of Montréal, 1986.

Britton, John N.H., and James M. Gilmour, *The Weakest Link,* Background Paper 43, Ottawa: Science Council of Canada, 1978.

Buruma, Ian, *Behind the Mask: On Sexual Demons, Sacred Mothers, Transvestites, Gangsters, Drifters and Other Japanese Cultural Heroes,* New York: Pantheon, 1984.

Carlson, Eugene, "Listing Top High-Tech States Depends a Lot on Definitions," *Wall Street Journal,* January 3, 1984.

Chira, Susan, "Business Schools, Japanese Style," *New York Times,* August 4, 1985.

Clarck, Lindley H., Jr., "There's No Way to Be a Little Protectionist," *Wall Street Journal,* September 25, 1984.

Clymer, Adam, "Polling Americans," *New York Times Magazine,* November 10, 1985, p. 37.

Coutu, Diane L., "European Nations Fret over Mounting Losses of Scientists to the U.S.," *Wall Street Journal,* October 21, 1983.

Daly, Donald J., "Weak Links in 'The Weakest Link'," *Canadian Public Policy,* 5/3 (1979): 307–17.

Drucker, Peter F., "Europe's High-Tech Delusion," *Wall Street Journal,* September 14, 1984.

Fauriol, Georges, and Andrew D. Kopperl, "U.S. Sugar Policy Rots Neighboring Economies," *Wall Street Journal,* September 17, 1985.

Freeman, Christopher, *The Economics of Industrial Innovation,* Cambridge, Mass.: MIT Press, 1983.

The Gazette, "Israel-Argentina Jet Deal Blocked by U.S. Report," August 28, 1985.

Ingrassia, Lawrence, "How Japan Sealed Deal to Build a Big Bridge Spanning the Bosporus," *Wall Street Journal,* May 20, 1985.

Jackson, John H., *World Trade and the Law of GATT,* Indianapolis: Bobbs-Merrill, 1969.

Johnson, Chalmers, "Introduction: The Idea of Industrial Policy," in Chalmers Johnson (ed.), *The Industrial Policy Debate,* San Francisco: Institute for Contemporary Studies, 1984, pp. 3–27.

Johnson, Paul, *A History of the Modern World,* London: Weidenfeld and Nicholson, 1983.

Kanata, Satoshi, *Japan in the Passing Line: An Insider's Account of Life in a Japanese Auto Factory,* New York: Pantheon, 1983.

Krauss, Melvyn, "Europeanizing the U.S. Economy: The Enduring Appeal of the Corporatist State," in Chalmers Johnson (ed.), *The Industrial Policy Debate,* San Francisco: Institute for Contemporary Studies, 1984, pp. 71–91.

Lewis, Flora, "Upside down Values," *New York Times,* February 9, 1986.

McNeill, William, *The Pursuit of Power,* Chicago: University of Chicago Press, 1982.

Murray, Alan, "As Free-Trade Bastion, U.S. Isn't Half as Pure as Many People Think," *Wall Street Journal,* November 1, 1985.

Nelson, Richard R., "Incentives for Entrepreneurship and Supporting Institutions," *Weltwirtschaftliches Archiv,* 120/4 (1984): 646–62.

North, Douglass C., *Structure and Change in Economic History,* New York: Norton, 1981.

Ozaki, Robert S., "How Japanese Industrial Policy Works," in Chalmers Johnson (ed.), *The Industrial Policy Debate,* San Francisco: Institute for Contemporary Studies, 1984, pp. 47–71.

Perlmutter, Amos, *Israel: The Partitioned State,* New York: Scribner's, 1985.

Pine, Art, "U.S. Gets a Protectionist Image in Brazil, But It's not Deserved," *Wall Street Journal,* December 16, 1985.

Reeves, Richard, "The Permissive Dutch," *New York Times Magazine,* October 20, 1985.

Roberts, Johnnie L., "Little Noticed U.S. Program Helps Firms Hurt by Imports," *Wall Street Journal,* August 13, 1984.

Robinson, Joan, *Economic Philosophy,* Middlesex: Penguin Books, 1962.

Safran, Nadav, *Saudi Arabia – The Ceaseless Quest for Security,* Cambridge, Mass.: Harvard University Press, 1985.

Samuelson, Robert J., "Pampering the Auto Industry," *Newsweek,* October 8, 1984. "How Do You Spell Relief?" *Newsweek,* October 21, 1985.

Sayle, Murray, "Japan Victorious," *New York Review of Books,* March 28, 1985.

Schlossstein, Steven, *Trade War: Greed, Power and Industrial Power on Opposite Sides of the Pacific,* New York: Congdon and Weed, 1984.

Science Council of Canada, *Forging the Links: A Technology Policy for Canada,* Report 29, Ottawa: Minister of Supply and Services Canada, 1979.

Sease, Douglas R., "Move to Fight Apparel Imports is Set," *Wall Street Journal,* December 17, 1985.

Shaw, Jane S., and Richard L. Stroup, "New Zealand's Free-Market Experiment," *Wall Street Journal,* December 2, 1985.

Smith, Adam, *An Inquiry Into the Nature and Causes of the Wealth of Nations,* Chicago: University of Chicago Press, 1976.

Stein, Herbert, "Don't Fall for Industrial Policy," *Fortune,* November 14, 1983.

Stern, Bernhard J., "Resistances to the Adoption of Technological Innovation," in U.S. Government Report of the Subcommittee on Technology, *Technological Trends and National Policy,* Washington, D.C., (June, 1937): 39–66.

Stocking, George N., and Myron W. Watkins, *Cartels or Competition?* New York: Twentieth Century Fund, 1948.

Tagliabue, John, "The Realignment in World Steel," *New York Times,* September 11, 1983.

Teitelbaum, Michael S., and Jay M. Winter, *The Fear of Population Decline,* San Diego: Academic Press, 1985.

Thurow, Lester C., "The Need to Work Smarter," *Newsweek,* October 3, 1980: p. 80.

The Management Challenge: Japanese Views, Cambridge, Mass.: MIT Press, 1985.

Thurow, Roger, "Playing Catch-up: West Europe Strives to Match U.S., Japan in High Technology," *Wall Street Journal,* May 8, 1985.

Viteles, Morris S., *Motivation and Morale in Industry,* New York: Norton, 1953.

Wall Street Journal, "Get Rich Quick," editorial, August 21, 1984.

Wall Street Journal, "A Little Principle," editorial, December 19, 1985.

Wiener, Martin J.L, *English Culture and the Decline of the Industrial Spirit 1850–1980,* Cambridge: Cambridge University Press, 1981.

Wolf, Marvin J., *The Japanese Conspiracy: The Plot to Dominate Industry Worldwide – And How to Deal With It,* New York: Empire, 1984.

Young, Michael, *The Rise of Meritocracy,* 1958, Middlesex: Penguin, 1973.

Name index

Abrams, B., 192, 193
Aharoni, Y., 141, 203, 205–6
Aitken, H.G.J., 138
Albertine, J., 39
Alchian, A.A., 178
Alsop, R., 94, 192–93
Alter, J., 184, 186
Anaxagoras, 117, 202
Anders, G., 182
Areeda, P., 189
Arieti, S., 182
Aristotle, S., 20, 40, 81
Armentano, D.T., 64, 187
Armstrong, G., 193
Arrow, K.J., 164, 189, 195
Asch, P., 33
Asinof, L., 195
Ataturk, K., 147
Austin, N., 101, 108, 179, 195
Avery, S., 176
Ayres, C.E., 189

Bachrach, I., 82
Backman, J., 187
Bailey, E.L., 106
Barmash, I., 185
Barnett, H.G., 111, 174, 177, 186, 194, 197–200, 202
Bartkus, R.E., 69
Barzel, Y., 185
Baumol, W.J., 8, 12–13, 74, 193, 206
Becker, G., 12, 54, 78, 81, 163, 205
Belshaw, C., 119
Ben-David, J., 198, 201
Benham, L., 95
Bennett, A., 175, 210
Bennis, W., 176
Ben-Yehuda, N., 115, 197, 198, 199, 200
Bergier, Y.F., 210
Berkowitz, P., 183
Berna, J.J., 44
Birch, J.J., 185
Bismarck, 129
Blair, R., 180
Bleakley, F.R., 184
Bleichröder, G., 38
Bonini, C.P., 52

Boorstin, D.J., 203
Borcherding, T.E., 141, 203, 206
Borden, Sir Robert, 129
Bork, R.H., 62–65, 67
Bowers, J., 50
Boyer, K.D., 23
Braithwaite, J., 30
Brenner, G.A., 29, 55, 77, 186, 191
Brenner, H., 90
Brenner, R., 26, 28–29, 31, 41, 43, 55, 66, 97, 119, 122, 124, 137, 150, 159
Bridenbaugh, C., 189
Britton, J.N., 148, 208–9
Broad, W.J., 201
Bronfenbrenner, M., 179
Brown, W.H., 33
Brown, Winthrop, 210
Browning, E.S., 200
Brozen, Y., 180, 192, 194
Brunswick, Duke Julius, of, 112, 147
Buchanan, J., 12, 26, 141, 176–77
Buruma, I., 210
Butterfield, H., 123
Buzzel, R.D., 195

Calvani, T., 72
Calvo, G., 179
Campbell, C.A., 153
Carlson, C., 102, 108
Carlson, E., 157
Carlton, D., 54, 55, 189
Carr, E.H., 99
Carr-Hill, R.A., 30
Carroll, L., 160
Carr-Saunders, A.M., 30
Carruthers, P., 201
Casson, M., 176
Cavanagh, R.E., 178
Cavendish, Lord Charles, 197
Chamberlin, E.H., 23
Chandler, M.A., 139
Chapman, S.J., 32
Charles, I., 100
Chevenement, J.P., 145
Chira, S., 210
Chiswick, B.R., 31
Choffray, J.M., 62, 106

235

Subject index